THE WHITE BUSHMAN

The White Bushman

Peter Stark

PROTEA BOOK HOUSE
PRETORIA
2017

The White Bushman
Peter Stark

First edition, first impression in 2011 by Protea Book House
First edition, second impression in 2017

PO Box 35110, Menlo Park, 0102
1067 Burnett Street, Hatfield, Pretoria
8 Minni Street, Clydesdale, Pretoria
protea@intekom.co.za
www.proteaboekhuis.com

Translator: Jan Schaafsma
Editor: Danél Hanekom
Proofreader: Amelia de Vaal
Cover design: Hanli Deysel
Typography and design: 11 pt on 13 pt Zapf Calligraphy by Ada Radford

solutions
Printed by **novus print**, a Novus Holdings company

ISBN 978-1-86919-413-0

A German edition of *The White Bushman* entitled *Der Weiße Buschmann* was published by Kuiseb Verlag – Namibia Wissenschaftiger Gesellschaft in 2003. The photographs in *The White Bushman* are used with their friendly permission.

Protea Book House would like to thank the following persons for the use of their photographs in this publication: Peter Stark, Nico Stark, Elke Müller-Brunke, Ute von Ludwiger, Immo Böhlke and Henning Barth.

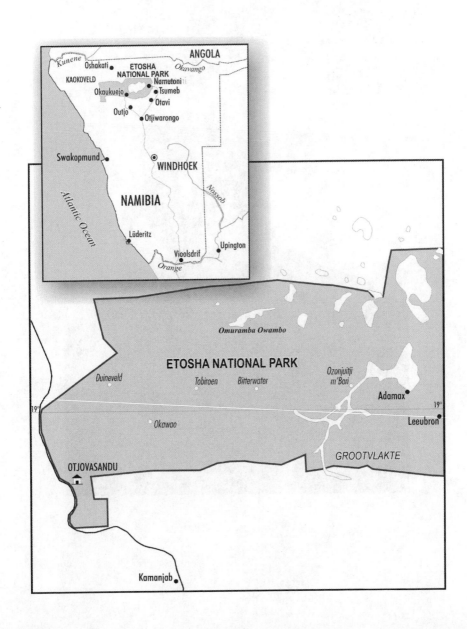

to Ondangwa

Ekuma

Poacher's Point

ETOSHA PAN

Andoni

ANDONI PLAIN

Fischer's
Pan

Great Okevi

NAMUTONI

Okerfontein

Omuramba Owambo

Twee Palms

to Tsumeb

Goas

Springbokfontein

Okondeka

HALALI (TWEEKOPPIES)

19°   19°

Leeubron

Rietfontein

OKAUKUEJO

Olifantsbad

GEMSBOKVLAKTE

GOBAUBVLAKTE

N

0   25   50 km

to Outjo

Foreword

The Etosha National Park spans some 2,2 million hectares. Proclaimed as a game park as early as 1907, little development took place before 1957, when roofed accommodation was available only at Okaukuejo. Following the restoration of the fort at Namutoni in 1957, tourists could be accommodated there as well.

During the tourist season current at the time (1 April to 30 October), game wardens also had to act as tourist guides. Vacation leave and the rainy season limited the time available for fieldwork, as the total staff complement at Etosha was only a chief game warden, biologist, senior and assistant game wardens, a mechanic and 26 Bushmen.

Complaints by farmers in the Kamanjab region about serious damage done by elephants prompted a decision by the Executive of the South West African Administration to cause a number of boreholes to be drilled along the 19th parallel. These were to be prepared in order to entice elephants from the Kamanjab region to the western part of Etosha. This decision resulted in the creation of another game warden post for the Okaukuejo region.

The requirements for the post called for an exceptional person. He needed some mechanical skills in order to erect the windmills, he had to be able to work with concrete in order to build drinking-troughs, needed to have a vast store of field expertise and the ability to work alone and without supervision for long periods, without any complaints about privations, discomfort, hard work and long hours, not to mention being brave enough to track and arrest poachers. Self-assurance was mandatory, because he would mostly have to make his own decisions, and act independently.

Peter Stark was the only candidate who matched all these requirements.

Essentially he was still a hunter. When he could no longer hunt lions, he hunted poachers with the same dedication. While he worked at that latitude, he had more than enough time for these extra duties.

Nature conservation offers field officers a very adventurous career. They usually experience their greatest adventures when they find themselves in an area on their own. Their tales can therefore very seldom be corroborated by witnesses, and readers may doubt their veracity. Parts may be omitted or added to in the telling and re-telling; no two people will have exactly the same recollection of an event.

However, I can vouch for Peter's work along the 19th parallel. It's still there, as testament to someone who, alongside others, did pioneering work at Etosha.

Stoffel Rocher
Former Deputy Director
Nature Management, South West Africa/Namibia

Introduction

I am an old man now. My body has been broken by many mishaps, operations and illnesses, but countless incidents have survived unscathed in my memory. For my entire life I was never rich in worldly goods, but nobody can take my wealth of experiences from me. I must thank my Creator for always protecting me. I am eternally grateful for this.

Unfortunately I must write a great deal about myself – something I never do with any relish. Still, I want to write not only about all the good things that happened in my life, but also about the dark days and events, and the many things I did which helped to shape me, and make me strong.

I have never liked writing, and have always shied away from it. Perhaps the new millennium helped to change my mind; perhaps it was the enforced boredom that came with old age and a broken leg.

My childhood

I was born at six o'clock in the evening of 18 April 1929. I know this because my mother always made me wait until six o'clock on my birthday before I could open my presents. My mother was very strict, typical of German officers' wives, precise and very proud. King Frederick the Great was her role model.

I cannot remember my father. He was a captain in the German security forces and came to German South West Africa (as it was called then) with my mother in 1903. He was a lawyer in civilian life.

I must have learnt tenacity from my mother. When my mother was eight months pregnant, she decided to participate in a horse race. She won, but the horse flashed past the post and simply kept on going. It was touch and go for my mother that evening, and I was almost born prematurely. She stuck it out, however, and the birth was quite normal.

My mother was crazy about horses all her life, and so I was taught to ride at quite an early age. She bought me three donkeys when I was six, thinking that riding them would turn me into a good horseman.

I usually rode Liese, the old jenny, who was quite calm. Along with Johannes, an Owambo, I careered about bareback every day

11

on our mountain property of some 20 hectares. One afternoon I decided that I would rather ride Johannes's jackass Jason. This was a spry and lively animal, and Johannes tried to dissuade me from mounting him. However, Starky wouldn't listen, and when I gave Jason a taste of my whip, he galloped full tilt straight towards a camel-thorn tree. I wanted to pass by on the left, but Jason preferred the right, and consequently my chin made rather decisive contact with the camel-thorn tree. When I eventually staggered upright, I was covered in blood from my throat to my legs, and Johannes had to carry me home. My chin was broken at the frontal fissure, and for a long time I was confined to eating only soup, something I didn't like in the least. My mother decided that the donkeys were no longer required, and sold the animals.

Gifts that shaped my life

Shortly after the donkey incident, my mother bought me a brown stallion and a single-shot Mauser .22 rifle for my seventh birthday. We named the horse Jupp.

Jupp and my .22 rifle formed the basis of my entire later life. For the rest of my life I chose my careers so as to combine horses and hunting. Money never mattered, other than that it sometimes proved an essential and useful evil.

My first riding lessons

My mother was very strict, as I said before. She was my first riding instructor, but I was more in love with my .22 rifle than horse-riding. In contrast, horse-riding was my mother's first choice, and so we did not always understand one another perfectly. Furthermore, the first riding lessons were round and round at the end of a lunge, without stirrups or reins, in order for me to develop proper balance. Feelings often ran high (both my mother and I had short tempers). When things became too much for me, I often jumped off the horse at full gallop and took off into the bush. Johannes, who always helped my mother, was then dispatched to find me. He was much faster than I and quickly caught up with me, dragging me back to the horse and dumping me into the saddle with little ceremony. When, in my mother's opinion, I could eventually ride well enough, Jupp and I were permitted to take to the bush and mountains by ourselves.

I thought this was wonderful, and as soon as my mother was out of sight, Jupp had to show all his paces with "Billy the Kid" as rider. When my mother realised that I had overtaxed Jupp, her horse-whip played a merry tune on my backside.

Hunting and horses in my childhood days

My rifle was my greatest love. I was up in the mountains at every possible opportunity, rifle in hand, looking for dassies (hyrax or rock-rabbits). Moses, an old Nama who looked after our dairy cows, taught me. Moses grew up on the farm Gochaganas and knew all about the veld. He was my first black friend and tutor – also with regard to the Nama language.

However, my horse-riding and hunting activities did not have a positive influence on my schooling, and my homework suffered most. Corporal punishment was still the order of the day, and the "Yellow Mamba", a vicious length of reed, often danced about on my posterior.

Our smallholding was in Little Windhoek at the foot of the Eros mountain range, some 8 kilometres from the school. I had to get up early every day, and then walk to school barefoot, at least for the first few years. I usually did my homework in class before school started, and made liberal use of my classmates' books – if they were prepared to lend these to me. I had almost no friends, because Little Windhoek was very sparsely populated in those days. My closest friend was Siggi Triebner, whose father had a large nursery some 6,4 kilometres north of us. His father and my mother agreed that it would be best if we were kept apart, as we both loved hunting. So we usually met secretly by all manner of backways, but paid the penalty on coming back home again. My worst punishment was when my .22 rifle was locked away for a week. Give me a hiding any time, but don't lock away my rifle! Siggi was always punished by having to do extra work in the garden.

Later, my mother devised a better plan for me. Miss von Eckenbrecher, a former schoolmarm, lived some distance from us. Miss Ecke, as we called her, agreed that I could do my homework under her supervision every afternoon. Miss Ecke had a lovely orchard, and I often visited it at night and helped her to clear her surplus of wonderful oranges and naartjies. Baboons were always blamed.

I had great respect for this strict woman. Apart from her strong arms, which were quite capable of dealing one some lusty blows, she also walked to school barefoot every day – and she was well into her sixties at the time.

My first hunting trophy

One afternoon, while I was wandering around in the mountains with rifle in hand, I saw an animal that looked like a large hare to me. I crept up to it very cautiously and shot it. When the animal fell, I noticed it sported a grand set of horns. I was as pleased as punch with my first buck as I carried it home.

The trophy was properly cleaned, the buck dressed, prepared and eaten piece by piece. As was the case with all the other spoils of the hunt I had shot, from a pigeon to a dassie, everything had to be cleaned properly, dressed and prepared for the pot. Moses always helped me with this. Apart from inedible vermin such as mongooses and wild cats, I was not permitted to shoot anything unnecessarily. My mother was a good cook, and she showed me how to prepare all the different game species and serve them as a tasty dish. Then I had to do it myself.

I carefully cleaned the skull of my first buck and mounted it on the wall above my bed. The buck I had mistakenly taken for a hare turned out to be a Damara dikdik.

My first big game

I was nine years old when Bitz von Eckenbrecher came to visit his mother. At that time he owned the farm Narachaams in die Outjo District in the Kaoko Mountains, which was regarded as one of the remotest corners of the world. There was a lovely bubbling fountain on the farm, and plenty of game. Lions sometimes loped from one side of the farm to the other.

Bitz managed to persuade my mother to let me spend a holiday on his farm. My mother saw me off at the train station when school broke up for the winter holidays.

What sticks in my memory about that first train journey was that I had to change trains from the Otavi Bahn to the narrow-gauge railway to Outjo. The last uphill before reaching Outjo proved too much for the locomotive. It gave up, and came to a halt in tremendous heat in the middle of nowhere. After a lengthy wait, a second locomotive eventually arrived, and after having endured many jerks and bumps along the way, we finally steamed into the Outjo station.

Bitz was waiting for me, with a sly grin on his face. "You got a proper roasting, hey?" he said when I alighted and asked for water.

We took off into the bush. Arriving at Narachaams after a long drive, Bitz showed me the fountain and the many game tracks that surrounded it. I thought Narachaams was a lovely farm, with mountains similar to those at Little Windhoek, and I immediately felt at home. Bitz introduced me to Albert, a pitch-black adult Damara man. Albert was fluent in German, and we quickly became friends. Albert was an experienced hunter and a very good tracker, and knew the veld like the back of his hand.

He was instructed to pick the four best donkeys and to keep them in a nearby enclosure. Albert was to serve me for the duration of the holidays. I was also introduced to Bitz's 8-millimetre Mauser. I was allowed to squeeze off a few shots at a target with the rifle rested, and was shown how to load and unload it.

Two donkeys were saddled the following day, and our equipment was loaded onto two pack donkeys. We took no food – a hunter worth the name finds his own! A hearty breakfast is quite enough for the day, and so Albert and I took off into the thick bush. The donkeys were well trained, and always moved at a good trot. After riding for about three hours, Albert suddenly jumped off his donkey and signalled that I should do the same. We tied the donkeys to some trees.

Crouching, I followed Albert. He led me to a rock formation, and from this shelter we peered at the ridges opposite us. Albert pointed out a beautiful kudu bull standing in the shade of a crag. The blood was flowing through my veins like fire, and my heart was thumping in my chest, the result of my first ever "buck fever". Albert noticed this, and got me to calm down before I rested the rifle on a rock. The shot was good, but too low, and I severed the kudu bull's right front leg just below the breastbone. The bull began to run, and I can still picture that leg swinging about uselessly. Albert grabbed the rifle and signalled that we should track the animal. We followed the wounded bull at a crouching run, and when we were close enough, Albert handed me the rifle and signalled that I should shoot. The next three shots all missed. My lungs were going like bellows, the rifle was too heavy, and every time I went down on my haunches, some or other bush got in the way. And when I fired a shot while crouching, the rifle's recoil put me flat on my back. It was a complete fiasco. I had only one round left, so it was now or never! We trotted up almost to the bull's side. I managed to put the fatal bullet into him, and ended his agony. I was dead tired, but boundlessly happy. Albert was pleased, and no doubt relieved.

The bull then had to be dressed, and this was quite a wearisome task for one and a quarter persons. The scrotum was cut off first, and a fire was made with wood from a thorn tree. The fire burnt out while we were slaughtering the kudu, and when the coals were ready, the scrotum and testicles were placed on them. "Hunters' food," said Albert. When the contents of the scrotum were ready, we ate them. It tasted a bit strange at first, but a hungry man will relish anything. The liver and marrow-bones followed. We placed a large slice of the liver on the coals, but not for too long; it still had to be pink and juicy inside. We cut out the long bones below the knees and hocks and heated them on one side of the heap of coals, and not for long, or the bones could split and the marrow would be spilt. The tops of the bones were then neatly removed with a hand-axe. The liver was cut into strips, covered with marrow, and eaten like bread and butter. A dish fit for a king!

Albert taught me all this on that first day, and I still owe him a debt of gratitude. By late afternoon we had finished the slaughtering and had securely loaded all the meat on the donkeys. One had to be careful here, or the meat would slide off. There was too much meat on that kudu bull's bones for the two pack donkeys, so our mounts had to carry their share as well. Albert led the one donkey, and I had to herd along the rest. We reached the farmhouse after dark, and Albert then unloaded and hung all the meat. I experienced it all as a tiring but wonderful hunt. Cat-thorns had torn my bare arms and legs, and even my face, almost to shreds, rocks had bruised and battered my toes, and donkey sweat made my backside burn. That night I slept like the dead.

The following day was spent processing the meat into biltong, smoked cuts and steaks. This job fell on Albert and me, but it's all part of a true hunter's tasks. It took us a whole day to process all that meat. Bitz would sometimes drop in and supervise and dispense advice, accompanied by appropriate comments.

16

When the meat and trophy processing was concluded, I could go out hunting with Albert once more. This time we ventured onto the flats, looking for zebra.

We came across a herd of zebra some time before noon. We stalked the herd, and when I saw a zebra standing within range, I aimed and shot. A very hollow sound indicated that I had hit, but Albert was very upset. "Stomach," he said reprovingly. "It's going to be tough."

The wounded zebra fled into a thick stand of mopani trees along with the rest of the herd. Albert tried to track it, but the wounded zebra would not leave the herd. We spotted a drop of blood here and there, but eventually even that petered out. The zebra herd stayed downwind, and always scampered off in time. We followed the spoor until late that afternoon, ending up on the neighbouring farm. Eventually Albert gave up. We returned to where the donkeys were tied up, feeling very disappointed. We rode back home, getting there only after dark. In the dark, thorns had taken their toll of all my exposed body parts once again. I felt shattered. That evening, at table, Bitz gave me a stern lecture on wounded game, the suffering of animals, over-hasty actions, poor shooting and incompetent hunters. I went to bed crying. I was confined to doing farm-work alongside Bitz for the next three days. To top it all, the neighbour informed us that vultures had led him to the half-eaten zebra carcass.

After three days of farm-work, Albert and I were once more allowed to saddle the donkeys in order to go hunting. That day I shot a kudu cow with a neat shot to the shoulder. I realised it paid off if you stayed calm and made sure of your shot. Bitz's sermon had had a valuable and profound influence on my future life as a hunter.

I stayed with Bitz on Narachaams for the entire winter holidays, and at the end of it I could tick off six kudu and four zebra. I learned a tremendous amount from Albert, and he laid the foundation for my big-game hunting for the rest of my life. The greatest influence was everything associated with the hunting process. The wind, the tracks, general awareness, stalking the game, staying calm, making sure of your shot, following up after the shot, skinning and butchering, packing the donkeys and night-rides.

To my mind the most pleasant ceremony was always lighting the fire on which to cook the meat. Learning how to cook the best cuts of meat was a close second.

When the vacation ended, I said goodbye to Albert and Bitz with a heavy heart and journeyed back home by train, laden with bags of biltong and a hunting logbook that Bitz had given me. Bitz had bound the book himself, in beautiful leather. Bitz showed me how to make entries on every animal I shot. Unfortunately, I never did this, and I regret it to this day. I hated sitting down and writing. Perhaps it was the result of my dark schooldays.

My first race

When I was twelve years old, the folk of Windhoek started having horse-races again. In the meantime I had acquired another horse, a half-thoroughbred named Kastor. He was a stallion, strong and wilful, and he threw me many a time. He was fast, and his very first race came about when my mother entered him against horses from various studs in South West Africa. It was a short race over 1 000 metres. All I knew about racing was that one had to go full tilt and try to stay in front. My outfit for that first race consisted of a khaki shirt, khaki shorts and *veldskoene*. An old professional German jockey who had ridden in Germany for years also took part in this race; a man of much experience.

The two of us were leading as we came into the final straight, side by side, stirrups almost touching. I was riding as hard as I could, in a blur of arms and legs. Over the last 100 metres he began hitting me with his crop, and I sustained more than a few cuts on my bare shins and on my toes. However, I refused to be put off by this, so we were neck and neck as we flashed past the post. It took a long while before the race officials declared him the winner by a short nose. His name was Hans, and he rode a black thoroughbred mare named Bayadere.

Much later I learnt from reliable sources that Hans had spoken to the judges and allegedly said: "The lad can't win his first race; I want him as my pupil, and he'll get a swollen head and then I'll have trouble with him." The race was a wonderful experience for me, and my mother was so proud of me.

After the race meeting Hans spoke to my mother and offered to train me formally in order to become a "decent jockey". It was agreed that I would go and visit him on the Claratal farm during the school holidays to be trained in all the finer aspects of racing.

My years as a jockey

My racing years were confused and hard, interspersed with good memories, but with a few dark events. These were my high school years, and my riding interests and schooling clashed. From the time of my first race I spent every holiday on the Claratal farm. I found it very difficult to ride with shortened stirrup-leathers, and had to cope with painful thighs, calves, back and neck. My legs were naturally long and not exactly suited to a jockey position, but I did master it eventually. Of course I had to train all the young horses, and practise in the mornings. Those young horses threw me many a time, to the sound of cracking bones. Hans was a hard and very strict taskmaster, and I learned a tremendous amount the hard way.

There were regular race meetings from then on, and I participated in all of them. The racehorses available at Claratal usually had to be ridden to Windhoek a week before a meeting, and back again afterwards, and I had to help with this task.

Inevitably it was a long 50 kilometres – in order to avoid leg and hoof injuries, the horses were only allowed to be ridden at walking pace. Hendrik, Hans's very loyal Damara, looked after the horses and riders.

I took part in my last public race at the age of 21. This was a long-distance steeplechase over 3 200 metres, and I won easily on a thoroughbred stallion named Lucky Stone.

My only drunkenness

Hunting fever burned in me ever since I shot my first kudu and zebra on the Narachaams farm as a nine-year-old boy. On Narachaams I learned how to skin and dress game and process the meat. There were many kudus in the Windhoek mountains. I discussed my feelings with Moses, our Nama cattle-herder, and he was keen. From then on there would be no lack of meat at home.

I had only a .22 single-shot rifle, and this left me no choice but to shoot well and accurately. One simply did not wound game.

The first kudu I shot in this manner was a young cow. The bullet must enter obliquely just behind the shoulder, slightly from behind, so as to penetrate the heart. If the shot is true, the buck will flee for 50 paces at most, and then fall down dead. If you are close enough, a head shot from directly in front into the brain, or a shot behind the ear, where the skull and neck join, or from the side, on the line between the eye and ear, may be equally effective.

When I had shot a kudu, it was a matter of honour to bring back home all the meat. One does not shoot an animal simply to take home the best cuts, leaving the rest behind.

One weekend, a long way from home, I shot a large kudu bull. I was on my own, as usual. I skinned and cut up the kudu as I was taught on Narachaams, and hung the meat in a tree to dry. As usual I hid the rifle in a crack in-between some rocks, because my rifle would be forfeit if I were caught with meat *and* rifle. Riding through the mountains, I took home as much of the best meat as I could. I then saddled one of my horses who was familiar with this work, and rode back to where the rest of the meat hung in the trees. I loaded the meat in such a way that the weight was distributed evenly on both sides of the horse. Then I led the horse back home. If any meat was left, I would have to repeat the process. I always planned my hunts to coincide with a full moon, or close to it, because it gave me the entire night to complete this task.

I managed to get the last of the kudu meat home early on Monday morning, just before I had to go to school. It was an icy night, and I was dead tired and half frozen, but dared not skip school. I went to class after a hot bath, but without breakfast. That was a difficult day in class, as my eyes would not stay open. Eventually I had to trudge back home on foot. I couldn't rest on my laurels that afternoon, because the meat had to be processed. As I was turning the meat mincer, one of my mates turned up. He helped a bit, and just before it was time to feed the horses, he suggested that we should have a party.

There was a cave in the mountains where I often slept overnight, and where my mates and I met to hold councils of war when we played cowboys and indians. My friend suggested rounding up a posse of pals for a jolly braai in the cave. If I brought the meat, they would supply the drinks.

Because it was such a bitterly cold night, my mother gave me a bottle of red wine, as well as spices, sugar and a recipe for Glühwein.

When I arrived with the wine and meat, a fire was already going, and the lads were busy making Glühwein. I had no idea what they had put in the kettle before my arrival – I only knew that it was sweet and smelled great. By this time I was dead tired, very hungry and thirsty, and I felt cold from all the hard work of the previous day and night.

My bottle of wine and sugar were added to the kettle, and we began braaiing. We tasted the kettle's contents, which was sweet and delicious and hot. I singed the sausage perfunctorily, and began eating it more than half raw, proving just how hungry I was. My mates showed much more moderation than I. They knew their liquor, while I had no clue, and they also knew what was in that kettle. They kept on encouraging me to have another swig.

As I was sitting there, I became aware that the fire was moving. It swept upwards, then downwards, and the walls of the cave came closer and then receded. I realised I was tipsy, and went all quiet, because I felt ashamed. I can still remember how my friends stared at me intensely, and poked one another with their elbows.

I tried to stand up, but couldn't stay on my feet, and I fell into the fire like a wet sack. Fortunately I was wearing a large sheep-skin jacket which protected me from burns. I rolled out of the fire in a flash, beating the glowing coals from my jacket.

Suddenly all my mates wanted to go home. Some of them tried to help me, but I refused. I felt ashamed and defiant at the same time. I sat there quietly until the last one had left. What followed, was a nightmare. I couldn't stand, but had to crawl.

I eventually made it to my bed, and I closed my eyes and tried to sleep, but everything churned and spun – and then my stomach protested. Even as a kid I had always puked with conviction, producing a sound like an ox caught by a lion. At first I tried to suppress that sick feeling, but when I could hold it no longer, I jumped up and stormed outside, roaring all the while. I then gave my own private recital in the garden. When it was all over I eventually went back to bed.

Mom came to my room very early the next morning with a cup of hot black coffee and a cheery call of: "Get up, get up, my friend, out of bed and off to school, and hurry, or you'll be late!"

I tried to ward off the inevitable: "Mom, I'm sick, I'm deadly ill."

"No, no, if you want to binge, you must also be prepared to work!" she replied. There was no way out.

That lesson lasted me the rest of my life. For years and years I couldn't stand the smell of wine or other alcohol.

My years as a pupil at Voigtskirch

I did not want to continue my studies after matric, and my mother decided to send me to old man Hans Wiese at Voigtskirch, at that time the manager there. Wiese was a blacksmith by trade, and was a farrier for the army in Germany for many years. He then came to South West Africa, working as a farm manager. He remained a soldier at heart, and most certainly never took anything lying down. My mother picked him to teach me manners, and when they reached an agreement on my appointment, he was naturally given the required instructions to take me in hand.

In the next three years of managing the Voigtskirch farm I learned about breeding stud horses, stud cattle and stud karakul sheep. If there was time, we went to the smithy where Hans taught me blacksmithing. Everything had to be made by hand. "You need a hammer, a chisel and tongs; you make everything else yourself," he always said. Welding equipment was unknown. I learned to forge iron with the help of a clean coal fire, and to make horseshoes, and tools for the farm and smithy. I liked blacksmithing very much, even though I sometimes suffered. Hans employed the work in the smithy as a means to soften me up. If he considered that I needed to be brought to heel a little, we went to the smithy early in the morning. I was then given a 7-kilogram hammer to do the rough work, while he indicated the rhythm by beating on the anvil with his small forge-hammer. Depending on his mood, we sometimes started in the morning and finished only in the evening. Initially I tired quickly, and when breath was in short supply, Hans simply asked: "But surely you're not a softy?"

I decided not to complain, and saw it through. When we finished in the evening, I stood before him, laughed in his face and left the smithy whistling a little tune, even though my arms and shoulders felt painful and numb. Others to whom he had spoken about me, later told me that he said: "I can't bring the guy to his knees, or tame him!" Apparently he said this with grudging admiration, something I did not expect from him. In his presence I was always a lowly private who had to suffer.

Voigtskirch is a cold place, perhaps the coldest in South West Africa. It lies at a high altitude, on the watershed east of Windhoek. Even in winter, at the break of day when it was still quite gloomy, the old man waited for me on the "parade ground", clean-shaven and dressed in clean jodhpurs, shining riding boots and a neat jack-

22

et, baton in his right hand and hands on hips. If I was not on time in the gloaming, the old man called out loudly and clearly: "Peta, where are you? I'm waiting for you! Have you fed the rams, are the horses fed? Quickly, wakey-wakey. You're taking too long, laddie!" I could judge his mood from his tone of voice. You had to spark and stand before him with a notebook and pen, and then repeat all the day's instructions verbally and write them down in your diary. He did not know the word "forget". You never heard the end of it if you said "I forgot" when you reported back in the evening.

One cold morning it was still dark when he called me, and I could clearly hear that he was upset. I had gone to bed late the previous night, and was in no mood for a lot of nonsense. In his opinion I had taken too long to present myself, and he had a lot to say about that.

I was feeling quite cross when I went into the feed-store to get feed for the rams. While I was bent over the bin, I unexpectedly felt a tremendous blow from behind, and ended up face first in the bran in the bin. When I surfaced again, quite chagrined, I saw a large thoroughbred ram standing there with a snotty nose and an expression on its face as if to say: "Hurry up, laddie!" My anger boiled over, and I grabbed his ear with my left hand and gave him a whack on the head with my fist that would have been enough to knock out anybody, but did not seem to bother the ram. I was ready to hit him a second time when the old man appeared around the corner of the gate. He approached me hastily, his baton ready. He stood in front of me and shouted that I should not take out my anger on the animals, nor glare at him like that before he had had his first cup of coffee. I felt my self-control slipping, and quickly walked away to my room. There I noticed that my entire body was trembling with rage, and I began to cry. I sat on my bed for some time until I calmed down, then went outside and continued with my work. Fortunately the old man was away (perhaps getting that first, very important cup of coffee). It was touch and go or we had tackled each other. Had we fought, it would have been quite ugly. Only respect for his age kept me at bay.

On another occasion I was dispatched to Windhoek with my workhorse Banner and a few other horses. I had to erect jumps for a showjumping course, in which Banner and I would later compete. Banner was a very difficult horse with a "cold back", who pranced about like a rodeo horse every time he was mounted for the first time every day. He was quite capable of prancing about in one spot for a full five minutes. When he leapt into the air, he turned his body a full 180 degrees. He also kept bucking in one spot, all the time bellowing like an ox having its throat cut.

I always ended up flat on the hard parade ground before he allowed me to ride him. Only when he had managed to get rid of you could you mount and ride him, but you had to be careful with every movement you made.

I went to stay with my mother in Windhoek. My old stallion Kastor (still a good racehorse and jumper) was kept in our stables in Windhoek. He was out of practice, but he still remembered everything I had taught him before I started working at Voigtskirch. I entered him in the same showjumping event as Banner.

On the day of the event I saddled Kastor with an old saddle which I kept in my saddle-store in Windhoek. The showjumping competition was one for "power-jumpers" where the height counted, and not the time taken. We jumped round for round, and eventually all the competitors apart from Banner and Kastor had dropped out. I had to jump against myself. The height of the jumps was increased after every round. I was in the middle of another round on Kastor when the cinch of my old saddle broke. I did not want to waste time, so I simply moved forward onto Kastor's withers without breaking his gallop, pulling at the saddle behind me and letting it drop to the ground. I completed the jumps without a saddle, and it was another faultless round. The spectators rose to their feet, cheering and applauding. Walo Suntheim, from whom I had bought Kastor, came running up with a new saddle, saddled Kastor and could not shower enough praise on me. After Kastor was saddled anew, I once more jumped both horses against each other twice, and each round on each horse was faultless. With the jumps at a record height, the officials asked me whether I wanted to continue with both horses, or would rather have both declared the winner. I was very proud of Kastor's performance, and because he was not trained for this, I decided to call it a day. Both horses were declared to be the winner of that particular event.

I felt like the luckiest person on earth. People came from everywhere to congratulate me. Old man Wiese wasn't there because he'd decided to stay on the farm.

The competitors and officials decided to get together for a party that evening. Then the telephone rang. It was old man Wiese.

"What happened?" he wanted to know bluntly.

"I won with both horses," I replied proudly.

24

"That's not the point! What about the saddle; why did the saddle break? You should have checked it."

"It was my old saddle," I replied.

"That doesn't matter, you should have checked it and prevented it from happening. If you had been with me in the *Wehrmacht* in those days, I would have confined you to the barracks for three days on black bread and water!" he answered.

Rage and disappointment rendered me speechless. I said only one word: "Perhaps." Then I put down the telephone.

I did not stay for the rest of the party, but sat on the back of the farm's pick-up truck, very disappointed and angry, until the people drove home. We got there at midnight, and the old man was already sleeping. The next morning, without any greeting, he told me curtly that I had to break 2 cubic metres of rock for building purposes every day for the next three weeks. The rocks were granite, and one really had to swing the heavy pick-axe all day to break up 2 metres of rock. Only suitable building-blocks counted, and much of the broken rock was simply rubble. For the next three weeks I trudged off to the quarry without breakfast to break rocks all day. Just the right thing to rid you of all your anger. Between ten and eleven every day the old man arrived on his dressage horse Distel. Without any greeting he looked down at me from his horse, and I stopped working, rested my arms on the big, heavy pick-axe, and looked him straight in the eye. Neither one of us ever said a word. This silent ritual continued for a full three weeks. Late in the evening, when I returned, I always waited for the old man to finish eating, and then I sat down at the table. Irmchen, his wife, usually came and sat next to me, and talked to me. She had a wonderful personality, and we understood each other quite well. She often tried to persuade me to apologise to the old man.

Later she told me that if I persisted with this attitude, the old man would dismiss me. My mother, who had come to hear of the situation, phoned me and begged me to make peace.

One evening, while the old man was sipping his glass of jeropigo, I buried my pride, walked over to him and started talking. I had hardly begun or the old man said: "Yes, it's all right, let's forget all about it!" That broke the ice.

From that point on we got along fairly well, and we had mutual respect for each other. He never told me this himself, but I heard it from other people.

The old man often used me to get some of his beloved jeropigo for free. The farm was known all over South West Africa as the place where the best and hardiest thoroughbred horses were bred, with warm-blooded imported stallions as the sires. The farm's outstanding eventing horses (showjumping, dressage and cross-country), with their great stamina, were equally well known. I had to train all the young horses and ready them for shows and subsequent sales. Amongst those young horses there were many tough ones, with all manner of quirks. The progeny of the imported Trakehner stallion Ermanrich were well known for their stubbornness. The worst amongst them rolled on the ground as soon as one saddled them, and tried to get rid of this burden on their back, all the while making a sound like a pig when it's caught. Almost all of them had "cold back" problems. One had to saddle these horses very carefully, keeping the cinch as loose as possible, and then lead them for quite a while, gradually tightening the cinch until the tension was correct.

Many foreign riders visited Voigtskirch. Aunt Irmchen usually met the guests in Windhoek in the afternoon, arriving at the farm in the evening. Old man Wiese was then mostly seen in deep conversation with them over a glass of pre-dinner jeropigo, talking about horses and riding. At the same time he probed the riders; he had good insight and could sum up someone quite quickly. If he thought someone was too ambitious, he assigned a particular horse to that person for the next day's ride.

I was given my instructions before the outride (regarding which horse was to be used, and how it was to be saddled). We had a good mutual understanding, and instructions were unnecessary. The three blacks who tended to the horses were also clued up. Fritz, the foreman of the stable-boys, had been in service for many years.

The saddled horses stood waiting for their riders on the "parade-ground" in a neat line. The cocky riders were hardly seated, or they were unseated again. "I thought you could ride?" the old man would then say, all innocence. If someone dared to suggest that the horse was unrideable, the old man said: "Come on, I'll put my young Peter on the horse, and nothing will happen." A case of jeropigo was then wagered, and I would have to ride the horse. Once a "cold-backed" horse has rid itself of a rider and has finished bucking, it is quite happy and will accept another rider.

The outride then commenced. In the rainy season the White

Nossob flowed through Voigtskirch, and one could really appreciate the natural beauty of it. Many eroded dry gullies and dry rivulets ran into it, and large indigenous thorn trees grew all along the river. There were also many thorn trees that have fallen down and that provided natural obstacles, interspersed with gullies as well as inclines and declines. Any eventer's dream. The ride always took place along the banks of the Nossob, and usually provided the riders with a great deal of fun.

Among our horses were also those who were naturally hesitant, and during the cross-country one had to be particularly vigilant. A horse sums up its rider very quickly, and reacts accordingly. If certain horses refused the jumps and the frustrated riders gave up, the old man usually said: "Well, I thought you could ride. I'll put my young man Peter on that horse, and he'll complete the jump at the first go. I'll wager a case of jeropigo, man!" Their pride hurt, the riders usually took the bet, and then I had to make sure that the horse cleared the jump at the first attempt. I knew the horses because I had trained them myself, and I knew what to do. In those days I earned £2.10s a month, and I could certainly not afford a case of jeropigo. If I failed, I would have had to buy the old man that case of jeropigo. That was our mutual agreement. As a result the old man often got his cases of jeropigo for free during these visits, and there was always enough in stock to last until the next visit.

Those three years at Voigtskirch were very pleasant. I had to work hard, but that never bothered me. The things I learned from old man Wiese served as a strong basis for the rest of my life. As a young man I made the most of my time at Voigtskirch. I usually made a deal with the local blacks and hitched a lift with them on their donkey carts to some remote outpost. I then slept in the veld and went hunting on foot the next day. If the hunt was for the pot, Aunt Irmchen usually took us out in a vehicle, in order to bag a kudu in quick time. That was for the kitchen and the blacks, and we usually shot a kudu cow. There were plenty of those. I didn't like this kind of hunting very much. I felt it was simply a "meat-producing" process.

Whenever I really wanted to experience nature, I struck out on foot all by myself. Game needed a chance to smell, hear or see you, and to flee. When the first game fled, it could take a long time before you saw anything again, because the game watched one another, and fled together. Furthermore, there were tattle-tales, such as baboons, grey louries and korhaans. Nothing is more frustrating than a troop of baboons following at a distance, on the hilltops, and telling the whole wide world of your every movement. Or a lourie flying from tree to tree directly in front of you, all the time repeating his penetrating "waaay" call.

Nothing gave me more satisfaction than hiking through the thick bush to find fresh game tracks, to follow the tracks and eventually, often after hours of tracking, managing to outwit the game. One is then able to bag the buck you want with a single well-aimed shot.

However, I was not there simply for the hunting. I also wanted to find bees' nests, and I often walked about in the veld for hours, armed with a knobkerrie, looking for bees' nests. There were bees' nests in hollow tree-stumps and trees, nests in abandoned anthills, in crevasses in the rocks and even in aardvark burrows.

In the mountains near Windhoek, on Miss Ecke's land, there was a bees' nest that was notorious for the aggressiveness of the inhabitants. You might be quite some distance from the nest, but they would come and enquire what you are doing in their backyard. The entrance to the nest was quite black from the smoke made by people who had tried to raid the honey.

I dreamed up a plan which in the end proved a failure. I put on an old Tommy helmet of my mother's, as well as long khaki trousers, with the bottoms tied off with string. Then came a thick army greatcoat and a piece of mosquito netting draped over the helmet and tucked into the greatcoat. To protect my hands, I put on thick leather gloves. I probably resembled someone trying to land on the moon, rather than a honey thief. I asked my friend Helmut Machts to come with me to help carry the basins and buckets – I was determined to take home a lot of honey.

The nest was 3 metres above the ground in a fissure in the rock, and it took some clambering to get there. I had decided not to make a fire or smoke, and that was a huge mistake.

At about 50 metres from the nest my friend Helmut decided that was quite close enough, and lay down in the tall mountain grass. I had to carry all the basins the rest of the way myself. As I was climbing up the crack, the bees came for me. I felt quite unconcerned, because the netting and clothing protected me quite well. Eventually I reached the entrance, and by this time the bees were peppering the Tommy helmet until it sounded like drops of rain. I still felt no concern. However, I had to force my upper body into the fissure to reach the combs. The large Tommy helmet scraped against the sides of the fissure, and when I bent forward a little more, I could hear the mosquito netting tearing. And then the bees really got to work on my face with their stings! I tried to hang on, but the burning sensation on my face became unbearable, and I made a very hasty retreat. There was no question of turning around inside the narrow fissure, and I had to crawl out backside first. Eventually I reached the rock face outside, and jumped the 3 metres down to the ground without any hesitation. Once on solid ground, I rolled around in the grass to get rid of the bees, but in vain. The enraged insects were all over me, and the dam in front of the house was my only salvation. I had to run around a knoll to get there. In the process I rid myself of the army greatcoat and shirt, because bees were covering my torso by this time.

When I eventually made it home, I dived into the dam without any hesitation, and stayed completely under water until I was forced to take a breath. Only then did the bees let up. I eventually stumbled inside and plopped down on my bed, a psychologically and physically shattered man. My entire body felt as if it was on fire, and I was whimpering like a baby with colic.

My mother carefully scraped the stings from my face, neck and torso with a blunt knife. She later told me that she had scraped off 62 stings.

My years on the Onguma farm

After working at Voigtskirch for three years, a Mr Böhme came to the farm to buy a stud stallion for his farm, Onguma. Mr Böhme was an elderly, lean and tall man, half blind and with only one arm. His left arm was crushed by a lion that was caught in a trap, but still managed to attack him. His weak eyes were the result, according to him, of using anti-malaria medication for many, many years. His farm, Onguma, was situated at the extreme edge of the northern farmland area. It lay to the west of the Etosha Game Park and to the north of the Manghetti region. These borders formed the Red Line. In those days everything north of the Red Line was Crown Land – a buffer zone between farmland occupied by whites, and Owamboland (Owambo today). It was still wild and untamed territory.

Mr Böhme stayed at Voigtskirch for two days. At night he told many stories about life on the unfenced farm of some 20 000 hectares. He was urgently looking for a young man to act as farm foreman. Everything he said convinced me that this was the place for me, and with the approval of old man Wiese I concluded a working agreement with him.

The years at Voigtskirch had been wonderful and educational, and working under old man Wiese had created a solid foundation for the rest of my life. It wasn't easy to take my leave of Voigtskirch and the people there, but old man Wiese understood.

As a parting gift he gave me my workhorse, Banner, as well as a large black stallion that threw me almost every day. Nobody would be able to ride him in any case. To get to Onguma, I had to take my horse to Tsumeb by rail, and then ride to Onguma, a distance of some 135 kilometres along a winding road across many farms.

The further north I went, the lusher the vegetation became. There were beautiful makalani palms on all the farms, and other trees that were new to me. The climate was noticably warmer. I arrived at Onguma on the afternoon of the second day. I immediately noticed five beautiful lion-skins draped on a wire fence. This must have represented an entire lion pride, because some of the skins were those of young lions. I was most surprised, because at Voigtskirch Mr Böhme had told us that he could no longer shoot lions due to his poor eyesight and one arm. When I asked him where the skins had come from, he replied: "I poisoned them. I was losing too many head of cattle." I felt very disappointed, because I abhorred poison.

In the evening, at table, there were always lion stories, and I asked Mr Böhme to stop using poison. I wanted to take full responsibility for the cattle, promising to track the lions in the bush on foot, and to hunt them honourably. He just laughed at my suggestion and said: "You'll never do it; the bush is far too dense, and the lions far too cunning." I immediately saw this as a challenge, but kept quiet. I thought to myself: we'll see.

My first lion

I had hardly been at Onguma one week, or I asked Willie, the Bushman, to come with me after work to shoot a few guineafowl and to show me part of the farm. I took the .22 rifle, and Willie, the dogs and I took to the bush. The dogs soon sniffed out the guineafowl and chased them into the trees, where I shot them one by one with the .22. When we had bagged enough guineafowl, we walked back to the house in a wide arc. Suddenly a herd of cattle stampeded past us at full tilt, bellowing all the while. One of the last was covered in blood pumping from enormous wounds on its rump. I looked at Willie quizzically, and he said: "That's the work of lions."

I immediately started scheming, and I asked Willie whether he would track the fleeing cattle's spoor with me the next day. He agreed on the spot. The sun was setting, and we went home, where we discussed the matter with Mr Böhme. He was very sceptical.

"Nobody has yet been able to shoot a lion in this thick bush. They are far too fast," he commented.

Willie and I left the house early the next morning. I was armed with my .303. I gave Willie a shotgun, loaded with buckshot, to make him feel safer. We followed the lion tracks over a long distance, and by 11:00 we reached a dense thicket of thorn trees. Willie proceeded very slowly and quietly. When I asked him something in a whisper, he simply looked around and put his finger to his lips.

We had brought along some dogs who ran slightly ahead of us. About thirty paces from us the angry roar of a lion sounded, followed by the panicky moans of fleeing dogs. I could see the tail tuft and ears of a lion in the bushes where the roar had gone up. The dogs stormed past us on either side. We were standing behind a bush, and I had to squeeze off a shot before the lion was upon us. I therefore took two paces to the left and forwards, with the rifle at my shoulder. Then the lion saw me, and came to an abrupt halt in a cloud of dust. He made a threatening growl, his tail flicking from side to side. While he was standing about 15 paces from me, undecided, I aimed at the dimple below his neck, and pulled the trigger. The lion collapsed and just lay there. It all happened in a flash. I wanted to walk towards the lion, but Willie grabbed my shoulder and said: "Wait!"

While we were waiting, Willie said to me quite calmly, but with admiration in his eyes and a smile on his lips: "You'll shoot many, many lions!" I will always remember his calmness and his words. This gesture served as an inspiration for all my other lion hunts. Stay calm, don't lose your head, think before you shoot, and shoot accurately. That became my motto.

While we were still waiting, a prolonged moan issued from the lion. When the lion was completely still, Willie said: "Let's go."

I would often hear this moaning sound, and every time I shot a lion, I would wait for it before approaching the animal. The hairs on a dying buck's back rise, and a dying lion says goodbye with a moan.

For the first time in my life I walked towards a lion I had shot myself. Before us lay a beautiful young male, and I looked at him with a great deal of respect. I took off my hat and said a brief prayer of thanks. I still couldn't believe it. It had all happened so quickly. We now had to fetch a mule cart to pick up the carcass and take it home. Mrs Böhme drove the only motor vehicle, an old Willys Jeep, and it wasn't used for hunting. At that stage I couldn't drive yet.

I went directly to Mr Böhme the moment we got home. It was during the midday break, and as usual the old man was digging in his vegetable patch in order (in his words) to make up for the time he had lost during the war in the Koffiefontein concentration camp. "I shot my first lion, Mr Böhme," I reported. He first looked at me with his penetrating blue eye, and then his jaw dropped.

"Is this true?" he asked, clearly not believing it, but then he congratulated me with that enormously large hand of his. "*Donnerwetter*, Mr Stark, that's wonderful! You must be a special shot!" And then I had to tell him all about it, in the smallest details. Then Willie and I harnessed the mules and fetched the lion's carcass.

Willie, my black father

Willie, the old Bushman, became my black father. He was much more than just a very good friend to me. I learned an immense amount from him, because even though he was "just" a simple Bushman, he was also a philosopher. Willie had phenomenal tracking abilities and knowledge of the bush. When I got to know him, he was already about 50 years old, and was born "wild" in the bush. He was a Heikum Bushman, and enjoyed enormous standing amongst the Bushman tribe as a medicine man.

The West Etosha region was overgrown, sandy and as flat as a pancake. There are no mountains to help in gauging direction, only thick bushes and trees. When we began hunting together, I simply stumbled along behind Willie like a blind mole, never knowing where I was. There were three large fountains on the farm, and no fencing. The entire western boundary abutted on Etosha. This meant there was never any shortage of wildlife. Many hungry mouths needed to be fed, and so we hunted almost every week. We usually shot three animals during every hunting trip – far apart and in different directions. We then walked home, inspanned two oxen to pull a wagon, and once more ventured into the bush to load the animals. Willie always led the oxen. We often had to skirt around particularly thick bush, but nonetheless Willie always managed to head straight for the carcasses, without any hesitation or sidetracks, even though the carcasses were many kilometres apart. It was often dark before we managed to get home. I often had no clue whether I was coming or going, but I never saw Willie hesitating. It made me feel hugely inferior, and I began to ask many questions.

"Look at that tree, it grew in that particular way. Look at that palm tree, look at that little flat area, look at that crooked anthill," Willie would then explain. "Always watch your shadow, so that you know the direction you're moving in. Watch the stars at night," he would always say. When I had some time to myself over weekends, I went into the bush and started practising, using Willie's methods. In this way I extended my knowledge of the bush and was able to orientate myself and determine directions, until I was able to take the lead and bring us back home safely. This proved of immense value in my later life as a game warden, particularly in parts of the park that were still completely unexplored. I always took the lead on horse patrols, when we often followed tracks through the bush for 100 to 130 kilometres every day, returning to various camps at night, and also determined our direction. I have Willie to thank for all this knowledge.

Willie's knowledge of tracking was phenomenal. At first I doubted whether he was in fact still following tracks. He walked upright and usually quite fast, and initially it seemed to me that he wasn't tracking at all. Even walking right beside him, I could often see no tracks at all, and then I would ask him if he was actually still following a trail. With the help of his little tracking stick he would then point out the tell-tale signs to me.

Early on I always became very angry when we were following a lion's tracks and Willie would suddenly veer off to one side or the other simply to pick off some edible gum or fruits, or to dig up some tasty roots or tubers.

"What about the lions?" I would ask him.

"They're still far away," he would reply, and Willie was always right. He never got angry, and was always ready with some carefully considered philosophy. I felt small and humble on such occasions, and kept my mouth shut.

Often when I was walking behind him on a lion's tracks, I would resolve: I'm going to see the lion first today! But it was always the same: Willie stood to one side and with his stick pointed at a thicket in front of us. And there the lions were. One could often see only their paws in the long grass while they were snoozing on their backs in the shade of a tree.

Tracking

When tracking, the following is important:
- Examine the spoor and form an impression of its character. Consider, in other words, the size of the animal, possible misshapenness, and the way it moves, etc. This may come in handy later, particularly with regard to tracks made by wounded animals.
- While following a track, try to see it as far ahead of you as possible. This eliminates unnecessary tracking, leaving you to follow quickly, with a view to catching up. In suitable conditions one can see tracks up to 20 metres or more ahead of you.
- Try to keep the sun ahead of you as much as possible. The tracks then produce their own shadows, and become far more visible than in the afternoon, with the sun behind your back. With the sun behind you, you sometimes have to look around to make sure you are still on the right track.
- Use your tracking stick. This is a light type of knobkerrie made in the correct manner from the correct type of raisin-bush (it is baked and treated with fat). It can also be a formidable weapon. This knobkerrie is about 1,5 metres in length, and is straight.

You can use this weapon to bludgeon an unexpected snake; to dig for roots or wild tubers; to help you carry meat; to kill young sparrows sitting in the trees; to dislodge mopani worms from high branches for a snack; to fend off troublesome thorn branches when making your way through thick bushes; to turn aside tall tussocks of grass; and to make an opening in thick grass. When running as part of a group that is hot on a trail, you can use the club to indicate the direction of a spoor, or to gesticulate, without words, to another tracker that he needs to concentrate on the trail to ensure that he can take over should you lose it. You might also need the club when arresting recalcitrant poachers or to motivate such a poacher to give himself up. In an emergency you could even fend off poison arrows with it.

I found such a club to be a psychological aid acting as a point of contact between one's eyes and the tracks, which helped me to follow the signs more easily.

The colour of the trail gives you a good indication of how fresh it is. Fresh tracks look darker, with fine dust visible around the edges. This dust puffs up when you tread on a footprint. Dung and urine patches are good indicators. Broken grass-stalks or leaves are also good signs, taking account of the heat on the day.

Resting-places under trees are usually an indication of where the sun was in the sky while the quarry rested in the shade.

When talking to Willie, he could say things which compelled you to think, or to burst out laughing. He had a tremendous sense of humour, and was always ready with a quick retort. He spoke good German, and I taught him some typical overseas German hunting practices, with all the right vocabulary. He used these words when he accompanied visiting German hunters. It always gobsmacked them to hear these words from the mouth of a Bushman.

He had the most amazing stamina. I was never able to tire him out, even at his age, as I often tired out younger Bushmen, who would then lie down for a bit and later join us at camp. He could carry unbelievable masses of meat over long distances – something I could never do, or could never face. Most Bushmen are masters at this, easily outperforming bigger and stronger men.

Once a buck has been cut up, and the meat needs to be carried to a certain point, they will get hold of a makalani palm stalk (preferably) and remove the sharp points on either side of the stalk with a knife. The malakani palm stalk is then placed in the fork formed by a side branch growing from the nearest tree-trunk. The carrying-stick for the meat is evenly loaded with meat on both sides, and will hang slightly below the carrier's shoulder-line. The middle of the stick is bare, because that part will rest on the bearer's shoulders. The Bushman will then look for a second suitable stick, usually his club. When everybody is ready to go, the men will all place a shoulder under the bare part of the meat-laden branch and lift it from the tree-branch so that it rests on the Bushman's shoulder. The other stick is then placed on the unused shoulder and positioned underneath the load of meat behind the man's back. By shifting the pressure on the second stick he is able to lift the load of meat from the loaded shoulder, and this automatically spreads the weight of the meat more evenly across both shoulders. The load of meat is too heavy for the Bushman to lift from the ground, and so he will always look for a suitable tree branch at about shoulder height in which to hang the meat-carrying stick with its load. In this way they are able to carry the meat for many kilometres before looking for a suitable side-branch from which they can hang the loaded stick. This gives them an opportunity to rest and smoke. The Bushmen all smoke pipe, but often there is only one pipe to a group, and then this pipe is passed on from one to the next. When they have finished smoking, each man will manoeuvre himself under his own load and continue the journey until they reach their destination.

All Bushmen who regularly carry meat develop hard, prominent callouses on their shoulders, almost like horns. The bigger these callouses, the better and more skilful the hunter.

Another outstanding characteristic displayed by Willie was his companionship. He usually carried a little leather pouch in which he put everything edible found in the bush. We ate when we rested in the shade of a suitable tree at about noon. Even if the pouch contained only one raw wild tuber or edible bulb, this was divided fairly and shared. Willie normally carried a fairly large water-bottle, and this water, too, was equally shared. The only thing I kept to myself was my pipe, but I was quite generous with my tobacco – something I always have a great deal of.

We often took no water with us at all, particularly in winter, preferring to sustain ourselves solely with so-called water-roots ("kambro"). Sometimes we were both pretty thirsty, and these roots scarce, but if we found one, we shared it like brothers. This is something where the blacks beat us whites by a mile. Not only where food is involved – family members, in particular, help one another as a matter of course, putting us whites to shame in this regard.

I'd briefly like to tell you about Willie's stamina. When we went hunting, we could count ourselves lucky if we had to walk only 16 kilometres to shoot something. Particularly when we were tracking lions, we often covered distances of some 60 to 80 kilometres. We walked all day, non-stop and at a stiff pace, mostly in deep sand, through thick thorn bushes that clutched at your clothing, with the hot sun beating down on you and sapping your energy. In summer it was often 42 °C in the shade, and that kind of heat takes its toll. Of course there were interruptions, for example when we dug up water-roots or dressed some game or skinned a lion, but even then we were doing physical work. When Bushmen accompanied us, they would often remain sitting under a tree in the afternoon, looking at my bare feet and saying: "Let those paws carry on; we'll come later." Willie and I then continued, and at the camp we would long since have made and drunk our coffee when the rest of the Bushmen stumbled in one by one.

During these severe walks I always wore only light, cheap tackies with the front ends cut off for improved air circulation. When we pursued lions, I took off the tackies so as to make even less noise while walking, and eventually I walked barefoot most of the time, even in deep sand when the heat was at its worst. My feet looked quite horrible. They were always dirty – almost black – with splayed toes and long, deep cracks in my horny soles. My footprints looked a lot like tiny elephant tracks.

Including a few breaks, I worked on the Onguma farm for six years. In that time I underwent advanced riding training in Germany (early 1956 to the end of 1957), and also chose bricklaying as a career. On conclusion of these breaks I always returned to my beloved Onguma bush farm, and the people there.

Poacher

I'm by no means ashamed to admit, now, that I shot 75 lions during my years at Onguma, because all those lions had had an opportunity to escape, or to attack and send me to meet my Maker. I've always regarded lions as kings, pursuing and treating them as such. Mr Böhme kept about 2 000 head of cattle, and before my arrival an average of 62 per year were lost to lions. Unfortunately lions and cattle-farming are not compatible. I knew no better, I was on my own, unmarried, full of life and adventurous, and hunting lions was my great passion.

The lions wandered across the Etosha boundary and caught cattle every now and then. Sometimes one lion would take up to twelve cattle, devouring the fattest briskets and leaving the rest. We couldn't allow this to continue. The neighbouring farms also suffered a great deal of damage, and I had to go and help out there every now and then. Most farmers used poison, but the only time I ever touched a bottle containing poison was when I discovered some of Mr Böhme's poison somewhere. I would then grab that bottle and bury it somewhere in the bush, making sure the hole was deep and far away. The old man often searched far and wide for his poison, but in vain.

Often when a lion ingested too much poison at a time, it would regurgitate it immediately, without dying. It would be very ill, but would live. Many farmers also set traps. The lions often freed themselves from such traps. If a lion had taken in poison at some stage but had not died, and had also freed himself from a trap, you knew you were dealing with a very cunning customer. They would bring down one or more head of cattle on a single occasion, finish feeding, and then disappear back into the reserve the same night, staying there for a few days and repeating the pattern a week later. In those days if you asked Nature Conservation for help, your pleas fell on deaf ears, because they simply did not have enough personnel. In any case, the relationship between Nature Conservation and the farmers was not of the best.

We often followed lion tracks, only to turn back at the reserve boundary. A week later the same lion would again catch cattle on the farm. Because we got no help, I helped myself.

Willie and I crossed the boundary at suitable places where the ground was hard and we left no tracks. We then picked up the tracks of that particular lion inside the reserve, followed it and shot it.

As I gained experience over time, and also had the use of suitable dogs, I took along a second tracker armed with a Remington .22 rifle. The lions usually fled in the direction of Fort Namutoni, where the South African Police and the game warden were stationed. There were many waterholes in the area around Namutoni, and game in abundance, so it was a natural habitat for the lions. Often we passed perilously close to Namutoni – so close that we could actually see people walking about there. It would have been disastrous to fire a .303 rifle so close to the fort. Yet I wanted my lions! This was where the .22 rifle came in. Eventually I had fantastic dogs, but usually took along only one or two. When the dogs had found the lion and were keeping him occupied (a lion normally worms his rump into a suitable thicket, fending off the dogs with its front paws, and trying to bite them), we crept up close to the distracted lion and killed it with a .22 shot to the head. This was only in exceptional cases, however; usually the .303 did the work. The police at Namutoni also employed skilled Bushman trackers, mainly to find Owambo deserters who had broken their contracts with farmers and then fled past Namutoni on the way to Owambo-land. We had to keep out of sight of these Bushmen.

If we were successful, and shot a lion or two, they were skinned, and the head cut off. We then covered the carcass with sand, branches and grass, and took home the head and skin. We walked on tufts of grass and hard soil as much as possible. At home we took the mule-cart and splayed open the skins in suitable places about 10 to 14 kilometres from home, salting them thoroughly and covering them with thorn branches to discourage jackals and vultures. We took the skins home again when they had been properly dried.

The carcass left behind in the reserve usually remained covered by the sand for two or three days before the jackals dug it up. As long as the human and lion scent is still strong, the jackals and hy-enas will avoid the carcass. Wherever the vultures gather on the ground, the Bushmen are not far behind, hoping to find some meat or marrow-bones. Then the truth was out: Namaquab (my Bush-man name) and his pal Willie had stolen another lion! By that time our tracks were too old and faded to follow. It often happened that Anton, the black policeman at Namutoni, would arrive at Onguma on his bicycle about four or five days after our visit to the reserve to do some shopping at the shop on the farm, and to carry out a rou-tine patrol. After his departure Willie would tell me about Anton's rather queer questions. None of the farmworkers were prepared to answer Anton's questions honestly.

Some of the Bushmen that the game warden sent out were mem-bers of Willie's family. They told Willie everything that happened at Namutoni. This meant that I knew what the game warden had in mind for us, and what he was planning. I therefore heard that the game warden was determined not to let us get closer to him than 50 paces – he would rather shoot the "bloody German" than risk confronting him and his big knife. I had made this knife from an old car spring-blade, and I still have it to this day. It became a cat-and-mouse game, and lions weren't the end of it. The challenge was simply too great for me. When the game warden was waiting for me at a certain spot, I entered the reserve with a few Bushmen, shot some game there, and carried home every last scrap of meat with the help of the Bushmen. One thing remained a strong principle for me my whole life long: One does not shoot game unnecessarily, and all the meat must be used.

I didn't shoot only in the reserve, but also on Onguma and the neighbouring Crown Land in the Mangetti area.

Bandy-leg

Bandy-leg was a large male lion I could never get at. He was particularly large, and the toes of his right paw were turned unnaturally to the right. Perhaps he had been caught in a trap, but managed to free himself. Certainly this lion had earned a degree in escapology, and eventually I developed the greatest respect for him. I have no idea how many kilometres I trudged on that lion's trail. When he was on his own, he usually walked a long distance and always lay downwind in order to have a sniff of our scent well in time. All we ever found, was his lair. At first we followed him beyond that lair, but always in vain. He found thick bush at the earliest opportunity and then circled around within it, with the result that we often followed our own footprints. I once saw him standing seven metres from me – a beautiful black-maned beast. But everything went wrong that day.

A bout of malaria had made me feel sick as a dog, and a severe headache made me wish for bed. Furthermore, I didn't have my .303 with me – the gunsmith was replacing the barrel. The old barrel was worn so much that you could push a round into the muzzle, with some play. I had taken my 8 mm Brenneke, inherited from my late grandfather. This weapon had a double hair-trigger, something I disliked a great deal. The rifle was very accurate, especially at long distances, but after every shot it was quite a struggle to remove the empty shell from the chamber. This weapon was totally unsuited to hunting lions at short distances.

Willie insisted that he had heard Bandy-leg roaring the night before and that he had seen fresh tracks in the morning. Although I was feeling rotten, I grabbed the Brenneke, and Willie and I took to the bush. Willie picked up the trail very soon, and we followed it into the reserve. We hadn't been walking long when Bandy-leg, who had heard us, stood up in thick bush. We hadn't expected him at all. I always shot very quickly. My method was to take up the play in the .303's trigger as I was aiming. As soon as the rifle-butt nestled against my shoulder, the bullet was sent speeding on its way. I wanted to do the same with the Brenneke on that day, but I squeezed the wrong trigger, and the shot sailed way over Bandy-leg's head. He needed no second invitation, and disappeared in a flash. Furthermore the shell once again stuck in the chamber, and I struggled to remove it. I blame my terrible physical condition for the whole sorry mess. I found my entire body shivering, something I had never experienced before. Anyway, Bandy-leg had stood only seven metres away from me in all his majesty, but was now gone.

On another occasion Bandy-leg was in the company of about twelve other lions. Mudschi, a large Owambo farm-worker, came to me one morning with tears in his eyes. He had trouble expressing himself. "The lions took all my goats. Come and help me," he said through the tears. I took my .303 and Willie, Mudschi and I went to the place where the slaughter had taken place. We came across 32 dead goats, Mudschi's entire store of wealth. Some had been partly eaten, others had simply been bitten and left for dead. The lions must have had a grand old time. There and then I decided that there would be hell to pay!

We found and followed the tracks of the lion pride. Bandy-leg was amongst them, and was walking at the very rear. About 13 kilometres out, we saw a lioness lying under a shrub and I shot her. The sound caused lions to jump up all over the place and flee. Willie grabbed my shoulder excitedly and gestured in the direction of the lions, but I simply loaded and shot, and within seconds it was all over. When we walked closer, three lionesses were lying dead. Willie asked me, with some reproach in his voice, whether I hadn't noticed Bandy-leg. "He was standing behind a bush to one side, and was looking at us while you were shooting," he said indignantly. Bandy-leg had once more escaped unscathed! We sent Mudschi home to fetch the ox-wagon, and Willie and I followed the tracks of the lions that had fled. We followed them to a large thicket, but had to abandon the effort at sunset.

We started tracking again the next morning, but immediately realised that Bandy-leg was no longer with the pride. He probably went his own way during the night. By two o'clock that afternoon we saw the pride again, and I shot another two. The other lions fled deep into the reserve, and we left them.

This is how it went for the rest of my stay at Onguma. We followed Bandy-leg on a number of occasions, but he outwitted us every time. He walked incredibly long distances, always downwind, choosing to sleep in impenetrable thickets. We saw his abandoned sleeping spots many a time.

To conclude the story of Bandy-leg, I must tell about the time when Bandy-leg was indirectly responsible for almost landing me in a big heap of trouble …

Hauled before the law

When I was appointed as a game warden at Etosha, I was given permission to keep two dairy cows and calves at Okaukuejo. I had to buy the animals from Tappie Sachse at Operet, and therefore had to drive through Onguma. I stayed there to have a cup of coffee and to greet everyone. As I was leaving, a group of my old hunting friends were waiting for me. They had seen my .303 in the pick-up truck, and asked whether they could borrow it. Bandy-leg had become very self-assured, as nobody was following him any more – and they wanted to bring me his skin. At that time giving or lending a black man a rifle was strictly prohibited. Furthermore, it was against my principles as a game warden to do something like that. Bandy-leg, however, was a great draw-card. Against my better judgement I gave Mudschi the rifle and a pack of ten .303 rounds; more than enough to bag a lion, too few to cause any other damage. I would come and fetch the rifle in about a month's time. I then went on to Operet, loaded my cattle and returned to Okuakuejo. Shortly afterwards it began raining heavily, and the roads became impassable. I could not go and get my rifle, so it was in Mudschi's possession longer than we had agreed.

One Sunday morning at Okaukuejo I was engaged in training my horses when a detective from Outjo arrived at my practice-ground. With little ado he asked me whether I knew a certain Mudschi and Bushman named Sam. I confirmed this. He then told me: "Sam is dead, Mudschi is in hospital, in a critical condition; both were bitten by a lion they were tracking." My blood turned to ice-water in my veins. It was alleged that the rifle found in their possession was my .303. He then asked me whether this was so. I could not lie, and explained the whole situation. He warned me that he would have to charge me.

Mudschi lived. He had been torn open from his shoulders to his buttocks, and three fingers on his right hand were badly mauled. The court case took place soon after he was discharged from hospital. His spineless brother, Kabobbie, had turned state witness. I spoke to Mudschi before the court case. He was wan and the pinky, ring finger and middle finger of his right hand were rigid. The great scars of the lion's claws lay upon his back. I asked him what had happened that day. Apparently he, Sam and Kabobbie had decided to go lion-hunting with my .303. They came across lion tracks and followed them. When they came upon the lions, Mudschi wounded a lioness and they followed her. The lioness turned on them and Sam and Kabobbie immediately ran away. The lion then overhauled Sam and bit him in the neck, killing him. She then left Sam and followed Mudschi. She caught up with him and raked open his back. While falling, Mudschi twisted around and shoved the rifle-butt into the lioness's mouth. They fought like this for a long time. Then Mudschi reached into the lioness's mouth with his hand and pulled her tongue to one side, which meant that if she bit, she would bite her own tongue. However, Mudschi sacrificed three of his fingers while doing so. Mudschi fought off the lioness for some time before losing consciousness. The lioness must have thought that she had killed Mudschi, so she left him and walked away.

In the meantime Kabobbie had run all the way home, and then went to the police at Namutoni to report the matter. The police accompanied him to the scene of the incident at Onguma. They loaded Sam's body and the wounded Mudschi, and took him to the hospital at Tsumeb. Mudschi remained in hospital for about a month before his wounds had completely healed.

I conducted my own defence, and decided to tell the whole truth. Representatives of Nature Conservation attended the trial, probably in hopes of seeing me behind bars, because the stigma of poacher still clung to me. I was given a fine of £30, with £20 suspended for three years. I paid the required £10, and was allowed to keep my rifle.

I still have that old .303, with the butt deeply scored by the lioness's teeth. I will never part with that rifle. One of my sons will get it as an heirloom.

High jinks at Onguma

There was another case of a lion taking a head of cattle at Onguma. I was at a riding meet at Swakopmund when a lioness took her chance, and on my return I investigated. The lioness was a loner, and judging by the amount of meat stripped from the carcass she must have fed to bursting. Then she wandered over to the neighbouring farm, Vergenoeg. However, it was too long ago to make any chase possible.

Vergenoeg borders on Etosha to the west, and the nearest waterhole was a fountain close to the reserve side of the border with the name Twee Palms. Twee Palms is about twelve kilometres east of

Namutoni, not far from Onguma. I knew with such a full stomach she would walk to Twee Palms at night to drink. It was almost full moon, which presented a good opportunity for waylaying her there.

A big birthday party was being held at Namutoni for former Sergeant Le Roux on that night. The Böhmes and I had been invited, but I preferred waiting for the lioness at Twee Palms.

At that time the gravel road from Onguma to Namutoni ran directly past Twee Palms. I told Mr Böhme what I was planning, and asked for a lift to Twee Palms; I would then be able to catch another lift on their way back.

At that stage I did not have a rifle with a telescopic night-sight, and because of its reloading problems my 8 mm Brenneke was unreliable on a lion hunt. I therefore borrowed Mr Böhme's old military 7 mm Mauser with a telescopic night-sight. However, I found this rifle to be very unwieldy because it was heavy, and had an unusually long butt. At that time I sawed off the butts of all my rifles to the same length to aid quick shooting, and the pressure point of all the triggers was the same. I practised daily with my .22 Remington; at the time I could not afford any other ammunition for practices. The Bushmen had to throw jam-tins into the air, or whirl them about on a long piece of string, and I then tried to hit these moving targets with my .22. I knew too well that quick and accurate shooting offered you the only opportunity to survive a lion hunt.

Armed with Mr Böhme's 7 mm Mauser, a hunting-knife and a blanket, I alighted at Twee Palms that night and sat on the ground with my back against one of the palm trees, about 20 metres from the waterhole. It was full moon; the very little wind there was, was in my favour; in the background the endless bone-white Etosha pan stretched out to the north. The little francolins were the first night visitors who came to the waterhole in little groups. Then the first squabbling zebra and wildebeest came to drink, accompanied by jackal. Then the giraffes and kudu. I sat waiting under the palm as quietly as possible, and the game was not aware of my presence. Eventually I tired, and stretched out on my back. My ears had to take over from my eyes – I knew that if a lion were to turn up, all the game would run away in panic. I lay like that for some time, listening to the animal noises. Suddenly the game scattered, coming to a halt some distance away amid much snorting and neighing; a sure sign that a predator or human was on the way. I sat up and looked in the direction in which all the game had retired. The lioness was coming from the direction of the Vergenoeg farm. Like a ghost in the moonlight; initially only the vague outline of a lion, and eventually very clear as the lioness approached. I aimed, and when the lioness lowered her head to drink, I slowly squeezed the trigger.

When the shot rang out, the lion leapt into the air with a roar, and spun about in front of me. I couldn't risk a second shot with her moving about like that, so I sat completely still, hoping that the lioness would not spot me.

I saw a vehicle's lights being switched on at Namutoni, which is situated on a hill in an area that is as flat as a pancake, so lights were visible from far away.

When you have a guilty conscience, you always expect the worst. Were the Böhmes returning from the party, or did someone else at Namutoni hear the shot? Sound can travel amazingly far on such a quiet night, particularly with the little bit of wind blowing in the direction of Namutoni. To top it all, the wounded lion lay down in the left track of the roadway. I was alternatively peering at the dying lion, then at the approaching vehicle. I hadn't yet heard the lioness's dying moan, so I wasn't sure whether she was dead.

I took a chance and slowly approached the lioness. She saw me, uttered a threatening roar, raised her torso and looked at me. A bad shot could be fatal at such a short distance. I tried to stabilise the cross-hairs of the scope on her forehead, but it danced about like a butterfly. The sense of shock following the lioness's roar, and the fact that she was still alive, as well as the vehicle which was steadily approaching, caused me to shake like a leaf. I stood completely still, trembling while I looked at the lioness. Then she sank down with a sigh. To make sure, I threw my hunting knife at her, but she was completely still.

By this time I could hear the vehicle approaching from Namutoni, and it certainly did not sound like the old Willys. There were four thin, scraggly thorn bushes about eight paces from me, but apart from the palm trees everything was bare. The thorn bushes had been trampled by the game and offered virtually no cover, but a drowning man clutches at straws. I quickly hid the rifle under one of the trees and rolled the lioness out of the roadway. I ran to the palm where I had been sitting, grabbed the blanket, sprinted back to the lioness and covered the carcass with the blanket. Then I huddled down and began covering the blanket with sand, hoping that it would resemble an anthill.

I was still busy when the vehicle's headlights began falling on me intermittently due to the bumpiness of the road. I had to get out of there, so I crawled back to where I had left my rifle. I fell on it and tried to make myself as small as possible. Very uncomfortably, with the rifle's bolt under my right hip, hands on head, I lay there under the thin little shrub, on top of the rifle and numerous devil's-thorns, trying to be as still as possible.

The vehicle came to a halt almost on top of the lion carcass under the blanket. A policeman in his dark uniform alighted. I thought this was it, but he walked to the waterhole some six paces away from me.

Then I heard the representative of the law calling to the people in the car to come and have a dip with him in the waterhole. I felt some hope. He wasn't there for me! Perhaps he hadn't even heard the shot!

A number of women's voices called back from the car: they couldn't possibly get out for a dip in a muddy pool. There was some argument, and eventually the policeman, a constable from Namutoni, returned to the vehicle. They sat smoking for some time, while I had to lie dead still with the rifle's bolt boring into me.

Eventually the constable took a turn around the waterhole in the vehicle and disappeared in the direction of Namutoni, spurred on by my fervent prayers of thanks. To this very day I cannot understand why he spotted neither myself nor the strange heap of sand. An hour later the vehicle containing old Mrs Böhme, her husband and their daughter Heinke turned up, and we loaded the lioness onto the Jeep. When I told them about my adventures, the old lady's pot-belly shook from laughing, and she seldom laughed. We brushed over the traces and drove home. The next morning, while we were dressing the lion, I made sure that it was the right one. It was indeed. There were pieces of red skin from the cow she had killed. It was touch and go, or I had had a brush with the law.

Catching game

Mr Böhme liked his tame antelope very much, and Mudschi (himself a good horseman) and I were delegated to catch him some eland calves and zebra foals. We were paid £3 for every live animal we delivered to him. We tracked the young game on horseback, chased them through the thick thorn bushes and then caught the calves and foals. We then used a lasso to tie the animals to a tree with a single trunk in such a manner that they would not choke or get tangled up against the tree. Willie and another Bushman usually arrived later on a mule cart, having followed our tracks, and then loaded the animals into crates on the cart. Then they returned home by the shortest possible route, leaving the animals in a boma. The eland calves were allowed to drink from our dairy cows, and the zebra foals from our jennys, until they were quite tame. Eventually the eland and zebras grazed in the open veld during the day in the company of the foster mothers, but late in the afternoon they were herded into a stout kraal to avoid the danger of lions. Eventually we fenced in a large camp with a game fence, and the animals were allowed to graze there day and night. Eventually we had gathererd a good number of game animals. Mr Böhme sold his game to game traders for £30 apiece.

This practice was a real thorn in the side of Nature Conservation, even though Mr Böhme had a catching permit.

One day someone sat on Mr Böhme's stoep, drinking coffee and talking. I could judge by Mr Böhme's voice that he was excited and irritated. After the man's departure Mr Böhme told me that this was the chief game warden at Etosha, and that he had alleged that I was taking game from the reserve. This upset me, and I was quite ready to let this chief game warden have a taste of my fists. However, Mr Böhme strictly forbade this. "There will be no fisticuffs on my farm, Mr Stark," he ordered. I felt a grudge against Nature Conservation in my heart, but little did I know that this very chief game warden would in later years be my boss. From that moment onwards I changed my main catching and hunting area to the northeast of Onguma, namely the Mangetti Crown Land. For the most part this is sandy area; the further northeast you go, the deeper you penetrate into the real Mangetti forest – beautiful, large trees with their characteristic thick trunks. Most of the trunks are hollow, and sometimes contain gathered rainwater. The wild Bushmen sealed these trunks after the rainy season, and for long periods they then served the hunters as watering-points. Only people living in these areas were allowed to use the water from these trees. The trees bear large numbers of oily nuts almost every year, and these nuts serve as a staple food to the so-called Mangetti Bushmen. The nuts are eaten raw, or lightly roasted or ground, with an oil-rich porridge prepared from the flour. Because Bushmen rarely wash (rain sometimes rinses them), the Mangetti nuts impart a characteristic odour, and the Etosha Bushmen maintain that the Mangetti Bushmen "stink".

Every year, just before the rainy season, the Bushmen burn down large parts of the Mangetti area. The grass begins to grow shortly after the first rains of the new rainy season, and this attracts herds of game, especially eland, but also wildebeest, zebra and gemsbok. Mudschi and I, and later also my wife, Elke, moved into the Mangetti with about ten dairy cows, dogs and three or four Bushmen, and stayed there for a month. We used the mule-cart, drawn by four mules, as our transport. Food consisted of maize meal, sugar and coffee. The cows supplied milk. We baked our own bread and churned our own butter. There was enough ammunition, four horses, tarpaulins and a light tent. Of course the pans had to be filled with water for us and our animals. We were very dependent on those pans, and if they dried up, we had to find new ones, or return home. We camped close to a chosen pan and quickly built a boma for the captured game.

As soon as the captured game had become tame enough, we put them into crates and took them to Onguma by mule-cart, left them with Mr Böhme and returned to the camp in the Mangetti. I regarded this existence in the wild as the best times of my life. Free, unfettered, a king in my own realm – yet it's not for everyone.

In the evening we sat around the campfire and most often roasted fat eland biltong, eating it with porridge or fresh bread. My wife played the guitar, and I accompanied her on a harmonica. We often awoke at night to the roar of lions, the plaintive sound of hyenas, or the cough of leopards. We often had to listen closely to determine whether we were hearing distant thunder, or the sound of a stampeding herd of eland or zebra that had been frightened by lions. The stars twinkled above us, as beautiful and bright as they can only be in the bushveld, and I sometimes lay awake for a long time, simply looking at that wonderful starry sky.

We always slept next to the fire, with a ground-sheet spread underneath the mattress, never in a bed. We had to use sticks to lift the corners and sides of the ground-sheet. This ensured that unwelcome guests like scorpions crawled underneath the ground-sheet, rather than under the blankets. A scorpion's sting burns like hellfire, and that means the end of any thoughts of sleep. And there are plenty of scorpions in that sandy terrain!

We saddled the horses early in the morning to go looking for eland. The eland were very tame at the beginning of the catching season. With the wind in our favour, we could approach to within 50 paces of a herd of eland at walking pace without scattering them. We could then pick a suitable eland calf at our leisure, and chase it with the horses. The more we chased the eland, the more wary they became. The horses enjoyed the chase, and as soon as they sussed out which calf was being followed, they took over the pursuit themselves. This sometimes landed the rider in big trouble. If the calf ran in between two intertwined thorn bushes, the horses, at full gallop, simply lowered their heads and followed the eland calf, with no worries about what could happen to the rider. You then instantly had to lower yourself onto the horse's neck, hold on for dear life, and hope you get to the other side of the thicket intact. What you looked like, was another matter. Usually there was blood streaming from your arms, legs and back where the thorns had raked you. This compelled us to wear a good deal of protective clothing, which created problems if you were out riding in the bush in the hot sun all day. We draped broad strips of leather on either side of the saddle to protect our legs and knees, and wore a leather jacket for the upper body. Of course you eventually looked like a real old-fashioned cowboy from the Wild West.

It was useless and cumbersome to take along a rifle. As mentioned before, I had made myself a short sword from a spring-blade. It was about 450 centimetres long, and about 10 cm wide at the back. It was always very sharp. Eventually this knife became my pocket-knife, dining knife, killing knife and if necessary machete, and it was a formidable weapon. I always wore it on my hip, and it eventually became part of my normal attire. The only thing I had to replace from time to time, was the leather scabbard.

When our supply of meat became depleted, I sometimes decided to kill for the pot. We usually picked a fat eland heifer, chased it in the direction of some large mushara trees, the horse running alongside the heifer, and then I plunged the knife into the eland's heart at exactly the right moment. Such an eland will normally run for another 20 or 30 metres before falling down dead. It may sound cruel, but compared to a well-directed rifle-shot, the effect is the same.

The eland comes to rest under or very close to a large mushara tree, and this is very important if one takes into account the hot weather conditions. One needs to slaughter quickly, drag the meat out of the sunlight and hang it in the tree branches as soon as possible. This is the only means of cooling that you have in the bush.

Still warm, the meat is then processed into thin strips of biltong, salted and hung in the shade of the branches to dry out. We also hung a few old rags or a shirt close by to scare off crows, vultures and other carnivores. As soon as the meat is dry enough, it is taken to the camp. There it is hung from the branches to cool off some more, and to dry out properly. Early in the morning the biltong is taken down, rolled into a blanket as a compact package and kept in the shade of a tree throughout the day. It is then hung again the next evening. Eventually the meat becomes bone-dry, and then it will keep for a long time. We normally roasted a piece of this biltong on the fire. When the biltong is bone-dry, you can grind it between two stones, eat it on bread, or cook it in eland fat in a three-legged pot, eating the mixture with maize-meal porridge. Very simple, but very tasty. An eland is a large animal, but we never wasted any meat. Every scrap of game was processed and eaten, and when everything was consumed, we hunted some more.

It may sound as if we massacred the eland. Of course not! I once specifically counted all the eland we encountered during the course of a single day-trip. We passed six different herds, and each herd was about 400–600 strong. Furthermore, we never subsisted only on eland meat. We alternated with zebra, gemsbok, kudu and warthog.

Very little meat can hold a candle to a year-old zebra mare or a suckling warthog. In this area I once shot a very lean warthog boar for his teeth. One tooth was 30,5 centimetres long, the other almost 23 centimetres. This boar's meat was useless to us.

Of course I also had many opportunities to hunt lions or leopards. It is almost more interesting to hunt leopard than it is to hunt lion. A leopard is smaller, but more difficult to spot because of its natural camouflage. It will also attack you from its lair far more suddenly than a lion would – without any warning.

One night I woke to the cough of a leopard. The next morning we decided to go and look for it. I saddled my horse Bento, a well-trained hunter; I could shoot from his back.

I took along two Bushmen as trackers, to test them. They were Owambo Bushmen, Stefanus and Hans (they later worked for me permanently). At that stage they were still *kaschoekoes* or beginners; I had only recently taught them to shoot, and in order to make them feel important, I gave them my .22 rifle. I took along my trusty .303.

We found the tracks of a female leopard quite quickly. She was hunting, because every so often the tracks led to the top of an anthill, or into a tree. The Bushmen showed good tracking skills. At one stage the tracks were indistinct, the ground hard and marshy, and the grass high. I dismounted from Bento to help with the tracking, and suddenly the leopard leaped up from inside an aardvark burrow and immediately ran away at full speed. One could only see the top of her head above the grass every now and then. I shouldered the rifle and fired at her head. I was leading Bento, who took fright at my sudden movement and reared. The horse pulled me backwards, off balance, as I was squeezing the trigger, and of course the sights were way off target. When the shot rang out, the leopard reacted by sinking to the ground with a brief roar, but kept on running. The leopard's reaction made it seem as if she'd been hit, but I first had to calm the horse, and couldn't reload quickly. The leopard disappeared into the tall grass.

A wounded leopard is not a comfortable companion. We followed the tracks very cautiously. In the meantime I mounted Bento with the loaded rifle across the saddle and the two trackers in front. Then the tracks disappeared into a stand of mopani trees. I rode around the stand, to see where the tracks emerged, but couldn't see anything. The Bushmen came to a halt beside the trees, but couldn't spot anything. I urged the horse forward, in the direction that the leopard had last been running, and then I heard a shot from a .22, the angry growling of the leopard and anxious shouting from the Bushmen: "*Hooeitere, hooeitere*" ("help, help"), they were calling all the while. I immediately turned Bento's head and was off in the direction of their calls at full gallop. Then I saw them. Like ostriches with wings outstretched, the two Bushmen were running across the plain with their open shirts almost billowing over their heads, and their heels almost touching the napes of their necks. The leopard was running behind them with great leaps, tail upright, roaring all the while. If the situation wasn't so serious, I would have burst out laughing. The only way of distracting the leopard would have been to position the horse between her and the flying Bushmen. I passed the leopard from the right at full speed, positioned myself between her and the Bushmen, then pulled up the horse and turned him in the direction of the leopard, feeling all the while that the leopard would be on my back the next moment. When I looked in the direction of the leopard, she had disappeared, but I could hear her angry growling from a nearby stand of mopani trees. Then I saw her lying there, facing me, about 20 metres away. There was no time to dismount, and I quickly shot from the saddle.

Quite unexpectedly she lay there, struggling. She couldn't get to her feet, and I dismounted and got in a quick shot to the head. The leopard lay still.

The Bushmen came trotting back from quite some distance away. Stefanus's entire body was shaking like a leaf in the wind, and both were quite grey from the shock. They struggled to say anything, apart from: "*Og, og ose kam te toke!*" ("Oh, we were nearly caught!")

We examined the leopard. My first shot, fired from the ground when she exited the aardvark burrow, had grazed her skull behind the left ear. The Bushmen's shot with the .22 had hit the leopard low in the stomach, which spurred her attack. My second shot, from the horse, was a bit high, just behind the shoulder, crushing her spine. Fortunately she was no longer able to get up after this shot.

It all happened in a matter of seconds. If I had not positioned myself between the leopard and the running Bushmen, at least one of them would have been killed or badly mauled.

Everything was recounted in great detail beside the campfire that night – again and again. Willie was rolling about on the ground and just could not stop laughing.

The ghost lion who would not die

One morning in the Mangetti, old Willie, Mudschi, Bushman Sam and I were on foot, looking for lions we had heard roaring the night before. Mudschi was carrying my 8 mm Brenneke, Sam had a short walking-stick and Willie was without any weapon that day. I had my .303.

By ten o'clock I heard the dogs making a racket in thick bush. They had tangled with a pride of lions. The thicket made it impossible to see properly. There was the sound of breaking branches, and a terrier shot obliquely past us, with a lion in hot pursuit. I could see the lion only for a fraction of a second, but it was enough to shoot. There was a dull thud, and the lion recoiled in mid-leap and disappeared into the thicket. Breaking branches could be heard everywhere as the lions fled after the shot. Then there was only silence. Of the six dogs, only the terrified terrier was left – the other five had been killed within seconds, and lay scattered about. We sat and smoked, waiting for the lion to weaken. It was an extremely humid, quiet day, and large rain-clouds were forming. I was concerned that it might rain and that we would lose the tracks.

It is almost suicide to follow a wounded lion through the bush without dogs, and we were all extremely nervous. For the most part Willie led and tracked. I was directly behind him, followed by Mudschi and Sam. We followed the footprints of the wounded lion slowly and silently. Then Willie came to a sudden halt, pointed ahead and turned his head as if he were listening intently, brushing his ear with one hand as a sign: I can hear the lion! Mudschi and Sam stood next to me. Mudschi and I were ready to shoot. About eight or ten metres ahead of us we could hear the lion breathing in a thick bush, almost like a dog that had been running. We could hear the slap of his tail, which indicated that he was waiting for us. We stood completely still, rifles at the ready, peering ahead. Not one of us could see the lion. Then the heavy breathing stopped: only the slapping of the tail could be heard. Still nothing happened, because the lion wanted us to come to him. Oh no, I thought, I'm not as stupid as all that. Using my hand, I motioned to Sam that he should throw his stick into the bush, and at that, the lion attacked. The bush ahead of us simply parted, accompanied by the lion's roar. Mudschi and I fired almost simultaneously. The lion flinched, turned tail with a hurt roar, and disappeared.

We had to start all over again. Once more we waited for a while, and then continued the pursuit. Once again we heard the breathing and tail-slapping after about 20 minutes. Once more Sam hurled his stick, and once more the lion attacked. Again the lion took hits, turned and ran away. This process was repeated another four times. After the fourth attack Willie stood ashen-faced and whispered in his language: "This is a ghost, not a normal lion, this is a ghost. Let's go back."

I tried to look calm, and grabbed his arm to encourage him to continue tracking. I was becoming desperate, and it took a lot of persuasion to go on. At that stage a small fork-tail took to the air from a branch ahead of us. Mudschi got such a fright that it looked as if he were about to turn head over heels. I was so startled by this that I almost gave him a thick ear there and then. We all suffered from nerves as taught as violin-strings. Following the fifth attack, the lion retreated a short distance, and when we approached for the sixth time, he could no longer stand up. Once again we fired almost simultaneously. Both shots went home side-by-side, obliquely from above, between the shoulder-blades, shattering the spine, and that was the end of the ghost-lion.

I have the skin to this day. It looks more like a sieve than a trophy. It was the most exciting lion hunt ever.

A close shave and the abandoned "tyres"

Wilhelm Hartmann, a coloured man, lived on one of Onguma's cattle-posts and was responsible for running it. He was the son of Mr Karl Hartmann, one of the famous six defenders of Namutoni when 600 Owambo warriors attacked the fort in 1904. In his day Wilhelm's father was a famous lion hunter in his own right, but was bitten by a lion on the farm Leeudrink, and died.

One morning Wilhelm came to us on Onguma, reporting that his post was experiencing a great deal of trouble from lions. We went to Grenspos by mule-cart and found lion tracks.

We followed the tracks for about 15 kilometres, and then came upon the pride. The lions were sleeping on the slope of a large ant-hill – one with its head on the shoulder of the next one. I aimed and shot at the top lion. Pandemonium broke out. The dogs who tried to block the lions' escape route were simply brushed aside, and the lion that had been lying half buried under the rest charged straight at us. I tried to reload, but is was too late, and I turned the rifle across my body to ward off the lion. When the lion was about two metres away from me, two fox terriers suddenly charged in between me and it. The lion bit the first dog on the neck, and pawed at the other at the same time. This gave me the opportunity to reload, and to shoot the lion at point-blank range. The other dog was lying at its feet, whimpering. He was mauled from his ear to his shoulder.

The first lion I had shot was lying about 20 metres away, with a bullet through his heart. All the other lions had disappeared, and so had Wilhelm Hartmann. During the pursuit he had maintained a respectable distance behind us. All he had left behind, were his two abandoned "tyres", forlorn under a large mushara tree. ("Tyres" were sandals made from old car tyres, the most common footwear worn by Southwesters at the time.) We called, and heard a rather frightened "Hey" from a tree. We looked up, and there was Wilhelm, swaying like a vulture in the top branches. It took a good deal of persuasion to coax him back to ground level. He told us shame-facedly: "I saw you shooting, and I heard the lions and the dogs, and I saw the lion coming, oh, I thought I'd be killed today, I left the shoes, oh, I climbed the tree!" Willie then told him his fortune, peppered with more than a few choice German expletives.

I realised that if it hadn't been for the two fox terriers, I may no longer have existed. The fox terrier in the lion's mouth was dead. The other had been deeply raked from his ear, across his neck and shoulder, to his right front leg. He lay flat on his side, and looked at me thankfully when I talked to him. This dog was named Poempie, and initially, on seeing those terrible wounds, I wanted to end his agony, but then I had second thoughts.

I gave instructions for Willie and Mudschi to skin the two lions, and left my rifle with them, in case the rest of the lions returned to look for their mates. Carrying Poempie, "Braveheart" Wilhelm and I returned to the outpost. I put the dog onto the mule-cart and returned to the farmhouse as quickly as possible. There I dressed the dreadful wounds with Datons Wound Powder, and sutured them to the best of my ability with khaki thread. I had no anaesthetics, and the nearest vet was at Tsumeb, 135 kilometres away.

Poempie lived, and became my most loyal dog.

I decide to become independent

A great deal of my work at Onguma consisted of building. We broke up large limestone blocks for this purpose. I was busy erecting a large feed-store with a saddle-room alongside it. I liked building with natural stone, because you had to use your imagination to pick the best blocks. The building was at window-height, and I had to stand on scaffolding to work. Willie was one of the assistants placing the large stone blocks onto the scaffolding. Part of this task was selecting suitable blocks from the heap. I asked Willie to hand me a specific block, but he began removing the wrong one. "No, Willie, that's the wrong one, it's that one!" I said. Willie's body language made it clear he wasn't very happy doing this work. He hardly looked up, and once more started removing the wrong block from the pile. Once again I tried to show him which one I had in mind. When, for the third time, he grabbed the wrong one, I lost my temper and shouted at him: "Willie, I want that stone, look at me, you damned arsehole!" Willie's reaction was typical. He stood up slowly, put one foot on the wheelbarrow, leant forward with an elbow on the knee of that leg, and stroked his scraggly Bushman beard. He looked up at me with a sardonic smile on his face, and answered very calmly: "You wouldn't be able to shoot a single lion without this arsehole!" Actually he is correct, I thought, and from that day on I took matters regarding bushcraft, hunting, direction-finding, survival in the bush and orientation at night into my own hands. In short, I learned to survive in the bush as a wild Bushman would.

I took to the bush on my own over weekends, and sometimes I got hopelessly lost, but eventually I would arrive at home or a camp, even if I were dead tired, thirsty and hungry. At night I used the moonlight to hunt with my dogs, spear, and bow and arrows. I tried to do everything the Bushmen could do, in my own way. I learned how to make Heikum Bushman poison, how to make arrows, bows and bow-strings. I learned bushcraft, and how to survive in the bush. When time permitted, I visited wild Bushmen in the Mangetti area and studied their way of life. It wasn't easy to become their friend, because many of them flee the moment they see a white man. Many of them had had brushes with the law, and were continually on the run. My knowledge of the Heikum Bushman language helped a lot to make friends with them. I always carried a supply of tobacco, which was much sought-after among the wild Bushmen. While I was catching eland, they came to visit me in my camps. Later on some of them began pointing out their hidden water supplies, which a wild Bushman regards as his greatest treasure.

My bushcraft improved, and it became easier to survive in the bush – often using only water-roots and other tubers. I gradually became more independent when it came to hunting lions as well. I continually practised my tracking skills, and later, when I worked for Nature Conservation, I often outsmarted the Bushmen. From the day that Willie told me my fortune on the building site, I began practising everything to the maximum.

One weekend Willie and I took to the bush with the mules, looking for a nice fat gemsbok. At some stage we saw vultures circling lower and lower. In order to keep any noise to a minimum, we steered the mule-cart close to a thick bush, lifted the shaft slightly to give the mules some respite from the weight on their necks, and tied the shaft to a strong tree-branch. The mules sometimes spent a whole day in the shade of a tree in this manner.

We cautiously approached the spot where the vultures were sitting in the trees, coming in from downwind. When vultures are still sitting in the trees, it means that predators or people were still in the area. Then we spotted the first lion tracks; a big pride. The

56

fresh carcass of an eland cow had been dragged under a tree, but the lions had gone. Judging by the amount of meat they had eaten, they could not be far away. It was a hot day, and the clouds were beginning to build up.

Lions don't like walking in the sun, and this presented me with a golden opportunity to hunt lions on my own. I asked Willie to take the mule-cart back to Onguma to fetch a trap that we could set near the eland carcass. I thought this was a decent way of getting rid of Willie for some time without raising any suspicion. Onguma was far away, and he would be gone for some time. Before he left, I pointed out a large mushara tree where I would be waiting for him.

As soon as I was sure he was far enough, I got up and followed the lion tracks. I wanted to make a success of it, and moved very quietly, shirtless and barefoot in order to make no noise.

After tracking for about six kilometres, I saw the backside of a sleeping lion about eight paces ahead of me. A shot from directly behind is very effective, and I aimed for the area below the tail, and squeezed the trigger. The lion leapt into the air with a frightened roar, and fled. The bush in front of me was suddenly alive with lions. I went down on my haunches and reloaded. When I looked up, a large lioness stood about twenty paces from me, growling threateningly. I aimed at the lioness's shoulder, and fired again. With a roar she leapt high into the air and also fled. Once again I reloaded rapidly and squeezed off a shot at a third fleeing lion. I hit this one, too, but obliquely from behind. All the lions were gone, and there was a deathly silence. I had to track three wounded lions, and I felt very, very alone. I pictured Willie finding my skeleton, picked clean.

To make the best of it, I walked to the tree where I had agreed to rendezvous with Willie. I sat there smoking for an hour to calm my nerves. Then I drew an arrow in the sand, indicating the direction I was going to take, so that Willie could follow my tracks when he returned.

The first lion I had shot from behind, was dead. The blue-bottles were already all over him. I didn't stay with him long, and was soon following the tracks of the large lioness I had shot in the shoulder. I found her carcass soon afterwards. The third wounded lion was still running quite strongly. I abandoned the trail, because I was afraid that the dead lions would begin rotting quite quickly in the heat. I went back to the big lioness. I rolled her into some shade, and began skinning her. It takes quite some time to skin a lion properly, because it's difficult to cut out the claws neatly. I was still busy when I heard a rustling in the bushes behind me. When I turned around, I saw Willie running towards me. "What are you doing?" he said, sounding relieved and reproachful at the same time.

I looked at him with a smile on my face and replied: "I wanted you to go away, so that I could get a chance to hunt on my own."

"Please don't ever, ever do that again," he said quite crossly, and repeated it: "Never, never again." I could see by his demeanour that he was very worried, even though he tried to hide his emotions. I loved Willie all the more.

We were still busy skinning the lions when the rain came down. This ruined any chance of tracking the third wounded lion, because the tracks would be erased very soon in the deep, soft sand. We went home in the dark and rain. We went out again early the next morning, and took along the dogs this time. It had rained virtually the whole night, and at the spot where I had shot the lions, vultures were sitting in the trees all around. We searched everywhere with the dogs until that afternoon, but the wounded lion had disappeared. I assume it was shot from behind in the haunch, without any bones being broken. Animals wounded in this way usually recover.

The best lion of all

A new rainy season had started, and it was time for ploughing. If one compares harvests in Namibia with those in South Africa, every Namibian harvest is a failure. Namibia is a dry country, with unpredictable rainfall. However, Mr Böhme was a firm believer in ploughing, even if it yielded only a few scrawny maize plants. The best crop was the very hardy type of runner bean which yielded a good supplementary feed for cattle when milled. To crown it all, Mr Böhme did not believe in a tractor. His single-share ploughs were usually drawn by oxen or donkeys. As soon as the first rains fell, the ploughing teams were busy everywhere, from early in the morning until late at night.

Experiments were conducted with zebra and eland as draughtanimals. A zebra was always placed next to a donkey, or an eland next to an ox. Mr Böhme wanted to prove to the other farmers that zebra and eland should be tamed for a useful purpose, rather than being shot. A donkey is not a good worker, but is useful; a zebra is almost completely useless. A zebra will use every opportunity to bite or kick, and simply falls to the ground as soon as it reckons enough is enough. Nothing can persuade it to get up again and carry on.

Eland have a good personality and are tamed quite quickly, but have very little strength or stamina when it comes to working.

Because Bushmen are by nature lightly built, and avoid confrontations with animals, Stark and Mudschi had to lead the animals, because we were big and strong, and not afraid.

I hated the ploughing season. Up, down, over the sods, through deep troughs, following in the footsteps of some stubborn animals. You were dealing with zebras or eland, newly trained young mules or donkeys, with one Bushman steering the plough, and a Bushman who handled the whip, and Stark or Mudschi leading from the front.

I often made a plan when all of this became too much. Using an old cream-can, I could produce a passable impression of a roaring lion. I also had a good collection of animal tracks made of plaster.

When the ploughing became too much, the lions were heard holding a concert very close to the house. They came to the cattle-troughs to drink, because that's where their footprints were found. Early in the morning Willie, all excited, then reported sighting these tracks. (Of course Willie was well informed the day before.) And Willie's judgement regarding lion tracks was never in dispute.

"*Na, Herr* Stark, I suppose you had better follow the lion tracks today to see whether you can bag one," Mr Böhme usually said. I was most eager to do this, and then Willie and I made a bee-line for the reserve. If we did not feel like finding lions, we soon shot a young warthog or springbok, had ourselves a lovely party in the bush, and came home late that evening, all "tired out". The lions normally made tracks directly for Namutoni, where we had to halt the pursuit. However, we did sometimes bring home a lion-skin.

Once I led two full-grown mules. At that stage I was the only one who could control them. I was soon on a short fuse because of the constant tugging at these big and strong mules. One morning, as I was struggling with them, Mr Böhme reprimanded me about the way I was handling them. I lost my temper at Mr Böhme's moaning and let him know in no uncertain terms what I thought of ploughing. I left the mules there and walked home. It was a Saturday morning, no less. Right there and then I decided that I'd had enough. I took my rifle and blanket, saddled my hunting mount Tankret, and rode to the Unizaub outpost without greeting anyone. Willie and another team were ploughing there. Unizaub is about 15 kilometres east of the house. I only got there late in the afternoon. Zampa, the Owambo manager of the outpost, gave me porridge and milk for supper, and I went to sleep a little distance away beside a fire. I had arranged with Willie that we would go into the sandy veld to look for lions, and he had agreed. The next day we ranged far and wide. Only in the afternoon did we see the tracks of a single large male. The midday heat had passed, so I did not think we would see the lion. Suddenly, however, Willie stood still and pointed ahead. A beautiful large black-maned lion was walking through a dense stand of wild quince trees (*Terminalea sericea*) about twelve paces ahead of us. It looked as if the red glow of the late-afternoon sun was being reflected in his thick mane.

As he was skirting a bush, he presented his side for a moment, and I fired. He collapsed with a strange "bo-bo-bo" grunt, and never got up again. When we reached him, he seemed to be the most beautiful lion I had ever seen. The sun was dipping low, and we decided to stay overnight right there. Willie collected some water-roots – our only water for the day. We were very hungry, and we skinned the lion by the light of the fire, and eventually roasted some ribs. Only our extreme hunger could make us force the lion meat into our stomachs, but I cannot recommend it! Quite apart from the predator smell, the meat is tough and rubbery, and the taste mimics the smell.

We rolled up the skin like a blanket the next morning, and took turns to carry it to Unizaub. The skin of a large maned lion like this weighs almost as much as that of a large ox. We reached Unizaub that afternoon. Zampa informed me excitedly that Mr Böhme had been looking for me all day. I simply showed him two fingers.

We rolled up the lion skin neatly and tied it firmly to the saddle. Tankret was then saddled with the lion's skin on his back. At first he snorted and rolled his eyes as if he were being paid for it. Very few horses will stand for a lion's skin on their backs. After I had led him some distance, I mounted and took the lion skin to Onguma.

I spread open the skin and salted it without saying hallo. I was still occupied with this when Mr Böhme arrived. "*Mein Gott!*" he said with admiration. "That's the biggest and most beautiful lion I had ever seen." He peppered me with a few questions, and then walked away.

After supper I had to tell about the lion hunt in all its details. The ice had been broken.

However, before we went to bed, I had to promise him that I would not simply disappear again without letting him know where I was going and what I intended doing. I later sold the lion-skin to an American film-maker for £50. At that time this was a lot of money – my monthly salary was £15.

I charged the American such a lot of money because he had angered me greatly the day before. He wanted to make a nature-film, and for this purpose we had to drive our tame herds of eland and zebra past his cameras again and again and again.

Eventually I became so cross that I simply left him, with his camera and crew, in the bush. And when he wanted to buy a lion-skin to boot, I saw an opportunity to fleece him with a take-it-or-leave-it attitude. He tried to negotiate for some time, but I wasn't interested. Eventually he bought it and paid cash.

The ghost in the night

One weekend in high summer, boredom once again spurred me on to action.

Willie, Stefanus and I entered the northern part of the reserve in the direction of the Andoni Plain Sandveld.

After walking for about three hours, we came across the tracks of two large male lions. After following the tracks for about another two hours, we saw a number of vultures circling ahead. Very cautiously, from downwind, we approached the spot where we expected an animal carcass.

Suddenly, about 20 paces ahead of us, we spotted two male lions under two low, green thorn trees. The lions immediately fled. I was able to squeeze off an oblique shot at the hindmost one, with a black mane. He collapsed and spun around. Then he came straight at us, but I shot him a second time, in the chest from straight in front. This slowed him down, but he still tried to advance. A third shot, from straight in front, next to his left nostril, was the end. It was a beautiful lion with a black mane, but not as large as the "best of the best".

The carcass of a large eland cow had been neatly dragged under the trees at the spot where the lions had been lying.

We immediately began skinning the lion, because it was an inde-scribably hot and humid day. Rain-clouds were already beginning to gather. While we were skinning the lion, Willie and I planned to spend the night near the carcass, waiting for the other lion. (Lions nearly always return to their fallen comrades.)

As soon as the lion was skinned, we folded the skin, and Ste-fanus took it home before returning for a night watch. Willie found some water-roots in the area, and that constituted the only food and drink for the day. There was more than enough eland meat, but we didn't dare light a fire – the smell of roasting meat travels a long distance.

Late in the afternoon we took our positions on the ground be-hind a bush, about twenty paces downwind from the lion carcass. We sat waiting in the dark, without moving a muscle, for about three hours. It was overcast, and some light rain began to fall.

Then the other male arrived. We could only see a grey shape; there was absolutely no sound at all. I could only shoot on instinct, because the rifle's barrel and sights were totally invisible.

When the shot rang out, the lion greeted it with an angry roar, and spun about. I did not risk a second shot, because that could have betrayed our position. It wasn't long before the lion fled, and we could hear the sound of his leaps.

When the tension became a little less, we began to feel the cold and wet. Fortunately Willie had collected some dry wood while it was still light. We managed to light a fire, although it was a struggle – Willie placed some wide strips of dry tree-bark over it to keep the burning wood dry. We sat waiting for the next day by a very small and smoky fire. It rained the whole night.

Every now and then we stripped, held our clothes close to the fire and put on the warm, steaming clothes. There was no question of sleeping, and our eyes were streaming because of the smoke. Eventually it was dawn, after what seemed like an endless night. The rain abated soon afterwards, and then stopped.

We tried to find the tracks at first light. The soft sand had been wiped clean, and we could see no tracks at all. We walked in ever widening circles, until Willie spotted very faint indentations in the sand. He was sure these were the tracks of the fleeing lion. We fol-lowed them very slowly, and with a great deal of difficulty.

Eventually the tracks became clearer, until we could actually see faint lion footprints. We followed the tracks until that afternoon. The lion had walked through the thick bush that fringed the Andoni Plain, further and further into the reserve. There were no signs of the lion resting, which meant that he was not badly wounded. By the afternoon I abandoned the quest and took the long road back. I felt tired and disappointed. I don't like leaving a wounded animal, but sometimes there is nothing you can do.

I still have the skin of that first lion to remind me of a horrible but unforgettable night.

Many lions, but no booty

One morning the foreman of the outpost at Ekaka came to Onguma to complain about being tormented by lions. His name was Kanjou, and he was Mudschi's half-brother.

Willie, Kanjou and I went to Ekaka by mule-cart. There we unharnessed the mules and left them in a kraal. The three of us then walked in the direction from which Kanjou had heard the lions roaring the night before. After walking for about two hours, we came across tracks, and soon after we saw vultures descending. The tracks indicated a large pride of lions, at least fifteen. Many vultures had already come to ground, so the lions had already left. We came across the stripped skeleton of a young eland cow. The lions had had their fill, so they would not be too far away. It was a winter's day, and not too hot.

We followed the lion tracks very cautiously and silently to a thick stand of yellowwood. We expected to come across the lions under a large, shady mushara or thorn tree. Willie carried my .303; I had my newly purchased 9.3 millimetre Husqvarna, and Kanjou, walking behind me, was armed with his knobkerrie.

We walked slowly and very, very silently, constantly looking for a probable thorn tree. At that stage the wind was in our favour.

I suddenly became aware of a strange feeling at my right shoulder, as if something touched me lightly. It was a feeling I can't really describe. I instinctively glanced to the right ... and saw a lioness's eyes about three paces away from me. She must have been quite as surprised as I was. You need to deliver a perfect shot at such a distance, or the lion will be at you in one leap. I lifted my rifle slowly and cautiously to put that bullet right between her eyes, but suddenly a shot rang out ahead of me. The entire thicket around us became a mass of lions, and then someone jumped on my back with screams of fear, I was thrown completely off balance and could

63

not shoot, as I was struggling to stay on my feet with all that extra weight on my shoulders. I eventually got rid of Kanjou only with some difficulty. I was very cross when I asked Willie why he had pulled the trigger. Reduced to stammering from the shock, he explained that he had almost trodden on a lion lying unnoticed in the tall grass behind a bush. He got such a fright that he instinctively pulled the trigger of the loaded rifle. Fortunately the bullet went straight up. He was probably as ashamed at his reaction as I was angry at him. He couldn't look me in the eyes, and his self-assurance was shot.

I found Kanjou's reaction to be inexcusable, and I was able to control my anger and disappointment only with great difficulty. It was all over in a matter of one second, and all the lions were gone. It was an impossible task to track them in the wild quince thicket. It would simply become another cat-and-mouse affair.

Kanjou was not used to this type of hunting, and regarded me as the only tree he could climb, as there were no other trees in the vicinity. When in doubt, climb the white man!

We felt very disappointed on the way home. The incident made me realise once again that on a lion hunt a frightened person was a greater danger than the lion itself. Avoid associating with such people!

The greatest distance at which I was able to shoot a lion during all my lion hunts was thirty metres; this was a lion running away from me.

The normal distance was between ten and fifteen metres. There was no alternative in thick bush. The first commandment of hunting was that thou shalt shoot quickly and accurately.

Great success, but little pride

On one of my last lion hunts at Onguma I experienced the exact opposite of the incident above. One weekend the Bushman Hans and I decided to look for lions in the eastern sandveld. Hans was in my personal employ, on Willie's recommendation. In his younger days Hans had lived in the bush, and he was no stranger to hunting, tracking and field-craft. Because he was relatively young, I could train him properly. Of course he also had to learn horse-riding, in order to help with catching eland. He was naturally brave and plucky, and his manner suited me. He also had Willie's sense of humour. On that day we walked a long distance before coming across some lion tracks, and it was already late in the afternoon. I had my new 9.3 millimetre with me. It could be loaded with six rounds – five in the magazine, one in the chamber.

The first lion we saw was a young male at a distance of about 17 paces, and he hadn't spotted us yet. My rifle was cocked, and I aimed and shot. I aimed for the spot where the neck and shoulder-blade meet – one of my favourite targets for a certain kill. However, it seemed as if the lion was about to get up, so I immediately reloaded. When I reload, I always look at the bolt to make sure the round actually enters the barrel. I shoot left-handed, and reload with the left hand. With enough practice you can do this very rapidly – you simply have to tilt the rifle a little to the left. When I looked, up the lion was still standing there. I got in another shot, but it seemed as if the lion was still just standing there, and I reloaded and squeezed off a third shot. I could clearly see the lion sagging. Following the third shot, I heard a lion's threatening growl to my right. It was a particularly large lioness, and I shot her. She leaped into the air and collapsed. To her left another lioness was trotting away slowly. She took a hit in her left side obliquely from the rear, and ran away. "There's another one!" Hans shouted, pointing to the rear. I could see a lion's head bobbing up above the grass with every step, but it was only visible for very short periods. I aimed at the spot where I would see the lion's head appearing next, and pulled the trigger. To my amazement the lion tumbled head over heels and disappeared. The magazine was empty, and while I was filling it with rounds, I said to Hans: "At least we've got four."

"No, we got six," he replied.

"How so?" I asked.

"There are three at the first spot, then the big lioness, then the other big lioness we still have to find, and one over there, shot in the head," he said. Quite flabbergasted, I walked to the place where the first lion was supposed to be. I found three, alongside one another, all in the same tranquil pose, looking as if they were sleeping. All of them were young lions, about two years old. As I looked down on them, even the great excitement could not suppress a feeling of regret. It was just too much. The shooting was a great feat, no doubt, but the result left me with no feeling of happiness.

We skinned the big lioness with the shot to the shoulder, and left the others. The sun was dipping towards the horizon, and we had to go home. We reached Onguma only late at night. We took the ox-cart out very early the next morning, loaded all the dead lions, and took them home.

The aggressive giraffes

I survived all my lion hunts unscathed. My first lion hunt gave me self-confidence, largely due to Willie's words: "You're going to shoot a lot of lions!" I developed a golden rule for myself: Never turn your back on a lion; try to kill the lion before he gets you. And of course one had to shoot accurately, with a good weapon.

I experienced far more trouble with other animals than with lions.

One day I was sitting on the stoep, drinking coffee, when a giraffe calf emerged from the bush and wandered past the house. I walked towards the calf to catch it. When I came near, I saw that he was a head taller than I was. I stood in front of the calf and tried to grab his neck. Just when I had him in a loving embrace, he gave me a vicious kick with both forelegs. This giraffe had kicked forward with his front legs – something I had never seen, nor expected. I was thrown through the air, landing in an umbrella-thorn with a thud. Umbrella-thorns carry the most vicious thorns of all, and it took me quite a while to extricate myself all in one piece. In the meantime the giraffe calf strolled on by, satisfied and perfectly serene.

When I was able to stand on my feet again, I was flabbergasted beyond description. I learned one thing very well: do not attempt to embrace a giraffe around the neck from the front with bare hands. He's a lot more powerful than you are.

I walked back home, gathered some Bushmen and restraining ropes, caught the calf and herded it into a kraal with tall walls. We fed the calf with bottles of cow's milk and green leafy branches, and tamed it well. When all our permits were in order, the calf was bought by an animal dealer in Okahandja, who came to fetch it. We discovered that the calf's mother had become entangled in a wire fence some distance away and had broken her neck in a fall. The calf was an orphan who had begun to wander about.

At full moon I invariably walked into the bush armed with a bow and arrows or a sharp throwing-spear. The dogs always came along. With the dogs cornering and distracting the game (mostly wildebeest), we approached as closely as was required, and I hurled the spear into the body behind the shoulder, preferably into the heart. This quickly killed the animal. It may sound cruel, but it is almost as efficient as a good rifle shot. We took along a rifle for emergencies, in case we encountered lions. Fortunately this never happened.

Four Bushmen and I visited the farm Vergenoeg one night. I should actually not have trespassed on Vergenoeg, because relations between its owner and Mr Böhme were rather strained. There was a soap factory on his farm, and he turned all the zebras he shot into soap. While hunting the zebra, they wounded a great many, and they often expired on Onguma. Mr Böhme often complained to Nature Conservation, but his pleas fell on deaf ears because Nature Conservation maintained that there was a zebra overpopulation.

We were quite far onto Vergenoeg land when the dogs surrounded some giraffes. There was a great hullabaloo – barking and yelping and the thud of giraffe hooves as they lashed out at the dogs. This was definitely not part of my plan, and I wanted to lure the dogs away from the giraffes as quickly as possible. I swopped my spear and my rifle, and crept up close through the bush. It was no use shouting at the dogs, as they would simply ignore it. I wanted to grab the dogs by the tail and drag them away from the giraffes, meting out some lusty blows to the ribs into the bargain. I was still crawling underneath a thorn bush on all fours when one of the giraffes decided to attack the dogs. Of course the dogs retired in the direction of their master. When the giraffe was almost on top of me, I raised the rifle and shot in his direction from a sitting position. I heard a dull thud, and then everything went quiet, apart from the satisfied grunt of the dogs tugging at something.

The giraffe's head lay on the ground about two paces from where I had been sitting. Then I realised: Stark, you've just shot a giraffe! Giraffes are specially protected Crown game!

The Bushmen stood about twenty paces away, dumbfounded and as still as pillars of salt. I called them. We all agreed that the giraffe had to be removed. If the farmer were to discover that the bloody German had shot a giraffe on his farm, I would end up in jail.

Willie offered to summon the entire Bushman location – old and young, big and small, to carry the giraffe to Onguma piece by piece. While Willie absented himself, the other Bushmen and I cut up the giraffe, skin and all. Then Willie arrived with his following. They were all loaded with as much giraffe meat as they could carry, and the whole lot left for Onguma. Four of the Bushmen and I stayed behind and cleaned up. We put the entrails and thick clots of blood in some aardvark burrows and closed them up. We covered the main pool of blood with sand, leaves and grass, took the last pieces of meat, and arrived home in the early hours of the morning.

I never said a word to Mr Böhme. For the next two weeks I constantly looked in the direction of the gate guarding the entrance to the Onguma farmhouse, expecting to see a police vehicle, but this secret remained secret.

The eland bull near Twee Palms and the "sacred" ox-wagon

One full-moon night in winter, itchy feet once again drove me to do evil. This time I went to Twee Palms. On the way there, I had to cross a piece of Vergenoeg land. While I was walking, I heard the click of an eland's legs. The legs of the big eland bulls make a clear clicking sound with every step. I sat and waited, and could clearly see them walking down a game trail about 120 paces away from me. There was a telescopic night-sight on my 9.3, and one of the big ones collapsed with a shot to the neck. I trotted back to Onguma and woke up Willie and all the other men who could help. We decided to take Mr Böhme's ox-wagon and oxen to bring the eland bull back home. This ox-wagon was Mr Böhme's pride and joy. He had ordered it specially made for him by Diekmann at Otjiwarongo. Mr Böhme was as proud and possessive of his ox-wagon as aunt Ella was of her Willys Jeep, and nobody dared use the ox-wagon without his express permission. He parked the wagon right next to his bedroom window in order to keep an eye on it. Under no circumstances was the wagon permitted to be taken into the bush – it was meant solely to go to Namutoni to fetch deliveries that arrived there by bus.

Very, very quietly we used all available man-power to push the wagon far away from the old folks' bedroom window. Fortunately the wagon had rubber tyres. We yoked the oxen at a suitable spot, and then went to look for the eland bull. On arrival we skinned and dressed the eland and loaded the meat onto the wagon. We camouflaged the signs of the butchery and erased all evidence of our misdeed. We were back at Onguma by midnight. We stacked the meat under a shelter, unyoked the oxen, cleaned the ox-wagon and pushed it back into its familiar spot under the old folks' bedroom window without making a sound. Then we began cutting biltong. Virtually the entire eland bull had been cut up into biltong strips by daybreak.

Mr Böhme, always an early riser, stood under the shelter looking at all the biltong, shaking his head and saying: "*Nanu*, where did all this come from?"

"Oh, I just brought home an eland bull," I answered. He stared at me for some time, quite bewildered, and then simply shook his head.

The eland bull and the Swiss army knife

We were catching eland calves in the Mangetti area, and over the weekend I saddled my hunting mount Bento and took to the bush to go exploring. I did take along my .303.

I was some distance from the camp when I reached a bare, pan-like flat plain. A fat eland bull was standing about two hundred paces from me. I reined in Bento, and looked at the eland bull, which looked back at me. I dismounted and took my .303 from the holder, simply to experience once more what an eland bull looks like in the gunsights. The sight was fixed on the eland's shoulder. I felt not a scrap of excitement, because I had no intention of shooting.

Quite involuntarily my left fingers began tightening around the trigger, and then some more, and even more, and suddenly the shot rang out. I got a huge fright, but it was too late. The bull leapt into the air, ran thirty paces and fell down dead. I trotted closer to the bull and stared down at it for a long time while I contemplated what to do.

It was very hot, and I took Bento to one of the mushara trees and tied him to it.

Back at the eland my hand instinctively moved to unsheathe my large half-sword to dress the eland, but then I realised I had left it at camp. I did have my Swiss army knife in my pocket, and at least I could use it to remove the eland's stomach. When I had finished, I felt so disgusted with myself that I felt I should punish myself for what I had done, but I also wanted to establish whether I would be able to skin and dress an entire eland using only an army knife. When the knife became blunt, I spread some sand on one of the eland's hooves and used it to sharpen the blade. When the eland was skinned, the major task (cutting the animal into sizeable pieces) lay before me.

Fortunately I knew how all the joints fitted together. So I started. I cut the one piece after the other and hung them all in the shade of a large mushara tree.

The haunches were too heavy to lift them as is. I cut them apart at the hip joint, dragged the loose haunches onto the carcass, crawled beside the carcass, underneath the haunches and lifted them onto my shoulders. With my last reserves of strength I stood up, carried them to the tree one by one, and hung them there. Eventually I looked like a vulture that had crawled into a carcass – blood and fat everywhere!

I felt quite apathetic as I rode back home, and almost fell asleep on the horse's back. I am very certain of one thing now: one can process an entire eland using only an army knife. Every time I see someone struggling with an animal carcass, I think back to that large eland bull and my little old Swiss army knife.

The wildebeest who refused to die

Sometimes one or the other of Mr Böhme's daughters came to visit, with their husbands and children. The men always went hunting with me, mainly to make biltong. One morning I was instructed to accompany one of the sons-in-law on a hunt for wildebeest. We were driving his vehicle. On the side of the Etosha Pan where large numbers of game are always to be found, he shot at a large wildebeest bull. The animal staggered under the shot, but did not fall down. He sat on his haunches like a dog, and shook his horns threateningly. The son-in-law had complained beforehand that he only had a small supply of ammunition for his rifle because it was difficult to get hold of those particular rounds. In order to work sparingly with the ammunition, I therefore offered to dispatch the wildebeest with my half-sword.

Something about the wildebeest's attitude looked suspicious, and I cocked my .303 and walked towards the animal. He was still offering a challenge by shaking his horns. At a distance of three paces I stood still, waved one arm, and said: "Get up!"

The wildebeest then stood up in a flash and made straight for me. I couldn't aim the rifle quickly enough, and was forced to shoot from the hip. I severed his right horn close to the skull, but that did not stop him. Instinctively I grabbed hold of his left horn and shoved my other hand into his mouth, just behind the incisors.

The wildebeest pinned me to the ground, with his head on my chest. I had to use all my strength to keep a hold on the bend of his left horn and his lower jaw; I simply tried to hold on and to stay as close to his head as possible, to prevent him goring me with his remaining left horn. From the corner of my eye, I saw Mr Böhme's son-in-law aiming while we were wrestling. The possibility of him shooting at us frightened me more than the wildebeest, and I kept on shouting: "Don't shoot, don't shoot!" The man stood there, paralysed by indecision. Then I shouted at him to grab the wildebeest by the tail and trip him up. Eventually he scraped together the courage to do this. When the wildebeest stumbled, I landed on his neck, pinning him to the ground.

I unsheathed my half-sword and cut through both carotids. However, I did not sever the spinal cord, because I thought the wildebeest was done for. Blood was pumping from the carotids with every beat of his heart. I quickly got to my feet because I didn't want to be covered in blood. The wildebeest did the same! I couldn't believe my eyes! The wildebeest came for me again, albeit much more slowly. I certainly had no wish to begin wrestling with the bloody monster a second time, so I turned tail and ran. This time I shouted: "Shoot, just shoot." The wildebeest collapsed after the second shot, and eventually died.

I had only some bruises and painful ribs, but was far richer as far as experience was concerned.

Wounded wildebeest are formidable opponents. During my stay at Onguma I lost quite a few dogs to wildebeest. However, I was able to rescue many of those dogs by treating them in time.

Encounters with gemsbok

Gemsbok are the most dangerous antelope in Namibia. Buffaloes are also dangerous, but I cannot write about them. I have never had the privilege of shooting a buffalo, as they were not common at Onguma and Etosha.

I had problems with my very first gemsbok. This was at the beginning of my stay at Onguma. I was eager to shoot my first gemsbok, and we walked to Palmvlakte (Palm Plains), because the Bushmen had said there was a number of gemsbok there. Hundreds of beautiful large Makalani palms grow on Palmvlakte, which is fringed by a dense wild quince forest.

A herd of gemsbok were grazing on the Plains, and we tried to creep up to them. One of Mr Böhme's sons-in-law, Hermann (an experienced hunter himself) was with me. But then the gemsbok saw us and fled. They were about 250 paces from us, and I decided to chance a shot. Judging by the sound of the hit, it was a shot to the stomach. The herd of gemsbok ran into the wild quince thicket, the wounded one among them. While we were tracking them, Hermann warned me that wounded gemsbok often attack, and that I should be wary.

While we were following the tracks, Willie suddenly stopped and pointed ahead. Behind a wild quince bush, about fifteen paces ahead of us, I could see the white stripes on the forehead of a gemsbok that was lying down, waiting for us. When the gemsbok realised that we had spotted him, he jumped up with a snort, and attacked. I couldn't shoot through the dense bush, and had to wait. Hermann simply shouted: "Watch out, he's coming!"

The branches cleared only about eight paces from us. When the gemsbok reached this spot, he had already lowered his head to gore us, but I then got in a good neck shot. I had to jump sharply to the right, because the gemsbok ploughed past to my left – dead!

"That was close," Hermann said quietly, but his breathing revealed that he must have been very tense. I immediately gained a great deal of respect for gemsbok.

On another occasion Willie, Kanjou and I were following lion tracks. This, too, was near Palmvlakte, and we had a few dogs with us on that day. While we were walking along the lion's footprints, the dogs cornered a gemsbok calf. The calf was bleating loudly, and I told Kanjou to go to the calf's aid and fend off the dogs. He ran ahead and caught the calf by the leg, and lashed out at the dogs with his stick. The calf was bleating all the time, and suddenly the gemsbok cow arrived at full speed. I didn't want to shoot, but I had to protect Kanjou. The gemsbok cow lowered her head to gore Kanjou, and I shot her in the neck.

We abandoned the lion tracks and caught the calf. Willie was sent to fetch the mule cart. We loaded the cow's carcass and took the calf home, where we reared it with the help of a milk bottle.

We succeeded in rearing it, but learned that it is much more difficult to raise a gemsbok calf than an eland calf. Eland calves will approach you on the second or third day when you arrive with the bottle; a gemsbok calf remains wild. It was always a struggle to catch the calf, and it was persuaded to drink from the bottle only with great difficulty. We sold the calf to an animal dealer as soon as possible.

The gemsbok and two leopards

On another occasion we saw how well gemsbok can defend themselves, and how determined they can be. Hermann, Mr Böhme's son-in-law, was helping me to deepen the well at Grenspos, because the level of the water was dropping. We therefore had to lower concrete rings into the hole to stop sand from filling up the well. The well's Bushman name was *Uriegeitsugutsaub* ("The Great White Night-well"): white because of the white sand, and great night-well because it was so deep that you could not see the bottom, and it looked like night down below. Kanjou and I had the task of standing hip-deep in the water to dig out the sand and to place one ring on the next to protect us from sand cave-ins. The work caused some sort of rheumatism in my left shoulder, probably as a result of standing in the water for such long periods. Yet I preferred this work above ploughing a hundred times, even though it was dangerous.

Wise men always stayed topside, giving learned instructions. Every now and then Hermann descended with the bucket and pulley to inspect, because he could see nothing from the top. I had to submit to him, as he had been a miner, with a great deal of experience. Also, he was older than I. However, whenever he went on too long, I let fly with a protracted fart, something I had a good supply of, thanks to all that meat-eating. It was usually enough to cause him to flee to the top, cursing all the while. Generally, however, I got on well with Hermann. At least he was no sissy, and joined in all the pranks.

Grenspos was a long way from home, so we camped there all week in a tent. One night we heard a leopard catching a buck. The next morning we looked for tracks in that direction, and found them quite close to the camp. We followed the leopard tracks and suddenly saw a gemsbok cow standing under an appelblaar tree (*Lonchocarpus nelsii*). She looked at us, then looked up, and then suddenly ran away. When she ran away from the tree, two leopard jumped out of the tree onto the ground and also ran away. We walked to the tree, and found a gemsbok calf lying under it. It had bite-marks to the head and throat, and was more dead than alive. We had to put it out of its misery.

Hermann suggested we leave the calf there, and set a trap. The leopards would return, he said. At that stage I had no experience of leopards.

We set a great lion trap near the calf's carcass, and went to have a look the next morning. I took along two strong knobkerries, a long one, and a short and heavy one. There was a leopard in the trap when we reached the tree. Hermann dared me to kill the leopard with a club. When we came close to the leopard, it was thrashing about and roaring. I was surprised at its voice, which would have done a lion proud. I approached the leopard cautiously. He went quite wild, and stormed me while dragging the trap. When he was close enough, I delivered a blow with the long club, and then two quick blows with the heavy club. The leopard was dead.

We set the trap for the second leopard. The next morning the second one had also been caught in the trap, and like the first, I dispatched him with some blows from my clubs.

When we examined the leopard, we discovered two punctures behind the shoulders, with the left-hand one a good deal larger than the right-hand one. I was surprised, because no one had shot the leopard.

Willie immediately said: "Those were made by the gemsbok's horns!" When the leopards had taken the calf, the mother must have attacked them immediately, causing them to find shelter in the appelblaar tree. Then the mother tried to protect her child by standing by him until she saw us, and ran away.

The wounded leopard's capacity for survival also astounded me. When we had skinned the animal, we performed a thorough post-mortem. The horn had penetrated the left side behind the shoulder, passed under the spine, and had exited behind the right shoulder. The leopard was quite lucky, in that no organs had been damaged, even though a gemsbok horn had passed right through his body. Furthermore, even though caught in the trap, he was as lively and aggressive as his friend the day before.

Goliath and the big leopard

One day Willie and I went after lions. We took along the dogs, but the lions sniffed our scent in time, and made themselves scarce. We gave up, feeling a bit down in the dumps, and walked home. It was a hot day, and most of the dogs stayed in the bush, preferring to come home during the cool of night. This happened quite often. Back home, a Bushman from the Ekaka outpost told me a hyena had been caught in a trap, and that both the hyena and the trap had disappeared. I asked him whether he was absolutely sure it was a hyena, and he confirmed it. I asked him why he hadn't killed the hyena with his bow and arrow, but he just shook his head and laughed. This Bushman was half off his rocker due to venereal disease, and it was useless trying to reason with him.

It was late in the afternoon, and we were all tired. Horseback was the quickest way of getting to Ekaka, and our mounts were always kept close to the house, ready to go. Heinke, Mr Böhme's daughter, asked whether she could come with us, and we set off for Ekaka at a steady gallop. Hyenas are capable of walking great distances, even when dragging a trap. I can remember a case when we followed a hyena on foot for about 50 kilometres before she crawled into an aardvark burrow. We had to loosen the soil with an assegai, scooping out the loosened soil with our hands, before we could get to her.

Tempers were rather short that afternoon due to fatigue and the prospect of another drawn-out session of tracking.

When we eventually reached the spot where the trap had been concealed, it immediately struck me as suspicious. A hyena will almost immediately make off with the trap; a leopard, on the other hand, will struggle with the trap, milling about in circles, biting at branches if it gets snagged, and moving in ever-widening circles, but not going very far. When the leg tissue starts to die off, they will gnaw off the leg to escape, and all that's left will be an empty trap with pieces of skin and bone splinters.

It's very difficult to identify the tracks because the animals struggle and trash about so violently.

However, I was quite confident this must have been a big, strong leopard, because it had twice climbed into and out of a tree with the trap in tow.

I was regretting not having brought along my rifle. To make matters worse, only Goliath among all the dogs had kept pace with us.

Goliath was my best dog by far; big and strong; a mastiff and bull terrier cross. He meant the world to me. Goliath was only some two years old, but already lacked proper canines, due to innumerable fights with wild animals.

While I was tracking, I handed Heinke my horse's reins, so that she could lead both horses in my wake. I soon heard Goliath's characteristic double bark in the bushes ahead of me, followed by the angry fighting roar of a leopard.

Heinke tried to restrain me, but I knew that the sooner I helped my dog, the better would be our chance of survival. All the time I was thinking of the canines missing from Goliath's mouth, wondering whether he would be able to hold the leopard. I immediately drew my half-sword and ran to the spot where the dog and leopard were engaged in mortal combat. They were there all of a sudden, and I could see what was going on. Goliath had fastened onto the particularly large leopard's left ear, and was shaking it with all his might. The leopard had driven the nails of its (free) left paw into the top of Goliath's head, between the ears. Howling and roaring, they rolled about with the leopard on top, and then the dog. Goliath was hanging on to the leopard's ear for dear life. No matter how frightened I was, I needed to react very quickly, because my dog came first. I grabbed the leopard's tail with my left hand, plunged the half-sword deep into his side behind the shoulder, and stood back. The leopard went limp, and died. I cannot describe my feelings as I stroked and praised my dog. He had some serious wounds to the head, but they were not life-threatening.

When I walked back to Heinke and the horses, she shook her head and said: "You're crazy, man!"

In the meantime it had become dark. We went to the Ekaka outpost and asked Kanjou to skin the leopard the next day and to bring us the skin. We then rode back home at an easy walking pace, with a smiling half-moon and sparkling stars above us. All the time my thoughts were with Goliath, my hero, and I felt extremely thankful towards the dog. The day had begun with great frustration, but had ended on a high. Can one give one's Maker enough credit at such a time? Today, some forty years later, I can.

My wife gets in a masterful shot

In the meantime I had been to Germany for a year and nine months, to undergo advanced riding training. I met my future wife, Elke, there. We were engaged before I returned to South West Africa, and she followed me a year later. We were married in Windhoek, and she then accompanied me to Onguma.

Initially she followed me everywhere, as young people in love tend to do. One of my first tasks was to teach her to shoot quickly and accurately, and to instruct her in general weapons handling.

One morning a Bushman from an outpost reported that a leopard had been caught in a trap, and we took off in the mule-cart. It was not long after we started following the signs of the dragging trap that we saw them entering a large aardvark burrow. We were still standing around, chatting softly, when the leopard began growling threateningly from inside the burrow. I gave my wife my cocked .303, because I wanted her to shoot her first leopard. However, the leopard first had to emerge from the hole. I then did something really stupid – the sort of thing only a newly-wed would do.

I squatted at the hole's entrance to see how far the leopard had retreated into it. I stared into two shining eyes not two metres in front of me. At that instant the leopard decided to charge. I jumped up to run away, but fell into another aardvark hole behind me. There was no time to get up again. Furthermore I was concerned that my wife would hit me, because I was between her and the leopard. I rolled away from the leopard as fast as I could, shouting all the while: "Shoot! Shoot!" I was still rolling when I heard a shot. I felt no pain, so she hadn't shot me! Neither did I feel any leopard claws or teeth. I stopped rolling and stood up, quite disorientated. My wife was still standing where I had left her, and the leopard was laying near the entrance to the aardvark burrow, blood and brain matter dripping from his forehead, shot neatly between the eyes. My wife could not have aimed a better shot than that.

Willie, standing a little distance away, turned his head to one side and looked at me for quite some time, a crooked smile on his face which revealed that he was thinking: "Stupid man, you asked for it!"

The remarkable nursing sister with the enormous fortitude

I have already mentioned that Mr Böhme had only one arm. His left arm was simply a short stump covered in a flap of skin from the shoulder. A long time before I came to Onguma, a Bushman came to Mr Böhme and reported that a lion had been caught in a trap. Because of his poor eyesight, Mr Böhme always shot with a telescopic sight on his rifle. He accompanied the Bushman to the spot where the lion was. It was one of those traps with two blades that opened outwards. I don't like those. Apparently the lion trap had pinned the lion in between two trees, and when Mr Böhme tried to shoot, the rising sun was shining into the telescope. He could see nothing from that position. He and the Bushman then decided to swop positions so as to have the sun from behind. As they were turning to walk away, the lion gathered strength and leapt towards them in attack. In the process he somehow managed to tread on both blades of the trap, opening them and freeing himself. He then charged with all his might. When Mr Böhme looked around, the lion was almost on top of him. He turned toward the charging lion and instinctively raised his left arm to protect his throat and face. The lion took hold of his arm. Mr Böhme had always been a strong and lean man; he was able to stay on his feet and grapple with the lion. Eventually he stood as still as possible, with his forearm in the lion's mouth. He looked the lion straight in the eye and saw the lion looking away to the left and then to the right. Suddenly the lion let go of his arm and trotted away.

Aunt Ella took her husband to hospital. Then something happened that went beyond anybody's comprehension. The doctor put the arm in plaster, but soon afterwards the bite-marks began to fester under the plaster. When Mr Böhme could no longer stand the pain, the plaster was removed, but it was too late. The entire arm had begun to rot, and had to be amputated just below the shoulder. Mr Böhme's entire body had, however, become poisoned. Nobody gave him any chance of survival, and in a short while he was a living skeleton, barely clinging to life. Aunt Ella sat by his bed day and night. The sisters did their best to keep Mr Böhme alive. But a miracle occurred, and he lived.

When he was discharged from the hospital at last, he extended an invitation to all the sisters to come and enjoy a free holiday on his farm whenever they wanted.

Many years later, when I started work at Onguma, Mr Böhme instructed me one day to fetch a sister from Germany at Namutoni. Apparently she had accepted the offer of vacationing at Onguma. Because there was no other transport, I had to go and get her in the mule-cart. I was in a morose mood when I harnessed the mules.

As a child and youth I often had contact with the nuns at the

Catholic Hospital in Windhoek. At that time it was the only clean and really good hospital in the capital. I remember the long clothing of the nuns, leaving only their faces open. Most of them already had their best years behind them and were very conscientious and dedicated to their work, but for the rest they were simply a bundle of clothing to me. They often reminded me of teachers, but not people.

On the way to Namutoni I wondered how such a sister would be able to board the mule-cart in her long attire, and how she would feel about the mule-cart as a mode of transport.

On reaching Namutoni, I asked the police whether a white sister had arrived.

"She's sitting on the steps under the shelter over there," said the sergeant with a smile. A middle-aged, slightly portly lady in a light blue dress was sitting on the steps. I introduced myself and immediately apologised for the mode of transport. "It's wonderful! It's romantic!" she replied with a laugh. I took her bag and we walked to the mule-cart. She boarded it in a flash, and the mules began trotting back home. We were hardly seated, or she delved in her handbag for a pack of cigarettes, and offered me one. "I smoke only a pipe, thanks." I couldn't fathom a sister smoking. Then she began chatting, all jolly and cheerful. She told of her years during World War II when she served as an army nursing sister at the various fronts where German soldiers were fighting. The worst was in Russia during the winter. This made me realise the suffering a soldier has to endure. She told her stories without bitterness, with a positive attitude. I gained a lot of admiration for her there and then, and the long road home on the mule-cart passed by in an instant.

I wanted to excuse myself the next day, because I was busy deepening the well at Ekaka. "I'll come with you," she replied. What would I do with a woman while I was digging sand from the bottom of a well? I tried using all sorts of excuses, but she simply replied that she did not feel like sitting at home with the old folks all day. I could not deter her. She went along, taking her crocheting with her, and sat under a tree crocheting all day, apart from the brief periods when I emerged for a quick lunch, or for a cup of warm coffee after standing in the cold water at the bottom of the well. We returned home in the mule-cart that night, with the dogs for company. I was amazed at her interest in game and hunting while we sat chatting on the mule-cart. She promptly said that she wanted to come along when I went hunting. At that stage I was still able to walk very fast, and most men soon lagged behind on a hunting trial. "You would never keep up," I tried to counter, "and you wouldn't be able to walk quietly enough." She then told me that she was the daughter of a German professional hunter. As a child she always walked through the woods with her father, and she knew how to behave during a hunt. I just could not shake this woman; she was always ready with a counter-argument. "Do you want to go shooting?" I asked.

"Yes, of course!" she replied.

"Can you shoot?" I asked.

"No, but I can learn!"

"All right, we'll try. Your shooting lessons begin tomorrow."

There and then I decided to take her on a stiff walk through the bush, to try to get rid of this persistent female.

The next day I was working at Ekaka again, and she went along. I stopped working a little earlier that afternoon so that we could start her shooting lessons at home. I did not go to much trouble, simply placing a piece of limestone, a little larger than an ostrich egg, on top of a sawn-off fence-pole. We took hundred paces back. I made Sister Ursula sit down on her backside under a tree, with her elbows on her knees and the rifle resting against the tree. I also told her all about aiming, breathing and so forth.

Then the truth came out. "I can't close only one eye – either both have to be open, or both have to be closed, but I have never been able to close only one," she confessed.

"Then you will never learn how to shoot," I answered with some relief. However, women are full of wiles. She quickly fetched one of her long silk stockings, pulling it over her left eye. She aimed for quite some time, lowered the rifle, took another deep breath and aimed again. At last the shot rang out. There was a cloud of dust above the pole, and the rock was gone. I couldn't believe my eyes. "Surely that wasn't the first shot of your life?" I asked in disbelief.

"I give you my word," she replied. "My father would never let me shoot because of this eye thing. It really was my very first shot."

The next day was a Saturday, and it offered the first opportunity to go hunting together. I maintained a stiff pace from the start, and she really needed to stretch her legs to keep up. I did not take along any water, because I wanted to quickly nib in the budd her lust for hunting. By early afternoon I spotted a wildebeest bull sleeping beside a pan. "We need to stalk it," I said. This was flat territory, sparsely vegetated. "To that little thorn tree," I gestured. "We need to go on all fours."

Like two large pythons we crawled 150 paces to the appointed thorn tree on all fours through quite vicious salt-grass. We eventually reached it, but while I was trying to position Sister Ursula in the correct position for shooting, the wildebeest bull became suspicious, scrambled upright, and turned towards us while making warning noises. He wasn't sure what was happening under the thorn tree, and was liable to take off at any moment. Sister Ursula was excited, and out of breath after crawling such a distance. And then there was the business with that damned stocking! First she pulled the stocking down to look with both eyes, then she pulled the stocking over the left eye, and aimed. It was a miracle that the wildebeest stood still, snorting all the while. I showed her where to aim for, right below the chin, in the middle of the neck. It felt like hours while she aimed, but at last the shot rang out. The wildebeest bull fell in its tracks and lay still.

I looked at Sister Ursula in disbelief. Once again I asked her whether these had been the first shots of her life, and once again she confirmed it.

On the way home I made her walk some distance in front of me to teach her how to keep direction. I noticed that she was walking rather oddly, almost as if she were treading on eggs. "What's the matter?"

"Oh, a blister must have burst," she replied.

"Take off your shoes!" I ordered. She sat down and removed her shoes. What I saw made me feel very sorry for this lady. Both feet were simply masses of loose skin from blisters that had opened. "Why didn't you say anything?" I asked.

"But I promised I wouldn't complain!" she replied.

At that moment I gained a great deal of respect for her. This woman deserved better treatment. My attitude towards her changed completely on the spot. First we had to heal those feet. We swopped her leather town shoes for comfortable tackies from the shop on the farm. Being a nursing sister, she knew enough to heal her feet herself.

I had to work at the well near Ekaka almost every day. She always went along, despite her painful feet, because she feared that she would miss something. Stefanus, a Bushman from our private camp, was with us. He was a young Owamboland Bushman, and I had trained him to maintain order in my camp, to prepare food properly, and to look after my horses. I also taught him how to shoot, mostly with the .22. He had to make sure there were enough grey louries, francolins and guineafowl for lunch. Particularly louries. Properly prepared and slowly roasted, they make the best poultry one can get. Stefanus was a master at preparing these birds.

I entrusted Sister Ursula to Stefanus's care to learn hunting and field-craft while I worked at the bottom of the well. As soon as her feet had healed, we took to the bush one weekend, and she bagged a zebra with a neat shoulder shot. The stocking still remained a big bother.

Almost daily Ursula begged me to give her a chance at a lion, but she was hopelessly too slow for that, and not fully fit.

Yet I did plan to give her the best possible chance. The only way would be a lion in a trap. So a wildebeest was shot and laid out as bait. We checked the traps early in the morning, but on the first two mornings we found only a jackal in one of the traps. On the third day I set out on my horse Tankret very early, checking the traps. I was still some distance from the carcass, suspecting nothing, when a lion suddenly pounced from the thick bush with an angry roar, and tried to attack. The trap on his leg inhibited him, however, and in the face of his charge the horse did an about-turn and started running. It happened so unexpectedly that I was almost thrown. I would probably have been dislodged if I wasn't so afraid of the incensed lion, but in the event I clung to the saddle for dear life, and regained my seat. I galloped off home on Tankret's back.

"There's a lion in a trap, let's go," I called excitedly to Ursula. The mules were quickly harnessed, and we went looking for the lion with the mule-cart, dogs, two rifles and Willie. We tied the mules to a tree some distance from the spot where I had my encounter with the lion, and proceeded on foot. It wasn't long before the dogs spotted the lion. The concert began. The lion was particularly short-tempered, and it ran into a thorn thicket, dragging the trap, and with the dogs close behind. With all that added noise, it was chaos. The lion could burst out of there at any moment.

Furthermore the sister, stocking and all, was bursting with excitement. We stalked the lion as best we could, but he moved to another spot every so often. Eventually we could see some of him. I sat down in front of Ursula and told her to rest the rifle on my shoulder. Eventually she let fly with a shot, after pulling at the sock a bit. It was a hit, and after a little while the lion lay down. The dogs were pulling at it from all directions, and we approached the lion cautiously. To make sure, I took my assegai from Willie, who had been carrying it, and pushed it all the way through the lion's body just behind the shoulder.

Just then some of the dogs started barking not far away from us, and we heard another angry roar. "The other trap has also been sprung!" Willie said. We left the first lion there, with the assegai in its body, and hastened to the second spot where the dogs were now baiting the second lion.

Once again we crept up to the spot where the dogs and lion could be heard, and after a fair amount of hassle Ursula shot that one as well. When we had made sure the second lion was dead, we returned to the first. As we approached, I could see that the shaft of the assegai that was stuck in the lion's body was moving. We stood still and watched very carefully. The shaft moved rhythmically with the lion's breathing. I gestured to Willie and Ursula to stand still; I cocked my rifle and walked closer to the lion's field of vision. He tried to get up with an enraged roar. He could get up on his front paws, but no more. I dispatched him with a quick shot to the head. I had to beg Ursula's forgiveness for that shot, but we may have had lots of problems if we had to go through her stocking business again. She understood.

The sister's greatest wish had been fulfilled. She had shot not one lion, but two. She was in her seventh heaven, and could not thank me enough. While we were skinning the lions, Willie made a very clever suggestion: "You must marry this sister. She fits in well in this environment, and there's always meat where she is!" Willie softly spoke to me in the Bushman language, all the while staring fixedly at the paw he was trying to skin as neatly as possible. (When the Bushmen say something of significance, they usually do not look you in the eye – they will normally stare at the flames of a fire, or seem to be occupied with something else.)

His Bushman logic was probably not wrong, and it cost me a great deal of persuasion to make him understand that this sister had important work in Germany, and, besides, that she was a good few years older than me. Willie was most reluctant to accept this. We were communicating in Heikum all the time, because Ursula was sitting next to me, taking hold of a body part whenever it was required while we were doing the processing, not knowing what this important conversation was all about.

Ursula's holiday came to an end, as do all things. In the same manner in which I had gone to fetch her, I took her back to Namutoni in the mule-cart, and from there to Tsumeb and the railway station on the railway bus.

Many years later, when I was in Germany undergoing advanced equestrian training, my fiancée (later my wife) and I visited her in Marbach in Germany. She was still working as a matron in a large hospital. Two lion-skins took pride of place in her flat. Her colleagues dropped in every now and then. They all wanted to know whether Sister Ursula had shot those two lions herself. Nobody had believed her.

In the meantime she had put on a bit of weight, and had, of course, also aged, but the same bright, sparkling blue eyes shone out from her matronly face. An unforgettable person!

My training in Germany

Just before World War II, Franz Schwermer ran a successful riding school on our plot. I was ten years old, and received training every day. He often asked my mother to send me to Germany to be trained at the Cavalry School. At that time this school was world famous. My mother refused because she wanted nothing to do with the Nazis who were in power at that time. Shortly after the war broke out, Franz Schwermer was interned in the concentration camp at Koffiefontein. The riding school went to pieces because the Germans didn't dare hold any meetings. He was then repatriated to Germany. He came back to South West Africa from Germany many years after the war – as a gardener.

While I was working at Onguma, he came to visit along with his sister, aunt Nolte. Franz and his sister had looked up my mother, and had asked her to send me to Germany.

And so it came to pass. My mother was already suffering from cancer at the time, and all her money went to operations and hospital expenses. She gave me a choice: to receive my inheritance, amounting to £600, in advance and spend it on proper equestrian training, or to buy the farm Vergenoeg for £600. At that stage the farm was in the market for that amount. To a certain extent the Hand of God was the decisive factor. I chose the training. Today Vergenoeg is a well-developed guest farm worth millions of rands, but during the Swapo bush war, two soldiers who were temporarily assigned to protect the farm were murdered in the house, and I would surely have been one of them. My choice of training in

84

Germany resulted in my getting good employ in the S.A. Defence Force as an instructor. I am now able to live to the end of my days on a good pension.

I travelled to Germany early in 1956. Aunt Nolte and her husband met me at Frankfurt's airport and took me to their home in Münster in Westphalia. The Noltes were very well off, with a handsome home next to their tarpaulin factory in Münster.

There was a well-known riding school in Münster where the best riding instructors in Germany received their training. Aunt Nolte had entered me for the course with the highest qualifications when I was still in South West Africa. We arranged the training with the head of the riding school, Major Paul Stecken. Aunt Nolte asked whether I would be able to sit for the State Examinations by the end of the year. Major Stecken had his doubts, because it was a three-year course, and nobody had ever done so. However, they would consider it because I was a foreigner. I was therefore placed in the most advanced class from the start. I really suffered during those nine months.

My biggest problem was advanced dressage, of which I had little knowledge. Theory was my greatest challenge. I had to buy stacks of books, studying night after night to catch up. Nevertheless I passed the final exams well. Major Stecken recommended that I should undergo one month's specialist training in showjumping and one month's specialist training in dressage before my return.

My first specialist training would be with Fritz Thiedemann in Elmshorn. Thiedemann was the greatest showjumping idol in Germany. I did not enjoy my time there, and was happy when it was over, and I had to move from the north of Germany to the south to be trained by Egon von Neindorff.

Egon von Neindorff, my dressage trainer-to-be, was a character in his own right. He gave me an old horse on my first day, telling me that the horse could do anything. I had to ride this horse and show him what I was capable of. He took a chair and sat in a corner of the riding school, just watching. Initially I found it difficult to get the horse going. A typical old riding-school donkey, I thought. I gave up after struggling for fifteen minutes, and rode up to him. "Is that all?" he asked.

"I don't believe this horse can do more," I answered.

The little man then exploded. Among other things he said: "It's an absolute scandal that the Münster riding school lets loose such products on mankind." Either I had to start from scratch, or I had to pack my bags. I really thought this man was nuts, but I bit my tongue, thinking that I would simply have to endure.

My training started that same afternoon. No stirrups, hands on hips, at a stiff trot, circling around him with the horse at the end of a tether. Every now and then he would repeat: "Sit, man, sit. Make those legs longer. Sit, man, sit. Make those legs longer." This went on for a full three weeks – all the while at a trot at the end of a tether – one horse after the next, for almost the whole day.

After the third week he said: "Let's have a bit of a circus." He gave me his best dressage horse, Silur, and we started off with the most advanced dressage exercises. At the end of that fourth week I was supposed to go home, but I realised: I can't ride a horse! If I compared myself to him and his former pupils, I was a complete dud.

"Can I stay on for another month?" I asked shyly.

"But of course you may, you are finally on the right path," he answered with a laugh.

"But my money's almost finished," I confessed.

"Doesn't matter, you can help me with the lessons, and handle the most difficult horses," he replied. We had made a verbal contract.

In order to save money, I immediately vacated my rented room at a café. Von Neindorff lived in a small flat above the stable complex – just him and his two dogs, because he was not married. I moved into an old stable, with a wooden bed I had made myself from old planks, covered in two blankets. And so we lived in that complex – he in his flat above, and I in a former stable. We worked every day for the next two months – seating lessons every day, and advanced lessons on Silur and other good dressage horses. In the afternoon we exercised the really tough customers – me on the horse, he on the ground with his long whip or buckets of water. In the late afternoon I helped in running his riding school, and giving lessons to those he did not feel like instructing.

In the meantime I got to know my future wife – only a friend at the time. Eventually she invited me to her home, and when I got to know her parents, they offered me a room in their house. I could live like a normal person again. They would not take any money, and I was able to save some more.

Eventually I became von Neindorff's master student, and I had to present special shows at equestrian meetings in southern Germany.

In the meantime the Hungarian Uprising had taken place, with a bloody suppression of the Hungarians by the Russians. There were a number of letters from my mother back home, begging me to return.

My money ran out, and after nine months with von Neindorff, I had to return. He tried to persuade me to stay with him. He wanted to train me for the next Olympic Games. I was torn. On the one hand there was the possibility of competing in the Olympic Games, and on the other there was a great longing for South West Africa and my sickly mother, who was missing me.

South West Africa won out. At the end of 1957, after a stay of one year and nine months in Germany, I returned to South West Africa. I had two shillings, one sixpence and a half-crown in my pocket. I wanted to surprise my mother, so I had not told her I was returning. Fortunately I bumped into Otto Fischer, an old school chum of mine, and he gave me a lift home.

My mother was greatly relieved when I arrived. Her illness had taken its toll and she was half her original weight.

Initially I wanted to open a riding school in Windhoek, but nobody wanted to support me financially. "First make others aware of what you learned in Germany," quite a few people told me.

I knew I would not thrive in Windhoek, and keeping in mind the Biblical verse: "A prophet is not without honour, except in his home town," I decided to return to Onguma, where they welcomed me with open arms. After a year of difficulties and waiting, my fiancée, Elke, followed me from Germany, and came to Onguma. She had to adapt to the circumstances there very quickly. It was an enormous adjustment for her, but thanks to her love of nature she managed it fairly smoothly.

Malaria almost gets the better of me

Malaria was fairly common at Onguma. In those years we medicated ourselves with whatever was available, and in summer you constantly needed to take prophylactic malaria medications. And yet one sometimes suffered malaria attacks.

One morning it was once again time to shoot the meat rations for the Bushmen. Vergenoeg had a new owner, with whom we got on very well. We inspanned the mule-cart and went to Vergenoeg to fetch a zebra from there. I felt nauseous that morning, and woke with a headache. The pain became worse on the way to Vergenoeg. I shot a large zebra stallion on the way. Willie and I first had to skin it, butcher it and load the meat on the mule-wagon. The headache was worse every time I bent over; eventually I sat under a tree to one side, and Willie had to carry on by himself. Then I began vomiting continually, my entire body shivered, and I was drenched in sweat.

One the way home on the mule-cart I found that I could no longer sit on the bench, because it felt as if my head would burst every time we hit even the tiniest bump. I had never had such an excruciating headache during previous malaria attacks.

Eventually I had to lift my body from the seat with my arms, and Willie slowed the mules to a walking pace to reduce the bumping. It felt like an eternity before we eventually reached home. I went straight to bed. Only Petrina the Bushman housemaid was there, because the Böhmes were on holiday in Swakopmund. She cooked me some food and brought me milk, but I could keep none of it down. I lost consciousness every now and then. After a while I couldn't see a thing, because everything was one dark blue haze. When I closed my eyes, it felt as if I were drifting far away on a great blue sea.

At one stage Petrina wanted to give me something to eat and drink, but I declined. She stood in the doorway, quite distraught. To this day I can still see her hazy outline standing there, with her right hand on her right hip. "But Boss, what can I do for you?" she asked, exasperated and hesitant.

"Bring me some water and my malaria pills," I answered. It had occurred to me that I should be drinking malaria pills. I wasn't quite sure whether it was malaria, because the headache had never been quite so intense during previous attacks. I drank my malaria medication. After a while it felt as if there was a slight improvement in my condition. I then realised, for the first time, that it *had* to be malaria.

Many people died of blackwater fever during treatment for malaria because they took an overdose of pills. Mr Böhme had often spoken about this, and had warned us not to drink too many malaria pills at once. I took another malaria pill only the next day, and then continued with the treatment in the manner he always recommended. My condition gradually improved. Still, I was dizzy for weeks afterwards. When I got up in the mornings, I had to sit on the side of my bed for a long while, supporting myself on my arms, before I could stand up. This continued for weeks. At the time I often wondered whether I would ever recover, and I fancied that I had sustained permanent brain damage.

But there's no good riddance to bad rubbish, and with help from Above, I made it through.

Mr Böhme told me that this had to be the kind of malaria that affects the brain in particular. One thing's certain: I had been at death's door.

The ant heap and the cheetahs

My only wheeled transport was a mule-wagon. We had wonderful mules, the hinnys, by horse stallions out of donkey mares. They were more slightly built than mules out of horse mares, but they were immensely tough, and had a better disposition. We used to inspan them in the morning, only outspanning them again in the evening or at night. They could keep moving at an easy canter all day when the shaft was properly balanced. In this way we never overtaxed the mules, and when they were outspanned, they still showed signs of liveliness.

Mr Böhme had a second farm called Kaijas. His youngest daughter, Maren, lived and farmed on Kaijas with her husband Hermann. Mr Böhme once instructed me to gather together all his horses and mules at Kaijas and to bring them to Onguma. Kaijas lay about 67 kilometres south-west of Onguma. Those horses and mules had never been handled or tamed. Everybody who could ride, went to Kaijas. We struggled for about a week to tame the animals to the point that we could lead them, then we tied them together three by three. We then returned to Onguma with a herd of thirty horses and mules. There were two beautiful horse-mules amongst them, easily 2 or 3 hands bigger than the hinnys. We did not touch them, because they were far too strong for any use on Kaijas, and broke things when we tried to catch them. The two large mules went along unfettered with the other horses we were transporting, because they were only used to horses.

Back at Onguma, we broke in all the horses which showed potential for riding. We kept the mules for last. Mr Böhme did not see his way open to tackling the two large horse-mules, however, and gave me instructions to shoot them for the Bushmen and dogs.

89

I took my .303 and went to the kraal where the two mules were cantering about. Both were already seven years old, but as I was standing there in the kraal, I couldn't help but admire their beautiful strong build and movements. They simply glided across the ground. There and then I decided to ignore my instructions to shoot the mules, and rather try to tame them. I went to Mr Böhme and told him of my intentions, but he just shook his head and said: "You'll never manage it. You're simply wasting your time!"

We had a very strong cattle-crush. We manoeuvred the mules into it, and put a strong ox-wagon draught-chain around their necks (though only after a titanic struggle), because they would have broken ordinary ropes or leather thongs. We then tied each mule to a tree with a single trunk, in the same way we always tied our eland calves. If handled correctly, there was only a very slim chance that they would injure themselves. We then began taming them. We tied a piece of cloth or an old sack to a long, thin pole and softly stroked or tickled the animals with this for hours until they stopped biting or kicking. This takes a great deal of patience and determination on the side of the trainer, because you must never lose your temper. It can easily take two to five days before you will eventually be able to approach the animal in order to stroke it with your hands, and, in time, to get it used to being led. Eventually we were able to lead the animals, and to harness them. They were first taught to pull a tree-trunk, and were then inspanned in front of a cart – one newly tamed mule together with a placid old one. Later both newly trained mules pulled together. As soon as the two horse-mules could be harnessed together, I received instructions to transport the clean river sand that came from the well at Grenspos by mule-cart to Onguma. The sand was to be used for building purposes. The long distances meant that we could not convey more than two cart-loads from Grenspos to Onguma per day, but it was good exercise for the two new mules, and an opportunity to tame them properly. And so we carted sand for days on end. We had an old metal trailer which we had made into a mule-cart. The disadvantage of this tin mule-cart was that it made an incredible racket on rough gravel roads, to such an extent that it often sounded like an entire orchestra of various types of drums. This tin trailer certainly did not have the most calming of influences on the newly tamed mules, and we often had to hang onto the traces and pull for dear life.

One day we were on our way with the two big horse-mules to

fetch the second load of sand of the day. The trailer was still empty. It was early in the afternoon, and the mules were cantering along quite calmly, because it was a hot day. As always, I had taken along the .303. The mules suddenly lifted their heads, became frisky, and looked to the right. I held the reins, and Mudschi was sitting next to me with a nodding head. When I looked to the right, I saw two animals that looked like lions lying in the shade of a thorn tree. I wanted to jump off the trailer to shoot the lions, and shouted to Mudschi: "Here, take the reins!" and quickly tossed them in his direction. He did not catch them cleanly. The mules immediately felt the relaxation in the customary contact with their mouths, and they sprang forward instantly. Mudschi grabbed the reins, but got hold of only one, and consequently pulled the mules to one side until they ended up in the thorn bushes by the side of the road. I was already on my feet on the seat with the .303 in my left hand, ready to jump from the cart, but I lost my balance and came down hard, flat on my back, in the cart behind the seat. I could only watch as the mules aimed straight at a large anthill at full speed. The next instant I heard a loud crash. I was thrown high into the air and then arrowed towards the ground head first. I instinctively put out my right arm to protect my head and neck, and lifted the .303 in my left hand to keep it safe. I landed on my right hand and felt a sharp pain in my wrist, and the clear sound of a bone breaking. I immediately sprang to my feet to attend to the lions.

The "lions", however, were still lying in the shade of their chosen thorn tree, looking at the mule-cart in amazement. I wanted to cock the rifle, but my right hand was useless. I quickly jammed the rifle in between my right upper- and forearm, and cocked it with my left hand. Then I lifted my right elbow up high and laid the rifle on this right elbow (I shoot left-handed), aimed a bit longer than usual, and shot. Fortunately it was a hit, because one animal stayed down even as the other jumped up and ran away. And then I saw they were not lions, but cheetahs! I then had to attend to the mule-cart. I followed the tracks of the mule-cart and passed the big ant heap with its top sheared off by the cart. Of course this ant heap was the reason why I had been propelled so high into the air.

Then I saw the mules, caught inside a large thorn bush. Behind the mules, the wheel of the overturned cart pointed towards the sky. I looked for Mudschi, but he was nowhere to be seen. I called a few times, and eventually there was a muffled reply from under the cart.

Fortunately the two mules were caught deep inside the thorn bush, or they would have dragged the overturned mule-cart who knows how far, and Mudschi could have been badly hurt. To prevent the mules from breaking loose, I securely tied one to the tree with the leather whip, which was lying next to the cart. I could only use my left arm, but fortunately I could lift the cart high enough for Mudschi to emerge with some difficulty. Fortunately he was not hurt, but quite grey from shock and dust. When Mudschi finally appeared from under the cart, we could set about righting it.

I had trouble with that right arm for a long time. We had planned to deepen the Grenspos well, and I had no intention of missing out on the activities at the outpost because of my broken forearm. I kept the fracture quiet from Mr Böhme and consequently did not have it put in plaster.

I will definitely remember the pain I had to endure when Mr Böhme greeted me with a handshake just before we left for Grenspos. Mr Böhme had an overdeveloped right hand. It was huge and powerful because he had to use it to do everything. When he greeted you by hand, it always felt as if he were pulling your arm from its socket. It certainly felt so, and more, on the day I left for Grenspos. I nearly sank to my knees when the old man greeted me.

During my stay at Grenspos I had to practise shooting with the rifle resting on my right elbow, but in the end it worked quite well.

My dogs

I have now told the most exciting stories about me and my Bushmen in my time at Onguma, but I also want to pay homage to my dogs; the most loyal friends I have ever had. No person will put his life in danger and willingly sacrifice himself as a dog does. I have experienced this time and again.

When I went to Onguma, there were more than twenty domestic cats and eight useless dogs. Initially I was a stranger to the dogs, but I have the ability to become good mates with a dog. I sleep badly, and in my early days at Onguma I hardly caught a wink at night, because the twenty cats had formed a rather raucous orchestra and choir. And who could blame them on such an isolated farm? They enjoyed their sex orgies to the enthusiastic accompaniment of the choir, and they were very merry and exuberant. I was the only one who disapproved. I've lost count of the number of nights I had to get up to disperse this orchestra with stones and knobkerries simply to enjoy a few minutes' sleep.

The dogs quickly sussed out on whose side this new master was, and we created a new underground movement. The password was: "*Katze, Katze!*"

After a while I simply needed to say this word very quietly, but with a hissing sound, and I had the full cooperation of the family *Canis*. The cats' choir would be interrupted, and concluded with a mournful miaow, and the next morning Mr Böhme picked up another cold, stiff, stretched-out cat carcass from the ground. Every time this happened, he was most indignant, and wondered what had got into the dogs lately, acting like that, little suspecting who the actual instigator was. The cat choir became smaller and smaller, until the last member was buried with full honours. Aunt Ella, to whom these cast actually belonged, had very little time for the dogs. But the air literally began to clear and the feline sex smells began to fade.

At the beginning of my stay at Onguma I went hunting guineafowl with the dogs nearly every afternoon. Mr Böhme's .22 Mauser hung outside on the verandah day and night. I had free access to the rifle, and after work I took it from its hook, cocked it a few times with an audible click, and softly said "*Katze, Katze*". All the dogs would bound around me quite madly, and couldn't wait to go to the bush with me. We soon formed a very close and unbreakable bond.

I have already told of how I shot my first lion when the dogs did not yet fully trust me, but in time this changed completely as they gained more experience in hunting. Eventually there were a number of casualties, and the ranks had to be filled with new dogs. We began breeding them ourselves; mostly bull terriers crossed with fox terriers.

Bull terriers were the only dogs that would attack a lion without hesitation, but they suffered great losses. I had to teach them, from a young age, to respect predators. This is why I first had the young dogs attack jackals caught in traps, and later to tackle hyenas in the same way. This experience came in useful when they later attacked cheetahs, leopards, wildebeest, kudu, gemsbok and eventually lions. Very few dogs reached old age; most of them were killed by lions, gemsbok, leopards or wildebeest. It was heartbreaking every time.

93

I had top dogs, many who were good, a few mediocre and some very bad.

The largest number of dogs I ever had at Onguma at one time was 21, but this number could change quite rapidly. The fewest I ever had to get along with, was four.

Goliath, the bull terrier–boer mastiff cross

Goliath was a big, strong dog and leader of the pack, even though, as a young dog, he was of rather average ability.

One day I was on Palmvlakte, looking for meat rations for the Bushmen. A herd of wildebeest ran past us at a distance of some 180 paces. I picked the biggest bull, but a dull thud indicated that the shot must have hit him in the stomach. A wildebeest can go far with a stomach wound, because it must surely be one of toughest game species. We only had three dogs with us on that day, because at that stage I had very few dogs left. After the shot the dogs ran after the wildebeest, and after some distance I could see that they had cut off the wounded wildebeest bull. As we were moving towards the wildebeest bull, I could see a white bundle flying through the air over the bull's head. I realised that one of my dogs had been caught by the wildebeest's horns; either Goliath, or his full brother Rollmops, considerably smaller, but sturdy and round.

We crept up to the fighting wildebeest bull, and I shot him dead. When we reached the carcass, Goliath was missing. I saw him lying under a tree some distance away, all covered in blood. An examination showed a large wound in his right shoulder. The wound was about 7,5 cm long and about 2,5 cm wide. Some of the dog's ribs were missing, and beneath the wound I could see his lung moving as he breathed. It was a terrible wound, and my first instinct was to give the dog the coup de grâce. I had already loaded, and was aiming at Goliath's head when it occurred to me that I had very few dogs left. I changed my mind. I had to do all in my power to get him through this.

I sent Willie to fetch the mule-cart, which was standing about 20 kilometres away at our camp in the bush. I stayed with Goliath and tried to comfort him all the time, but asked myself whether I was doing the right thing. I could see he was suffering a great deal of pain.

Eventually Willie arrived with the mule-cart, and we loaded the wildebeest carcass and the dog on it and journeyed to the camp. On arrival I thoroughly cleaned Goliath's wound, disinfected it with Datons Wound Powder and sutured the wound as best I could. There were no anaesthetics, and the Bushmen had to hold Goliath down. Then I placed a large wad of cotton-wool, liberally sprinkled with wound powder, on top of the wound and kept it in place with bandages wound round his body. My tent was pitched beneath a thorn tree. I tied Goliath to the tree, almost next to my bed, and made up a bed for him from old blankets in such a manner that he could hardly move. I gave him food and water.

I will never forget the first three days and nights. Goliath yelped in pain virtually day and night, and I got almost no sleep. The thought often entered my mind that I should shoot the dog, yet I stuck with my decision. The surface wound closed after a while, and I began leading Goliath for short distances. I took off the chain after about two weeks to enable him to move about freely. The dog got well, apart from a permanent deep hollow under the skin.

In this regard something remarkable happened. When it was time to go home, I struck my tent underneath the thorn tree, loaded it on the mule-cart with the rest of the baggage and took it to Onguma. I left my large three-legged pot with cooked meat near the fire-place to make sure there would be food when we came to fetch the next load in the afternoon.

On our return I looked for the camel-thorn. It served as an excellent beacon amongst the yellowwoods, as it was the only tree to provide a bit of shade. But I couldn't see the tree's crown anywhere, no matter how hard I looked, and it took a long time to find the camp.

The torn camel-thorn crown was lying on the ground, next to a short, broken-off stump. The middle part of the tree was missing, but pieces of camel-thorn wood were scattered all about. Close by, my three-legged pot rested on the cinders of coals that had been doused by rain. That very morning, the tent had stood under that camel-thorn to which Goliath had been chained for a very long time. We had hardly left, or a bolt of lightning from a passing thunder-storm had hit that very tree. To this day I ask myself: was this an act of Providence?

After the incident with the wildebeest, Goliath's skills developed even further. He hunted carefully and judiciously, and never lost a hot trail. Whenever a wounded buck fled, I often saw Goliath chasing that animal down. While running, he then ran in between the animal's forelegs, or took it from behind, grabbing the animal by the nose, and slamming on the brakes. Most of the animals then went head over heels, landing on their backs. In a flash, Goliath would then take them by the throat and throttle them. Animals that managed to stay on their feet often hurled him into the air, but in such cases he never let go of the nose, until the animal eventually fell over, which gave him the opportunity to grab it by the throat.

Goliath was at his very best with lions. He often came with us of his own accord when we went in pursuit of lions. The lion spoor often looked quite fresh, and then I wondered when Goliath would give them some attention. Initially he always walked behind us, and I often got cross because he wasn't ahead of us.

Time and again Goliath quite casually slipped past us at the right time, began sniffing at this branch or that tuft of grass, and then disappeared. Five or ten minutes later we would hear his double bark, always followed by the angry roar of a lion. It would then become quiet for a while, and eventually Goliath's double bark would sound, followed by the lion's grunt or roar when he charged the dog. We often had to run long distances in the wake of the dog and lion until we finally caught up and had a chance to shoot the lion. If we were close enough, we often crept up close to this business to see what was going on.

It was almost the same procedure each time. When the lion tired, it burrowed into thick bush with its behind, and pawed at the dog. Goliath then circled around the lion at a safe distance, and waited for us. Only occasionally would he give his double bark, and he never gave up on a lion. Later I took only him on lion hunts; he was more effective than all the other dogs put together.

Goliath meets an unexpected end

One day a Bushman reported that a trap set for jackals had disappeared.

"There were lion tracks near the trap, so I rather came back," the Bushman said. It was quite some distance from home, so we hitched the mules to the cart and went to the spot where the trap had been set. We tied the mules to a tree and continued on foot. I took all the dogs with me on that day. On the one hand it was a mistake, because the more dogs there are, the less cautious they become, and the greater your losses are. We followed the drag-marks for a long while, and eventually found the lion. It was a large female. She was very aggressive from the start, and chased the dogs this way and that. We had to run to keep up, and then Willie shouted: "I think she's free, you must shoot her quickly, or she'll get away!" He was right. The lion had shaken off the trap and was chasing the dogs at will. Eventually I got a chance to shoot the lioness amongst all the dogs. All the dogs started sniffing and pulling at the dead lioness. It seemed as if none of them had sustained any serious injuries. We put the lioness on the mule-cart and went home, with the dogs in tow.

The next morning I was busy training a young horse for Mr Böhme when Sofia, the young Bushman servant, came over and said: "Your dog Goliath is dead!" I could not believe what I had heard, and asked her to repeat it.

"Goliath is there, under that palm. He's dead. Come and see for yourself" she said, and turned away. I steered the horse over to the palm tree where Goliath was lying curled up, as if he were sleeping. Bluebottles were swarming all over him, however, and he wasn't breathing. It hit me like a thunderbolt; I could not accept it.

I removed my saddle from the horse and walked back to Goliath's body. He was already cold and stiff. Intestinal fluid had dripped from a small wound to his hindquarters. The lioness's canines must have punctured his belly and torn the intestines. While we were bringing the lioness's carcass home the day before, I could remember Goliath favouring one of his hind legs when he was walking, but I had paid it no attention because I could see no blood. All alone, quietly, without complaint, Goliath had died an honourable hero's death.

I asked Willie to bury him. Only Willie had the required dignity to perform such a task.

I walked over to Mr Böhme and told him about Goliath's death. I felt a great lump in my throat. At first he looked at me as if he hadn't understood what I was saying, and then asked: "Goliath, dead?" He could see that I was greatly affected, and then said quietly: "Well, Mr Stark, I know how you felt about that dog; you need not work today ..."

Under one of the large thorn trees beside the Etosha Pan, where I sat many a night in the moonlight when I wanted to be alone with my Creator and nature, I cried long and hard. There was a pain in my chest I had never felt before; I think it was what one calls "heartache" ...

Poempie, the mongrel

Second on my list of favourite dogs was Poempie, a scrawny little wire-haired mongrel. I've already told of the narrow squeak we had with the abandoned "tyres", when Poempie and his late brother almost certainly saved my life. I told of the great tear from his ear to the bottom of his shoulder, and how we carried him home and nursed him. From that day on, this little dog and I were inseparable. He wanted nothing to do with lions any more, but he was great where other game was concerned. He was quite aware of his immense status in my eyes, and his attitude reflected it. He never stood back for any other dog, no matter how big and strong, and I often had to wade in when he became involved in a fight with another dog and was not having the better of it. Of course the other dogs were very jealous of him.

He met his end while I was in Germany for advanced riding training. During my absence a young man who stood in for me went hunting guineafowl one evening. The dogs chased a large black mamba into a tree, and the young man then shot the mamba with the .22, but instead of shooting the snake in the head, he hit the body. When the mamba fell out of the tree, the dogs grabbed it. Three of my best dogs, Poempie amongst them, bit the dust that evening through the stupidity of an inexperienced hunter.

Hekse, the bull terrier bitch

Among my bull terriers there was one who was particularly good for all types of hunting. She lived a relatively long life, and was a dog we bought when she was still very young. Our bull terriers came from a farmer in the Outjo District, and they were all outstanding dogs.

One day we were out hunting wildebeest for meat rations; a cow. She did not die instantly, and fought the dogs. We were riding home after I had given her the fatal shot, and we had loaded her onto the wagon. On the way back I noticed something hanging from Hekse's stomach. We stopped, and I saw that her intestines were protruding from a gaping wound behind her chest The intestines were not perforated, but the belly fat was covered in grass, sand and gravel. I once again took a chance, turned her on her back, took her in my arms, clambered aboard the cart, and gave Willie the reins.

She had to undergo a serious operation when we arrived home. We put her on a table, and told a few Bushmen to hold her still. I then cut away the soiled belly fat with a pair of scissors and pushed back the uninjured intestines bit by bit into the stomach cavity with my thumbs. It was a lengthy process, which must have been extremely painful for the dog. She was yelping, moaning and grunting all the time, and her tongue turned blue from pain. The intestines kept falling out again, and I had a hard time keeping them inside. Eventually I pushed back the last piece of intestine and quickly sutured the wound with khaki thread while the Bushmen struggled to control the squirming dog. I think one will only be able to perform such an operation on a bull terrier – any other dog would have driven you mad with its yelping. I used copious amounts of Datons Wound Powder, spread a thick wad of cotton wool over the wound, and kept all in place with bandages wound around the dog's body. I kept the dog chained up for a few days and tended the wound daily until it had healed.

Moritz, the fox terrier, and the large cobra

Moritz was an ordinary fox terrier of the large type. He always came along just for the ride. He was only interested in birds and mice, and when it came to lions, he was always way back in the queue. I therefore paid him very little attention.

One Sunday afternoon I was walking from my outside room to the verandah of the main house to have some coffee and cake with the Böhmes. Aunt Ella baked cake every weekend, and Mr Böhme and I never missed a crumb.

After the coffee and cake I dawdled back to my room. Moritz was lying in the middle of the footpath some distance away from my room, as if waiting for me. When I got close, he suddenly stood up and jumped up against me with all four paws, as if he were trying to push me away. When he landed back on the ground, he immediately turned around and made off in the direction of my room at full speed. Then I saw a very large striped cobra (known as a zebra snake) lying in front of the room's door. He attacked the zebra snake without hesitation. However, he grabbed the cobra too far behind its neck, and I could see the cobra biting him several times. I had nothing in my hands, and needed to run past the two struggling animals to get hold of a knobkerrie in my room. When I returned, the snake was dead. Moritz was still shaking the snake in anger.

I fetched the snake-bite equipment and injected the dog according to the instructions. However, I could see that the snake had bitten the dog on the head and neck. There was very little chance that the dog would survive.

The next morning he lay there stiff, cold and dead. The brave little dog was very much in my thoughts that night, and I immediately had a great deal of respect for him – but too late.

I buried my dog with full honours; it was all I could do for him. One thing was certain: that dog was fully aware of the snake! He tried to push me away from the snake, and did not hesitate to sacrifice his life for me. It really makes you think.

Satan, the large bull terrier

Satan was Hekse's brother and a very good hunting dog, just like her. He went through all the stages of training for the hunt, survived and became a full-grown dog. He was a very strong dog, and completely without fear. I mostly admired his way of dealing with lions. While the other dogs distracted the lion, he would jump on it obliquely from behind, and then fasten onto its neck, just behind the ears. His paws then hung down on either side of the lion's neck. He was quite literally riding those lions. I always had to make very sure of my shots to avoid hitting him. I saw him riding a lion like that a few times; it was no coincidence.

Piekie-Pieks, the miniature fox terrier

Piekie-Pieks was a small, short, round fox terrier, a real scamp, naughtier than most. He always maintained a safe distance of about five metres between himself and me. He had known many a knobkerrie or stone to whistle past his ears, and he was the instigator of mischief amongst the pack.

When we harnessed the mules, he had the irritating habit of standing before the mules, barking excitedly, which resulted in a great barking chorus. The young bull terriers then often saw their

100

way open to attack the mules, and before you knew it, a young bull terrier was hanging on a mule's nose. This created great consternation, because the mules reared and jumped, and a broken harness was often the end result. When you eventually managed to leave the yard in the cart, Mr Böhme's large oxen and dairy cows by the side of the road were next in line. Piekie-Pieks simply barked, but we often had to rush to where we could hear an ox or cow mooing. When we got there, the animal was often on the ground with the young bull terriers at its throat, nose and ears.

I had to act decisively and very forcefully in the case of the bull terriers, no matter how much I loved them. The cudgel then sang its merry tune, and I had to hurl the terriers as far away from their victim as I could, because they simply attacked again and again. While you are getting rid of one dog, the next had already gone for the throat. Eventually all of them learned to distinguish between wild and domesticated animals, but what a struggle it was! And Piekie-Pieks's trouble-making certainly did not make things any easier. Many's the time that I grabbed my .303 in anger to put an end to Piekie-Pieks's tricks, but Willie always grabbed my arms and would not allow it, as he had a very soft spot for the little dog.

Piekie-Pieks also enjoyed great favour among all the lady-dogs, young and old, big and small. Whenever a bitch came on heat, Piekie-Pieks arranged matters so as to be the first to win her affections. He usually instigated a fight amongst the big dogs, and while they were occupied in this manner, he grabbed his opportunity to make it with the lady.

He would rather endure the punishment afterwards meted out by the big dogs than leave a bitch alone. In the end I helped him whenever murder was on the menu.

The little fox terrier wasn't just about mischief. He had some good characteristics too. He had endless stamina, and was always the last to give up when some wild animal was cornered.

Simba, father of the bull terriers

Quite near the end of my career at Onguma, we bought the parents of all the bull terriers we had acquired, as the farmer was no longer interested in breeding. We then also got old Simba, the forefather.

He was already old, with no canines any more, and his left eye

101

was missing. Apparently he had lost the eye while hunting porcupines. He and his wife, the original breeding female, were almost deaf, which usually happens with elderly bull terriers.

Simba quickly adapted and was a good hunter. Because he was so old, I always let him run behind the mule-cart for short distances only, then helped him aboard. He enjoyed riding on the cart very much, and he always had standing-room on board.

One day we quarrelled, however. I had to take a large load of salt-lick to various outposts. The mule-cart was heavily laden, and because we had to cover such a distance, I did not want to take any of the dogs with me. But how do you explain this to a half-deaf bull terrier? When undertaking trips like these, I always put the dogs in a special holding-pen. Not without great difficulty, of course, because you had no sooner wrestled one dog inside, than another sneaked out again, as they all wanted to go along, of course.

While I was busy with the dogs, Simba had already taken his place on the cart. I picked him up and put him on the ground. I had hardly done this, or he was on the cart again. I lost my temper when he did this for the third time. I grabbed him by the tail and wanted to pull him to the ground. I should not have done that! He turned around in a flash and was at my throat with an angry growl, and held fast, as bull terriers do.

In order to prevent further injury, I fell to the ground with him, and lay on top of him. I immediately grabbed his throat with my hands and choked him. If I tried to tear him away, I could have been badly injured, perhaps tearing an artery in the process, as his jaws were clamped on either side of my neck. Fortunately I was still able to breathe – my throat was not entirely closed off.

And so we lay on the ground, with my body on top of his, and both my thumbs pressing hard on his Adam's apple. Willie wanted to help him, but I shook my head to indicate he should not interfere, because I knew Simba would have to give in at some stage. Simba's tongue turned blue, and then he began to urinate. When his jaws relaxed, I extricated my neck without serious injuries. He had to endure a number of hard blows from my fist for his aggressiveness towards me, just to make sure he knew which one of us was the boss.

I was never actually cross with Simba. He was an old dog and wasn't brought up by me, so I forgave him quite soon. One should not pull such a dignified figure by the tail!

My first encounter with elephants

In all the years I worked at Onguma, there were never any elephants. Deep pit traps had been made in the limestone around the
Onguma, Coantzas and Harib waterholes. They were about 3 to 4
metres deep and about 5 to 6 metres across. It must have taken an
enormous effort to dig those pits, because they had all been made
in limestone. Taking into account the tools the people of those times
had at their disposal, it must have been an enormous undertaking.

When I asked who had dug those pits, and why, Willie told me
the Owambos had come down from the north many years before.
When elephants came to drink, they frightened the animals, herded
them into the pits and then killed them with their primitive weapons. Willie had heard this from other old Bushmen, but had never
seen it himself. In all the years that Mr Böhme had owned the farm,
there had never been elephants, but the pits were there.

There was a large, good field of lucerne just outside the outbuild-
ing in which I slept. It was Mr Böhme's pride and joy. No animal
was allowed to graze near that field. The lucerne was cut daily, and
Mr Böhme then fed it to all his favourite animals, for example the
tame eland and zebra. Banner, my horse that I had brought with me
from Voigtskirch, was not one of his favourite animals, and always
came off second best. I used the opportunity and let Banner into the
lucerne field at night. In the evening I heard Banner running about
in the lucerne field, snorting quite excitedly all the time. I thought
lions were about. It was a pitch black night. I grabbed my .303 and a
torch, went to the lucerne field and searched for the lions, but saw
nothing. After a while Banner calmed down, and I returned to my
room.

Early the next morning, as I was drinking a cup of coffee on the
verandah, I saw Hanjama, Stefanus's elder brother, running about
in the lucerne field, looking at some tracks. Every now and then
he shook his head. I asked what he was seeing. He answered in
the Bushman language: "There were elephants here!" The word for
"elephant" was not yet in my vocabulary, and Willie, who had heard
the conversation, interpreted. When he mentioned elephants, I
was eager to see them, and I immediately asked Willie whether we
would spot them if we followed the tracks. He said yes.

We quickly finished our coffee, and were off. When we walked
past Hanjama to look for the elephant tracks, he said: "Leave the

dogs at home, because they will annoy the elephants!" However, I took the dogs along, because I was convinced they would leave the elephants alone.

Willie and I followed the tracks west, in the direction of Etosha. We travelled through the bush for about 8 kilometres, following the tracks, when we saw the Etosha Pan stretched out before us, on the other side of the river bank of the Omuramba Owambo, flowing south from Owamboland and Angola and disgorging into the Etosha Pan. There are deep permanent pools near the river mouth, and three large elephant bulls were bathing there. I wanted to see the elephants from closer by, and walked in their direction. Suddenly my dogs followed the elephant tracks and began running in their direction at full speed. I immediately realised that this meant trouble. The elephants began trumpeting, and I saw my bull terriers jumping to grab hold of the elephants' ears, while the elephants were brushing them off their ears with their trunks like ticks, hurling them high into the air.

Only when the dogs realised what strong animals they were dealing with, did they come back to me.

We had no rifle with us, there was no shelter to be seen, and we had to make sure we got back home in time. Willie and I turned tail in a flash and began running home. To crown it all, a light east wind was blowing, and home lay in the east.

After a while our legs just couldn't carry us any longer, home was still far away, and we had to walk. I looked back while we were walking, and about 30 metres behind and a little to the side of us I spotted a large elephant bull emerging from the bush, walking along our tracks. His trunk was pointed downwards, just like a Bushman tracker's stick as he followed spoor. It was a hopeless situation, and we had to get downwind. Our only salvation would be to run at an angle in the elephant's direction, round him from behind in a semicircle, and then head for home in a wide arc. It was a difficult situation, but we had little choice; we simply had to get downwind.

I gave Willie a hand sign to show he had to follow me, and our flight started again. Our legs felt as heavy as lead, we were completely out of breath, and the sound of breaking branches and the elephant's trumpeting had a paralysing effect on me.

We now had to run home parallel to the elephant, in other words using a deviation in order to get downwind. This is very difficult

104

when you are tired and counting every step, but it was our only chance of escape. I could see the elephant hesitating as we were running, so we ran as fast as our legs could carry us.

Eventually we reached home and fell down on the verandah's stairs like two wet rags. I felt as if my lungs were dancing about in front of my mouth like two glowing bellows, and I had absolutely no power left in my legs. Willie was not much better off, and we lay panting on the cold concrete floor of the verandah.

As we were lying there, I made up my mind that the elephants had treated us most unfairly, and decided to take revenge. I wanted to teach these elephants a lesson and make them run as fast as they had made me run.

In-between the panting, I asked Willie to call Stefanus. When Stefanus arrived, I instructed him to saddle my horse Banner as quickly as possible.

When Stefanus brought me the saddled horse, I took my old 12-bore shotgun with bird-shot shells. I gathered the available dogs who had in the meantime arrived, and we returned to the elephants. When I passed through the thicket on the shore of the Etosha Pan, I could see three bulls walking back to Namutoni. I caught up with them at a lively gallop, and passed in front of them. They lifted their heads and trunks in surprise and tried to determine who was so bold as to get in their way. In the meantime some of the dogs had caught up, and the show was on again. I rode into the wind, and when they caught my scent, they charged. This was open country, and I had no trouble in staying ahead of them. I drew them towards Onguma's border. When they tired, I rode very close in front of them, and when they charged, I rode away ahead of them. Eventually two of the younger bulls lagged behind, and I let them be. The larger, older bull, which I recognised as the one that had chased us when we were still on foot, kept on coming, even though he was quite tired. The dogs did their bit, biting his feet here and there. Every now and then one of them sailed through the air, but bull terriers can take that. In this way we reached the border of the Etosha Pan.

The elephant had long since ceased to be overly aggressive, and I became the hunter, and the elephant the hunted. If he started walking too slowly, I let loose a shot in the air above him. In this way I was driving him like a steer. Eventually he was so tired that he sought out the shade of a large mushara tree and just stood underneath it. He must have felt the way I felt a little while ago on the verandah of Onguma's homestead. The dogs, too, were exhausted and sought out the shade under the trees closest to the elephant.

Only one dog was still going strong – Piekie-Pieks. He sat in front of the elephant, barking and trying to bite the elephant's trunk every now and then. He was too quick for the elephant, and eventually the elephant had twisted his trunk around his right tusk. Piekie-Pieks then began biting the elephant's feet again. The bull shifted his feet. In the end he devised a plan which worked quite well. He used his trunk to break off a large branch from the mushara tree, and swatted away the dog below him with it. Piekie-Pieks's angry barking roused the other dogs, and they helped Piekie-Pieks for a while. Then the elephant swatted away the whole lot with his branch.

During all this commotion I saw the dust-cloud of a vehicle approaching from the direction of Namutoni; the Böhmes had returned. I quickly rode to the road, heading them off, and said they should come and look at the elephant I had tied to a tree to welcome them. They drove to where the elephant was, and their amazement knew no boundaries. In the meantime I had begun feeling sorry for the bewildered elephant, so I whistled for the dogs, waved goodbye to the bull with my hat, and we all went home in triumph. Little did I know that this incident would form the basis of what would later become a large part of my work as a nature conservationist.

I did realise one thing, however; you do not walk in the direction of an elephant without a rifle!

The kudu cow, the zebra stallion and the elephant bull

One day I had to go to Namutoni to fetch a load of goods for Mr Böhme. I always went ahead on horseback while the ox-wagon, drawn by six or eight oxen, lagged behind. The goods had to be off-loaded from the railway buses at Namutoni, and I had to acknowledge receipt.

From Namutoni the water from a fountain runs along the road to Onguma for about a kilometre. It draws a wide variety of game that come to drink there, and on this day there was a large herd of kudu. The ox-wagon was not far behind me. I rode back to Willie and told him I was going to catch a kudu – he had to follow my spoor into the bush. He was reluctant at first, because we were far too close to the Fort. However, as it was mid-day, and everybody was probably resting, I decided to risk it. There is a bare plain near the waterhole, but there are bushes and trees a kilometre to the south. Once you have disappeared into those trees, you have also disappeared from the sight of the Fort.

I drove the kudu into the bush at full speed, and after a while I overtook a fine cow, and grabbed hold of her ears and lower jaw until Willie and another two Bushmen reached us with the ox-wagon. They quickly hobbled the kudu with some thongs, and lifted her onto the wagon. I instructed Willie to move through the trees alongside the pan to Onguma, and I rode ahead again.

About halfway to Onguma, there was a herd of zebra in the pan, amongst them a fairly large foal. I once again told Willie to follow my trail, and I went for the zebra in the direction of the trees at full tilt. When I overtook the herd of zebra, I discovered that the distance had caused me to make a mistake with regard to the foal's age, and that it was probably close to a year old. I only managed to control it with a great deal of effort, but I hobbled it with a leather strap. The ox-wagon arrived a bit later, and after a huge struggle we loaded the young zebra stallion alongside the kudu cow.

A little shy of Twee Palms we came across a herd of seven young eland bulls of about 18 months old – properly weaned.

Because we were almost at the border of Nonguma and far removed from Namutoni, I decided to catch an eland on the pan, rather than chasing it into the trees. Eland are not great runners, and after a short ride I was in amongst them. When I grabbed the nearest eland bull by the horns and was preparing to jump off my horse, I felt my one foot catch in the stirrup. I did not want to land on the ground head first, so I let go of the eland's horn, and grabbed the ring on Banner's snaffle in a flash. I took firm hold of his mane with the other hand, and was left dangling by his side. Banner immediately began whirling in a circle, while snorting and bellowing like an ox, and then changed direction in tight turns. Every time he did this, I was hurled outwards. Eventually the riding-boot which had caught in the stirrup burst open along the seam at the back. My foot slipped from the stirrup, and now both legs, being free, swung in circles as the horse turned.

I let go of the snaffle-ring and the horse's mane at the same time, and I was hurled free without getting a kick for my troubles.

I had scarcely stopped rolling across the plain or I was on my feet, one of them stockinged. My first thoughts were of the eland, and I eventually caught up with them. Every time I tried to grab hold of an eland bull's horns, he simply swung his head to one side, and I missed. After a while I began panting wildly, and grabbed the eland's tail in desperation, knowing that I was in danger of getting kicked in the teeth. And so it happened. I had grabbed the eland's tail as close to his body as possible, and hoisted up my entire body. I was hanging on to the eland with the whole weight of my body. After a few vicious kicks, the eland's hind legs began to sag. I had no strap or thong with me; they had been used to subdue the kudu cow and zebra stallion, so I could only use my belt. I fixed it so that it passed around one of the eland's horns while the other end was tied to one foreleg, above the knee. This prevented the eland from getting up or running.

I then left the eland, because I was exhausted. I had struggled with the kudu, then the zebra; I had had to cling onto my horse's neck, then chase down the eland, and finally wrestle it to the ground, and all this activity had taken its toll. I sat by the eland until Willie arrived with the ox-wagon. He was laughing loudly and clapping his hands, shouting all the while: "*Aure agatse! Aure agatse!* You're the man! You're the man!" As everything had occurred on an open plain, they were able to witness the entire proceedings. We loaded the eland bull onto the wagon with great difficulty – and loaded me as well, as my horse had disappeared! We only caught up with Banner at the gate in the boundary-fence, where he was standing and waiting for us. The reason why my foot had caught in the stirrup like that, was that my boots were second-hand, re-soled riding boots. The new sole had come unstuck, and the stirrup had slid underneath the front end of the sole, getting stuck.

If I had not reacted as quickly, clinging to the horse's snaffle and mane, Banner would very probably have kicked or dragged me to my death. He went completely crazy if something went slightly wrong on mounting or dismounting him.

He was a difficult horse when I began working with him at Voigtskirch. He threw me almost every day. Even though he was almost 17 hands, he bucked like a rodeo pony. He jumped straight up, and turned almost 90 degrees with every leap. If you sat on him, there was nothing in front of you, as his head was between his forelegs, and almost nothing behind you either.

He would stand almost on the spot, bucking like this and turning, while making the most horrible groaning sounds.

I almost succeeded in staying on him one day. I managed to get into his bucking rhythm quite nicely on that day, and began feeling quite safe – until I noticed the saddle loosening up beneath me.

It happened again. While bucking, he suddenly fell down. I landed in front of him, with the saddle between my legs, and on landing, I had also pulled the bridle over his ears. I lay there with the saddle between my legs, the bridle in one hand. Quite remarkably, the girth had not broken or loosened – Banner had simply left it. Still bucking like crazy, he disappeared over the horizon with a bare back.

At Voigtskirch old man Wiese and I nearly always rode to the various outposts together to check whether the cattle were all right. One day we rode to the Ovio outpost, about ten kilometres south of the farmhouse, along the Nossob River. Old man Wiese loved riding along the river, even though there were many side-streams and fallen tree-trunks. I had to jump all these obstacles on my young horses.

Near Ovio there was a garden belonging to the black foreman there. As was the custom, the house was enclosed with thorn branches to ensure that the goats and cattle do not come inside. Old man Wiese thought this was just the right jump for Banner and I – those two hard cases. "*Na*, Peter, I wonder if you can do it?" he said in his usual challenging way. I really had no choice.

Banner and I sailed over the obstacle at the first try, but because the fence was so high, a thorn branch got stuck in Banner's tail. He first pulled in his haunches, with the thorn branch between his buttocks. Then he went completely haywire. He began bucking unbelievably high, and kicked out with his hind legs at every jump. I remained seated for a long while, but eventually I had to vacate the saddle. I landed behind him and while I was still in the air, he hit me with a haymaker on the back of my head, exactly where the head and neck come together. It felt as if my whole head was exploding. Everything went dark, and my body felt numb. In my subconscious I heard old man Wiese shouting all the time: "Peter, Peter, stand up, stand up!" My vision cleared only some time afterwards, and eventually I was able to stand up, though I felt very wobbly. Banner was still in the kraal, and so I was able to catch him. We removed some of the branches from the enclosure, led Banner out, and I mounted him again. We returned home at a very sedate

walk. I had an unbearable headache, and everything was hazy before my eyes. Aunt Wiese sent me to bed for the rest of the day.
After a night's rest, I still had a slight headache the next day, but at
least I could see. Everything returned to normal after a while. Old
man Wiese tried to avoid talking to me as much as possible, but he
mentioned (to other people) that he had been very worried, and
thought the horse had kicked me to death. He was about thirty metres away, but could clearly hear a loud crack as Banner hit my head
with his hoof. "Like when you hit a table with a hammer," he would
explain to those people.

The end of Banner

While Banner and I were at Onguma, he developed into an exceptional horse. He left most of his bad habits behind, and I often took
him to shows where he won dressage and showjumping competi-
tions. It was part of my work to take Banner and three or four other
horses from Onguma to Tsumeb station on my own. Mr Böhme's
dressage horses always went along, too.

I tied the horses together on short leads, and from the outermost
horse a control-rein fixed to his bridle ran to my right hand across
the other three horses. In this way all the horses moved together
neatly, in echelon, and I could decide whether to walk, trot or gallop. I covered the distance of 135 kilometres in two days, saddling
and riding a fresh horse every now and then.

Eventually Banner developed into an outstanding game captur-
ing and sporting horse, and became virtually indispensable. I forgot
all about the days of wrangling and being thrown at Voigtskirch,
and my initial grudge against him turned to love and respect.

One day I was riding him to catch eland. We were soon on the
trail of a herd of eland, and I was driving the herd through the
bush at a gallop. When the eland changed direction, I wanted to
take a short-cut to catch up to them quicker. A large old ant heap
with a young makalani palm on top was in my way. I steered Banner straight at the ant heap, with the intention that he should jump
right over it. While the horse was in the air during the jump, I saw
a large aardvark hole right in front of us, exactly where the horse
was supposed to land. I could not change the horse's direction in
the air, and I lifted myself from the saddle in order to land next to
the horse. As I was rolling on the ground, I heard a heavy thud,

and everything was hidden in a cloud of dust. When I got up and looked at Banner, he was lying on the ground, his neck twisted to one side quite unnaturally. On closer examination I saw that he had broken his neck. He was still alive, but was groaning in pain all the time. I had to walk home, fetch my rifle and come and relieve my horse's misery. It wasn't easy. I had to give my best friend the coup de grâce.

I had been working for Mr Böhme at Onguma for six years now. In that time, I spent one year and nine months in Germany undergoing advanced horse-riding training, and I learned bricklaying at Swakopmund and Windhoek for nine months, following which I returned to Onguma. My period as a bricklayer apprentice was a misery – monotonous and frustrating. Eventually I signed a contract for three years with Mr Weigmann's building firm, but I lasted only nine months. In my whole life this was the only job that I deserted from. I had no problem with my colleagues, but could not get on with other people. I was involved in a fight with a new immigrant, a young German, breaking his nose and jaw with two punches, and felt that Windhoek was not the right place for me or my short temper. I asked Mr Weigmann to cancel my labour contract, but he refused. I was a very good worker, and he did not want to let me go. When I said that I would go anyway, he threatened to sue me for breach of contract, and to have me locked up. However, I found the daily grind of bricklaying so frustrating that my temper became shorter and shorter. One Friday after work I packed my tool-box and took it home. I can still remember the carpenter who always gave me a lift home after work looking at me askance and saying: "Piet, you're intending to run away!" I answered that he should not wait for me if I'm not at our usual pick-up point on Monday. On the Sunday of that weekend I took the bus to Tsumeb, and from there I telephoned Mr Weigmann to tell him about my decision. The next Monday Aunt Ellie came to fetch me in her Jeep, and I was back in my little kingdom. Instead of prosecuting me, Mr Weigmann sent me a glowing reference, which I still have.

My farewell to Onguma and the transition to S.W.A. Nature Conservation

During my sixth year of working at Onguma, the same man who had upset me terribly two years before, namely the chief game war-

111

den of South West Africa, Mr De la Bat, arrived one day, but this time he came in peace. He called me when I walked past the verandah where he and Mr Böhme were drinking coffee.

After we had talked for a bit, he suddenly asked me whether I would not rather work for them than against them. My first question was: "What kind of work would I be doing?"

"You would mainly have to catch poachers. You know that sort of work well," he replied. I immediately felt enthusiastic. "You may have to wait for a while, because your post would have to be created and advertised, but I am interested in you." Little did I know of all the red tape associated with the creation of a post and advertising it within the S.W.A. Administration at the time. We arranged for me to start working for Nature Conservation at Okaukuejo at the start of the new year.

That evening Mr Böhme did everything in his power to keep me. Double the salary, my own house, and permission to keep 30 head of cattle of my own were not enough to dissuade me from my decision to join Nature Conservation. In the end Mr Böhme was extremely cross with me, and I felt I had to press ahead with my intention.

The date for my resignation arrived, but all was quiet from Nature Conservation's side. I was too proud to ask Mr Böhme whether I could stay a bit longer, so I rode on horseback to Uncle Tappie Sachse, on the farm Operet. He worked on a mine, and returned to the farm only on weekends. I asked Uncle Tappie whether I could stay on his farm until I received notification from Nature Conservation. He was delighted, because I had helped him before whenever there were lions on his farm. He could supply me with milk, but not pay me a salary, as he himself was working for a salary.

So I went to Operet with two Bushmen, Stefanus and Hans, two dogs and three horses, the most basic clothing, firearms, of course, and my wife. We lived in Uncle Tappie's house for the first 17 days. He did not want to put me to work because he could not pay me, but I could see no sense in simply hanging around on Operet, twiddling my thumbs. I therefore decided to move to my old hunting-grounds, the Crown Land in the Mangetti area. I arranged with Uncle Tappie that he would let me know when Nature Conservation had accepted me. At Namutoni I arranged that they would let me know via Operet.

My wife Elke and I, together with the dogs, horses and Bushmen, entered the Crown Land with a bag of maize meal. It was summer, there had been good rains, the pans were filled with water, and we took along a light tent as protection against the rain. In the company of the Bushmen we lived off the veld for the next months like Bushmen. It was the life of Riley; harsh, certainly, but thinking back on it, probably the highlight of my life.

We drew water from the pans for the humans and animals; our meals consisted of maize meal and meat. Occasionally, over weekends, we would ride to visit Uncle Tappie at Operet, just to ask whether Nature Conservation had not yet made any contact.

After visiting Uncle Tappie for a short while, we would then return to our bush camp loaded with butter, milk and eggs from the farm. For about three or four days our diet would then vary a little bit.

We baked bread and even a type of bush cake, and we had sugar for our coffee. We had to earn some money for the Bushmen's salaries and for essentials such as sugar, coffee and bread flour. A few eland bulls had to pay for this with their lives. I made leather thongs from their hides, and Uncle Tappie sold these for us at Tsumeb. We had no other source of income.

It was too far to ride to Windhoek, there was no money for a train ticket, and someone had to mind the horses.

Almost every day my wife and I, sometimes accompanied by either Stefanus or Hans, would ride into the bush to explore and hunt. On some days we walked, following lion or leopard tracks, or simply for some exercise. On a few occasions I met some wild Bushmen, and studied their way of life. At night we listened to the sounds of the various animals, and sat around the campfire for hours while my wife made music. In short, it was a free, unbound, happy life, which I spent mostly in studying the Bushmen. Yet these three happy months, too, passed. I received the message one weekend: "Your appointment to Nature Conservation has been approved. The game warden at Namutoni will fetch you at Vergenoeg on Tuesday, to take you to Okaukuejo." I had reached the turning point in my life, and the wolf would be turned into the shepherd.

My work as game warden

On that Tuesday, my wife and I were at Vergenoeg at eight o' clock in the morning. We had made prior arrangements with Uncle Tappie to leave the horses, dogs and baggage at Operet until we could arrange for transport to take the lot to Okaukuejo.

Mr De la Bat had given me permission to take along my horses to use in my work. I would not have accepted the job without my horses.

Elke and I had to start walking from Operet in the dark in order to be at Vergenoeg in time; a matter of some kilometres. Like Bushmen, Elke and I bundled up the bare minimum of clothing and carried this with the support of a rifle over the shoulder. On arrival at Vergenoeg, the game warden was waiting. He did not look too friendly, because I had been a real thorn in his flesh up to that moment. The farm-owner later told us that when Elke and I emerged from the bush, the game warden said: "Here comes the worst poacher in South West Africa. I can't imagine why my boss appointed him." He took us to Okaukuejo, where Mr De la Bat welcomed us.

At that time Okaukuejo consisted of a police station, a temporary prefabricated house for Mr De la Bat, and five "luxury" huts for VIP tourists. The VIP huts consisted of one small room with a porch in front for sleeping on. There was a fireplace with a grid outside, serving as our "kitchen". This would be our "house" for the next two years. The lions had trodden a well-worn path in front of our house to come and drink water from the swimming-pool. You dared not wander about the camp at night, because you were liable to blunder into a pride of lions at any moment. The grass huts in which the tourists slept were clustered around the Okaukuejo waterhole. This may have been romantic, but certainly not very wise, because it interfered with the drinking habits of the animals, and posed great danger to the tourists. Hyenas and jackals often carried off pots and personal belongings that the tourists sometimes left outside their huts.

The workers consisted mainly of indigenous Bushmen who had their own living area, where they had built their traditional shelters of wood, about 1½ kilometres from the tourist camp. Such were the living quarters of the Okaukuejo civilisation at the time.

Because Elke and I were used to life in the bush, we did not complain. We experienced problems only later, when my wife became pregnant and experienced the discomforts of any pregnant woman. When she felt nauseous, she had to hurdle over my bed to storm outside, and then I had to stand beside her with my rifle at the ready to ensure that the lions did not drag her away. The toilets were simply too far away from the huts. I always baked my bread in a hollow next to the fireplace, and prepared our food on the grill.

We could ride to Outjo once a month to do the shopping for the whole month. One had to plan carefully, because money was tight. My starting salary was £63.10s per month.

Apart from myself and Mr De la Bat, the Strydoms lived in an old police house near the police station. Louis Strydom was a qualified motor mechanic, but apart from his vehicle repairs he had to perform a great deal of development work, particularly erecting windpumps and other installations.

At that stage the three of us were the only white staff members, and Louis's wife was the tourist officer. My very first job was to learn how to drive a motor vehicle. I knew as much about driving a vehicle as a cow about Latin. Louis took me into the bush to gather firewood on my very first day, in an ancient Austin two-ton truck. He explained the various gears, and how to use the accelerator. I had to drive for a short distance to where the wood had to be offloaded. There was a cream can filled with some of the slightly salty Okaukuejo water on the back – drinking water for myself and the Bushmen. The Austin's radiator leaked slowly but surely. In the Austin's cab there was a very important piece of green soap, used to stop the hole in the radiator from time to time. There was no time to remove the radiator and solder the hole. It was extremely hot in the Austin, and the smell of petrol was almost unbearable, so the front windscreen had to be dropped and held in place with a piece of binding wire to ensure survival. I had to fetch the second load of fire-wood on my own, with the Bushmen to help. Louis dismissed my protests that I could not yet drive with a laugh, saying: "Swim, fishie, swim!" Fortunately there was a tame Bushman named Simon who knew a little more about vehicles than I did, and he was very helpful. The two of us managed to bring back one load of fire-wood for the tourists after another, and the Austin kept on going.

The Austin was my truck. I had a blue one-ton Fargo as a service vehicle. Even if it did look as if it had come ashore in Jan van Riebeeck's ship, it somehow managed to run. It was far lighter and faster than the Austin, and early on I didn't quite make it around a bend, and ended up in a ditch. The bend was then forever named Stark's Bend. One had to accept the struggle with humour, which made things more bearable. The police stationed there watched me with eagle eyes, and constantly asked me when I was going to do the driver's test. I had to know all the road signs and regulations current at the time in order to do this. The day I had to do the test, I stood a little behind the testing official and quickly read the answers when he himself was not too sure, and looked up an answer for his own benefit. This meant it was quite easy to get my driver's licence, and for a heavy vehicle to boot!

Initially there was little in the way of catching poachers. There was too much other work. A zebra or wildebeest had to be shot every Wednesday and Saturday for the lion party. These lion parties were presented as a special treat for the tourists. There was a pride of about 12 lions at Leeubron – sometimes more, sometimes fewer, and sometimes none at all. In that case one had to sit around until eleven o' clock at night, or face sending home a bunch of very disgruntled tourists. We used the Fargo to carry the game carcasses to Leeubron, hauling them from the truck with the aid of an anchored chain. Old Kastor, a calm old beast, was the master of the pride at that stage. Isabella was the queen of the pride, and she was a really temperamental old lady. On the days when her hormones were all scrambled, she could easily attack your vehicle from far away, and that meant you had to make special plans to remove the carcass from it. Because we game rangers were not permitted to shoot anything at all for ourselves, all the carcasses first underwent some surgery. I always removed a good piece of fillet or meat from the hip, and then carefully sewed up the skin again.

Apart from the lion parties, there was always much work to be done. Windpumps had to be checked and maintained regularly. New signposts had to be put up, viewing points built, rubbish removed, general tourist patrols undertaken, fires brought under control, game counted by moonlight at the waterholes, day camps erected for tourists, with the necessary latrines, and so forth. Every day was filled with twelve working hours, and sometimes a lot more. I liked the work, feeling that it wasn't really work as I was out there in nature, amongst the wild animals, every day.

After a while my first son, Udo, was born.

One of my priorities at Okaukuejo was building the stables. Initially I built four stalls. A lion-proof fence had to be erected around the stable complex, because the Leeubron lions came to visit almost every night. Two houses for two Bushman families were also built at the stable complex. They had to raise the alarm should the lions become too bold. My service vehicle was parked near my house. When the Bushmen raised the alarm at the stables, I had to race over there to chase away the cheeky lions with the vehicle. Some nights I had to do this up to four times, as they found the smell of the horses irresistible. Once I encountered a particularly bedevilled lion who refused to budge. I had a one ton four-wheel-drive Ford bakkie at the time. The lion charged the bakkie as I was driving slowly in his direction. When I reached him, he stood up on his hind legs, slammed the nails of his front paws into the bonnet, bit the right front light to pieces, and left great holes and rents in the mudguard below the light. When Mr De la Bat saw the battered bakkie, I had a lot of explaining to do.

As horses had never before been used at Nature Conservation, I first had to prove that they would be useful in this type of work. At my own risk I had to use my horses for all kinds of tasks, and had to buy feed and tend to the horses myself, out of my own resources. This was very difficult, given my salary at the time.

When the stable complex was finished, I had to erect the exercise facilities. Two dressage areas, a lunging ring and a number of jumps inside a well-fenced camp had to be created. In the meantime some of the whites and Bushmen had to be trained as horsemen and horse handlers. I started with four young Bushmen, and they showed great progress.

My first test

There were still a few wild Bushman families in the Etosha Game Reserve who were living there illegally. I was instructed to round them up and bring them in. A certain Bushman named Agarob was related to them, and knew the veld and their circumstances well. He had to go with me. They were located in the bush about 65 kilometres south-east of Okaukuejo.

We first drove to the Du Toit family's farm Grensplaas ("Border Farm"), where I introduced myself to Uncle Danie du Toit. In time the Du Toits would become our best friends. At Grensplaas, Agarob was told at which waterholes the wild Bushmen were staying. We left the vehicle at Grensplaas and struck out into the wilderness on foot.

A young Bushman named Swart Sikspens ("Black Sixpence" – there were two Sixpences at Okaukuejo, the one black, the other yellow) came along with us. After walking for almost 20 kilometres, we found the Bushman spoor and followed them in the direction of the Gumses waterhole. On arrival at Gumses, we saw that water had recently been scooped up there. We followed the fresh trail, and Agarob warned me that the group included one full-grown young man who was very dangerous because he would not allow himself to be captured, and would not hesitate to shoot any white. Everybody was scared of him. Suddenly the operation became very interesting. While following the fresh tracks on the trot, we suddenly spied a large group of Bushmen walking in single file some distance away.

I told Agarob we needed to surprise them, and we ran after the group as silently as possible. They kept on walking, suspecting nothing, and I was able to reach the very last Bushman, a fairly old man. There was a quiver full of arrows on his back, and a bow over his shoulder. I grabbed hold of the quiver full of arrows and told him in Bushman language to sit down and surrender. He got the fright of his life and sat down immediately, calling out to the other Bushmen in front of him: "Sit down, all of you, we have been caught!" They all got an enormous fright and cried out in amazement: "Oh, we've been caught!" I explained the situation to the eldest and told them not to make any trouble, so as to avoid trouble for themselves. Agarob immediately asked where Nabekub was, namely the Bushman who had said he would never surrender. The captured Bushman pointed ahead and said that he, his wife and their child had walked on ahead. I left Swart Sikspens in control of the captured group, and Agarob and I followed the spoor. After some three kilometres we saw Nabekub and his wife walking ahead of us, suspecting nothing. We ran as quietly as possible in the direction of Nabekub, who was walking in front. Behind him his wife was carrying a 15-litre tin of water on her head, and a child in a skin on her back. When we were eight metres from them, I stumbled over a rock because all my attention was concentrated on the people in front of me, and I was somewhat tired from running. The woman heard the sound, looked around, and saw me. She got a real fright, threw the tin of water from her head and shrieked hysterically: "*Jloeee*, there are white people!" Nabekub was probably as shocked as she was. He tore the bow from his shoulder, and drew some arrows from his quiver with his other hand. I shouted at him not to shoot.

"No, I won't shoot!" he shouted back, but at the same time he slotted an arrow onto his bowstring. I drew my .38 Special Ruby. Agarob was carrying my .303, and he, too, began yelling at Nabekub, who aimed at me with the arrow, and let fly. The arrow, aimed at my heart, would most certainly have hit me, but there was just enough time to turn my torso. I had my pipe in my breast pocket, and the arrow penetrated the right-hand pocket just below the pipe. It flew past my chest inside my bush jacket, and exited the bush jacket near the left-hand breast pocket of my shirt. I fired two quick shots from my .38 on either side of his legs, shouting all the while in Bushman language: "Don't shoot, don't shoot! Stop shooting, stop it!"

Nabekub immediately shot a second arrow at my stomach, and I jumped to the left. The arrow missed my hip by a fraction. I squeezed off two more warning shots to either side of him. At the third arrow, I jumped to the right. The arrow opened up the side of my left wrist, and once more I squeezed off two warning shots on either side of him. Then, from the hip, Agarob shot into the ground below his legs with the .303, covering the Bushman with dust, because he was crouching at that moment. However, he did not allow this to distract him, and he shot at me once more. I ducked down and fell over a rock in the process. He shouted: "I've got you, you fucking bastard!" and then turned and fled, still crouching. I wanted to kill him because he had cursed at me, but I had spent all my revolver's bullets.

I was still sitting in the grass, looking at the fleeing Nabekub when Swart Sikspens and the group of captured Bushmen came trotting up. Nabekub's uncle, Xosahdonab, immediately grabbed my left arm and began sucking the poison from the arrow wound on my wrist. He shook his head, repeating in indignation: "Oh, oh, that's not right. Nabekub has done wrong."

When he no longer tasted any poison, and the wound had been cleaned to his satisfaction, he stopped sucking. I now had to explain to the Bushmen that they were in the reserve illegally and that I was forced to arrest them. We walked to their huts, where a great deal of eland biltong was hanging out to dry. At the camp there was an ancient but still well-built Bushman named Tarretauseb ("Thickneck") with snow-white hair, together with his wife. He was Nabekub's grandfather, and the old man and his wife were busy looking for mopani worms. On our arrival he was quite jovial, and said with a smile "I greet you, white man."

We had to walk to Grensplaas with my prisoners in order to get to the service vehicle. In the meantime it had grown dark, and most of the prisoners were locked up in a storeroom for the night. Xnahdanab ("Grassy Head") and Tarretauseb ("Thick-neck") lay on the ground around the campfire with us. We talked around that fire in the Bushman language until deep into the night. All the Bushmen had been born in Etosha, and had grown up there. They had worked on neighbouring farms for a while, but during the severe droughts the farmers had moved away from the frontier farms to look for grazing elsewhere, and had left the Bushmen behind. The farmers simply did not have enough money to keep them.

The Bushmen therefore returned to their birthplace inside the nature reserve.

The next morning early, after a cup of coffee supplied by the Du Toits, we loaded all the prisoners on the bakkie and drove to Okaukuejo. I thought a great deal about the lot of the Bushmen during the night, and felt very sorry for them after hearing everything the old man had told me. I felt that they were part of the reserve, and belonged there.

At Okaukuejo the chief game warden instructed me to take all the Bushmen to the police station at Outjo and to charge them.

Before arriving at the Outjo police station, I talked to the Bushmen and explained the court procedures to them. I told them that they would get an opportunity to state their case before the court pronounced judgment. I said that they should draw the magistrate's attention to the fact that Etosha was their birthplace, that a severe drought was raging, and that they were unable to obtain work as a result. I repeated that they should not be afraid to state their case, and that they had to talk.

I then handed them over to the law. One of them I did not hand over, however, namely Xosahdonab. He was Nabekub's uncle, and Nabekub was still at large. I wanted him! I had to use Xosahdonab in order to get hold of Nabekub without spilling any blood. I wasn't angry at Nabekub; in fact, I had great respect for him. He had the courage to defend his freedom against two men with firearms while armed only with a bow and arrows.

I gave Xosahdonab the choice of looking for and bringing in Nabekub. If Xosahdonab chose to run, I would pursue and find him and Nabekub, dead or alive. Xosahdonab promised that he would bring in Nabekub.

As I was loading the vehicle, a message arrived from the Outjo police station that Nabekub had given himself up at Outjo. They were not certain that it was Nabekub, but a Bushman had apparently arrived there, had placed his bow and arrows on the counter and had told the police the following: "I shot dead a white man, but my wife and my entire family were caught. I give myself up. Here

I am." We drove to Outjo to identify Nabekub. It was him. When I asked him why he had done what he had done, his excuse was that he had been badly frightened because he thought we wanted to shoot him dead. He was in leg irons and handcuffs, and was being charged with attempted murder.

Just before the magistrate was about to deliver his judgment and sentence, he asked the accused whether they had anything to say. The Bushmen needed to speak now, but they simply sat there with their heads bowed. Because I knew Bushmen well, I also knew this was the end. They would not defend themselves. I quickly raised my hand and asked the magistrate whether I could say a few words on behalf of the Bushmen. The magistrate looked at me in amazement, but allowed me to enter the witness stand and speak, I then told the magistrate about the birthplace of the Bushmen and the reasons why they had returned there.

When I had finished, the magistrate looked at me intently for a long time and then simply said: "Thank you. You may go, Sir."

He thought for a long time, and then pronounced his judgment: "The eland hunters must go to jail for a minimum of six months. All the old people and women must stay at Okaukuejo. The state will look after them by giving them indigent rations. When the hunters have completed their prison sentences, Nature Conservation must employ them and create positions for them." I felt greatly relieved. It was fair punishment. The Bushmen had a future. I loaded all the old Bushmen and drove back to Okaukuejo. Only the three hunters had to serve their sentence. On arrival at Okaukuejo, the chief game warden immediately walked over to my vehicle, even before the Bushmen could get out. He asked me what was going on, with a frown on his face. I told him what the magistrate had ordered. "Over my dead body!" he replied angrily. "Load them again and dump the scum outside the reserve. If I catch them inside the reserve again, I'll shoot them dead!"

I was gobsmacked. I couldn't believe my ears. I wanted to defend the Bushmen, but he quickly silenced me and ordered me to execute his instructions.

Then I had a plan. I kept quiet, loaded the Bushmen, and drove to the Ombika gate. The Bushmen had to alight there, on farmland. Then I gathered them all together and said: "I can't help what I have to do. Go in peace to where you are happy. Don't fear me from now on. I will never, never catch you again. If you see me, don't be

121

afraid, I will always bring you something. Don't run away from me. From now on, I'm your friend. Just be wary of strangers!" Those were my parting words.

They would have to spend the night somewhere in the bush without any shelter, blankets or food. I was certain of one thing – Bushmen can do that.

Nabekub's case was heard a few weeks later. He was accused of attempted murder. The case did not last long. He repeated that he was frightened because he looked around and saw a white man so close to him. He thought I was trying to kill him, and so he tried to defend himself. Nabekub got three years in jail – the greatest punishment for a Bushman. If they are in jail for longer than three years, there is a great risk that they may die for longing.

I have never been able to feel hatred or any bad feelings towards Nabekub, although many people could not understand why I did not shoot him dead. I simply felt admiration for him because he defended himself armed only with a bow and arrows against two men with firearms.

I never saw Nabekub again. I believe he began working on farms after serving his sentence.

My first elephant

In the wake of the foot-and-mouth-disease epidemic which had ravaged South West Africa for a long time, it was necessary to erect a game-proof fence around the Etosha Nature Reserve. The erection of this fence created a great many problems. The fence had to be patrolled and maintained constantly. As the fence progressed, I was given more and more work and responsibilities. On completion of the fence, I was responsible for 290 kilometres of its length, from the farm Renex to Otjovasundu. The main culprits who constantly damaged the game-proof fence, were elephants. The elephants broke the fence as if it were simply a spider's web. They often caused even more damage on the neighbouring farms by pushing over windpumps and trampling fences. We had to shoot these elephants, and following a good deal of trouble on Grensplaas, I was instructed to destroy a particular bull elephant. I had never shot an elephant before, and I could not understand how one could fell such a mighty animal with a rifle.

We reached the breaches in the fence, left the vehicle there and followed the elephant tracks over hills and ravines. Tobias, a middle-aged Bushman, was an excellent tracker with wonderfully sharp eyes.

At one stage we were on top of a high hill and could see the elephant below, in a gorge. I tested the wind, and we began to stalk him. The wind was fickle, because it often blows in a different direction on top of a hill than below in the gorges. Eventually, after having to change direction a few times, I was close enough. I tried a brain shot from the side at 30 metres, slightly above the cheekbone, a hand's-breadth in front of the ear. The bull elephant collapsed as if hit by lightning, enveloped in a huge cloud of dust, and lay still. I had shot him with my 9,3 millimetre, which is enough to drop an elephant on the spot, if the shot is true.

It went completely against my grain to waste meat, so we started an enormous butchery. The ears, trunk and feet had to be neatly severed. We cut biltong from more than half of the elephant. The trees surrounding the carcass were black with meat. On the third day we had to pack up and return to Okaukuejo. The rest of the carcass had begun to smell unbearably. Uncle Danie du Toit carted away loads of biltong for his Bushmen. The elephant hunt gave me no satisfaction. I felt sorry for these giants who for years were in the habit of trekking to the mountains, but could no longer do so because of the fence. With this fencing, the Etosha Nature Reserve had become a giant game farm.

Horses are employed usefully at Etosha

I appreciated the problem posed by the elephants, and because there were few elephants at Etosha at the time, I decided to herd the elephants that had wandered onto the farms back to Etosha.

Following my adventure at Onguma, I was quite up to this. However, it was specialised work, and not every rider and horse could do it. The horsemen had to be particularly well-seated, and the horses particularly obedient and properly trained, or this could become a deadly game. There were situations where you had to flee before an attacking elephant through thick bush at full gallop. If you fell off your horse, you could be dead. Eventually I trained a team of four specially picked young Bushmen. Almost all of them had been my personal horse-wranglers from an early age. All of them had first learned to ride without reins or stirrups at the end of a lunge-rope, until their balance and confidence were such that they could go along on an elephant hunt.

The horses needed to be very obedient. I did basic dressage with all the horses to ensure that they obeyed any rider's commands. They had to get used to someone shooting from their backs. They needed to master the usual obstructions and ditches without hesitation. They had to be able to gallop through thick bush, also without hesitation. They had to be taught not to be afraid of elephants. It involved systematic, thorough, purposeful training for both horses and riders, but it proved very successful, rewarding and satisfying.

The system for hunting elephants varied very little. We could transport three horses at a time, using a home-made horse-box. We usually transported the horses to the various camps or stations. A station consisted of a small construction of corrugated iron, large enough for a few bags of feed and all the necessary harness. There also had to be enough space for three people to overnight in, in case of emergency. There were six corrals for the horses alongside the house, each about four square metres, enough to allow six horses to overnight, each in its own corral. The corrals were very sturdily fenced, and the fences were high, to ensure that the horses would not break out should unwelcome visitors like lions or other predators come prowling about. At night we usually slept on either side of the corrals next to large fires to make sure the horses were safe. We were never permitted to keep dogs, which was a rather foolish decision by the higher authorities, because a good dog which would warn one in time would have been of great value. Therefore, we had to do a dog's work, and rely on the horses. At the first warning snort given by a horse, you had to throw off your blanket immediately, and investigate with torch and rifle in hand. The lions would then already have surrounded the camp, sometimes as close as five metres from us. In some cases the lions pulled blankets off people, and in one case a Bushman was grabbed in his sleep and dragged off.

In my fifteen years as a game warden I did not lose one horse or person on any of my patrols, but only at the cost of any ability to sleep.

Where the elephant problem was at its worst, I erected a horse station every 20 kilometres along the game fence, because it was almost impossible to get about in a vehicle in the rainy season. These horse-stations were all along the boundaries of the farms Grensplaas, Renex and Mara. Along the northern boundary between Etosha and Owamboland we eventually had a horse corral every 50 kilometres to combat poaching.

We drove to a station with the trailer, and patrolled the fence every day. Where elephants had broken through onto the adjoining farms, we followed their spoor until we reached them. If the elephants were on the march, we rode up-wind to make sure they were aware of our presence. We rode as close to them as possible, sometimes as close as ten metres. On my hand signal we all began shouting as loudly as possible, shooting into the air at the same time. Normally they fled. You then had to stay close on their heels, shouting and shooting all the while. In this way we persuaded them to change direction and flee back to the reserve along the shortest route.

It wasn't always as easy, and there were cases, many involving solitary bulls, where they immediately attacked us. You always had to ensure you had an escape route for this eventuality. An elephant blunders over bushes and small trees like a horse running over tufts of grass. This means an elephant always had an advantage over a horse, which has to run past a bush or tree. This is not serious in areas where mopani trees predominate, but in thickets of thorn bushes this can be a real problem. Horses are very hesitant here, and you often resemble a freshly slaughtered pig, not to mention the damage in the form of torn and tattered clothing! The entire eastern and northern boundary of Etosha is mainly covered in thorn bushes, and this is where one had the most trouble.

We were often unable to follow the fleeing elephants quickly enough, and then we lost sight of them from time to time. That meant going back to tracking. Something we often observed was that the bull elephant leader would hide behind a tree, standing dead still in order to ambush his pursuers. In such cases we often saw nothing but his tusks and trunk as he waited for us. At first I thought it was purely coincidental, but when it happened almost every time, I came to realise this was a carefully thought-out tactic of such bulls. If you blundered blindly into such an ambush, it would be your last elephant hunt.

If you identified such an elephant, and tried to herd him any further, his reaction was almost always an angry charge. The hounded animal would attack with a deafening trumpeting sound. In almost every case the elephant simply pushed over or trampled the tree behind which it was hiding. I think this is a display of power which fires him up for the charge. Like dogs baring their teeth before a fight, the elephant breaks trees to pump himself up, and to frighten his opponent before joining the fray.

It certainly has a tremendous effect, especially on the horses. The rider has usually already spotted the hidden elephant, but the horse is unaware of his presence. When the elephant then suddenly pushes over the tree and charges with an ear-splitting trumpeting, the horse swivels round and tries to run away in panic – and few things are as dangerous as riding a horse that is fleeing blindly. You need to apply all your expertise to gain control of your horse, all the while trying to avoid whipping branches. You cannot use nervous horses for this work.

I never allowed such things to put me off my stride. Elephants never pursue a rider for too long. As soon as they realise the horse is faster than they are, they give up the chase. Once the horse has been brought under control, we turn around and continue the pursuit of the elephants until they have left the farmlands behind and once more find themselves on the reserve's territory.

Herds with cows and calves react quite differently. When you start shouting and shooting into the air, they become very agitated, and are only concerned for their calves. Once they have identified the intruders, they usually attack on a very wide front to chase away the pesky noise-makers. It's actually quite impressive when a whole herd of elephants comes thundering towards you. The calves usually slow down a charge of this nature, but the noise is tremendous. You are treated to a trumpeting symphony, accompanied by the sound of breaking branches.

When they eventually calm down, you try to get them moving in the opposite direction once more. You need to keep them moving at the slowest possible pace, because the little calves tire quickly, which is reason enough for the elephants to turn around again and give you the charge. We often followed large herds of this nature at an easy canter. The herds learn quickly, and once they have been removed from a farming area, they seldom return. The solitary bulls were the problem animals, as they often returned. They also caused a great deal of damage on the farms by crushing everything in their way. They become very wilful, and must eventually be shot.

The wilful elephant meets his match

We patrolled along the Renex boundary on horseback because the elephants had become bothersome again.

It was a morning after some heavy rain, and the going was so wet and slippery that we decided to patrol part of the fence on foot. When we reached the water pans along the Renex boundary, the fences looked like the middle part of a concertina. A lone bull had trampled the fence, had returned a little way off, and had crossed over again at another spot. One wilful elephant had caused seven fresh breaches of the game-proof fence. I was most upset, because we had fixed the border fence the previous day.

While my team of Bushmen were repairing the breaks, I decided to follow the elephant's trail together with Stefanus (who had followed me from Onguma to Okaukuejo) just to give him a fright. At that stage I was already suffering from back pains and a weak left leg, and could walk only with some difficulty.

Stefanus tracked the animal, and I followed with my old .303. We had not walked far when we saw the animal grazing about 50 metres in front of us. The wind was not in our favour, but I simply wanted to shoot into the air above the elephant to frighten him.

When the shot rang out, the elephant stood there with his trunk in the air, testing the wind. I knew this meant trouble. When the elephant got our scent, he lowered his head slightly, spread his ears high above his head, trumpeted angrily, and charged in our direction with his curled trunk held up high. I realised this was a determined charge, and shouted to Stefanus to run. He was out of there like a whirlwind. I followed with my gammy leg as best I could, at little more than walking pace. While trying to get away, I reloaded the .303. To top it all, I reached a dead end in the form of a slippery pool. The elephant was almost on top of me. At the last moment, at a distance of about 15 metres, I turned around and instinctively fired a shot in the direction of the elephant's head, without really aiming. The elephant hit the ground beside me with a sound like a clap of thunder. He lay still, and only the end of his trunk moved up and down for a while I couldn't believe that the elephant was dead. As I looked at the elephant, shivering and disconsolate, I involuntarily mumbled a little prayer while Stefanus came up cautiously. He was an ashen colour, whistled through his teeth and kept shaking his head. He then looked at me for a long while with all kinds of questions in his eyes, as if he could not grasp what had happened. I realised I had not done this; only help from Above had miraculously saved me at the very last moment. On closer examination I could see the .303 bullet had entered the skull just above his left eye, causing his death.

A close call at the Onguma boundary

The elephant problems never went away. It was mid-summer, very hot and dry, and the elephants went to drink at the Guamkas waterhole on Onguma. The fences were being trampled all the time.

On a scorching day we arrived at a break in the boundary fence and decided to camp there. We had not yet built paddocks for the horses, and these had first to be erected. Unfortunately the Onguma boundary fell outside my area.

We offloaded the horses and tied them to some trees, quickly built a fire and cooked a pot of mealie-meal porridge. As we were eating porridge and sour milk, we heard a tree breaking in the nature reserve. The Bushmen and I looked at one another significantly, and Stefanus mumbled: "Somebody's full of himself; he's liable to land himself in trouble soon."

Stefanus quickly gulped down a few more mouthfuls of porridge, and then, with much enthusiasm, went to saddle our horses. I buckled on my belt and two revolvers, we each mounted our horse, and we were off. The rest of the Bushmen had to build enclosures for the horses, because I wanted preparations made for a stay of at least two weeks. We went straight in the direction of the noise of breaking branches, and found a large old solitary elephant bull, occupied with completely destroying a tree. The manner in which he was breaking off the tree's branches indicated that this elephant was greatly upset, because he was ripping off pieces of the tree, but not eating anything. He must have caught our scent when we were having our lunch, and it obviously put him in a bad temper. I was equally short-tempered, because I had no intention of chasing elephants through thorn bushes in the heat of the afternoon. Being thick with acacia thorns, the terrain was most unsuited to such activities. All I wanted to do, was to fire a shot in the air to set the elephant in motion, but it didn't turn out that way. I had hardly fired the shot, shouting at the elephant all the while, or he began flapping his ears in anger, and then charged us. Stefanus and

With another lion I had shot.

Supervising the training of Bushmen and the horses that were used to track elephants.

The horses had to overcome their fear of elephants. Riding Blitz, I am 3 metres from an elephant.

During a riding lesson for the Bushmen.

One of many encounters with an elephant.

The other way round, this time!

As game warden with an animal that had died of anthrax.

Gemsbok at Etosha.

A common sight at Etosha.

Elke and I at one of our camps.

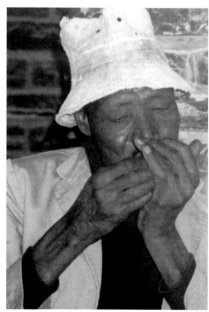

Paul Doodvreet.

At the height of my career as a game
warden.

Elke, Heiko, Ingo, Peter with Nico, and Udo.

We shod our horses ourselves.

Two lions in Etosha.

Herding zebra foals.

Ostriches at Etosha.

Zebras at Etosha.

Kudu on the savannah plain.

A wary lioness with her cub.

An elephant and a giraffe at dusk in Etosha.

Elke reared many animals by hand.

A colleague and I with a sedated elephant.

A kudu cow at one of the drinking-holes.

Giraffes were protected game in South West Africa.

Sunset in Etosha, with a tree full of nests in the foreground.

Ute – for many years one of my riding pupils – and I.

Me as a soldier.

Me today.

In July 2011, I spent three weeks in Namibia, camping and hunting with my children and grandchildren.

My family today, almost all of them, during a hunting trip in Namibia, 2011.

On one of the donkeys my mother bought me.

Long before I began hunting lions.

With Jupp, my first horse.

On my horse Alarich before the South African championships.

Rudolf and Ella Böhme of Onguma.

Willie with one of our horses.

Mudschi with my horse Banner.

Wilhelm of the abandoned "tyres" (standing) and Willie with a gemsbok.

Stefanus, Willie and Mudschi after a hunting trip.

An "Onguma Mercedes".

The palms at the Twee Palms waterhole in the west of Etosha.

In my younger days.

In Germany, undergoing advanced riding training.

I each took off in a different direction, and after a brief pursuit the elephant bull stood still, uncertain about whom he should follow. We also halted and began shouting at him again.

This time he picked me as his target, and charged. Had I mentioned that I was short-tempered that afternoon? I reined in my horse, Blitz, and aimed a shot at the approaching elephant's ears. Blitz was a very obedient but somewhat nervous horse. The bull charged through the thorn bushes with loud trumpeting and crashing noises. I let fly with one shot after the other close to the elephant's ears, but there was no stopping him. When the elephant was 20 metres away, Blitz could no longer stand it. He reared, and then jumped to one side, trying to escape. I was off-balance, because Blitz turned towards my weakened left leg. As the horse reared, I leaned forward and let go of the reins to make sure Blitz did not fall over backwards. His turn to the left caused me to lose my balance, and I almost fell off. Fortunately Blitz had a long, thick mane, and I clung onto this for dear life. As I was hanging on to Blitz's side, I had no control over the horse. The horse fled from the elephant bull with great bounds. In normal circumstances I would have fallen off long ago, but fear made me cling on with all I had. The elephant was almost upon us, his great yellow tusks sweeping across the horse's haunches, accompanied by his ear-shattering trumpeting and the sound of breaking branches. One lacks the words to describe it. The thorn branches cut across my face and bare arms like swords.

Eventually I was able to regain my balance, in the process also regaining control of the horse. The elephant gave up his pursuit after a while, turned around and walked back in the direction of the game reserve. Stefanus rejoined me as I brought the horse to a halt in order to reload my revolver. Blood was dripping from his cheeks and ears as well, and he kept saying in the Bushman language (with a very tremulous voice): "That's Satan, that's Satan, let's leave him alone!"

Although I had feared for my life a few minutes before, this fear had given way to a determination to make that elephant pay. The elephant was in full retreat; perhaps his painful ears had persuaded him to take this course of action. We followed him at a good gallop. Eventually he tired, regurgitated water from his stomach, sucked it from his mouth with his trunk and used it to moisten and cool his body. He did this repeatedly. I could not believe my eyes the first time I saw it. He must have been very tired. We were far enough into the game reserve and I began to feel sorry for him. I judged that enough was enough, so I let him be.

I now know that one manages to do the impossible if you are fearing for your life!

A game warden miraculously escapes death

I practised elephant herding of this nature for years, usually with my three Bushmen of choice, namely Sam, Hebakoib and Stefanus. Later, Mudschi also resigned from Onguma and joined me at Namutoni. Because I was achieving such good results with my horses, all my horses, apart from Alarich and Scipio, were taken over by the Administration. In the meantime the Etosha National Park was divided into four wards, namely Namutoni, Halali, Okaukuejo and Otjovasandu.

Namutoni, Halali and Otjovasandu each gained a game warden and two horses, and I kept four horses at Okaukuejo. Two of them were my own, and the other two were service animals. I mainly used my own horses for advanced equestrian sports, and the two service horses for nature conservation work. However, there was so much nature conservation work that my own horses went along in most cases. These horses played a significant role in combating poaching.

Early in 1972, after I had been herding elephants from farming areas for years, Anglia Television asked to film the whole elephant herding process. They had to use helicopters for most of their activity, because a vehicle would never have been able to transport the entire film crew. (The film was titled *The Fence*.) The bush was too overgrown, and it was decided that the entire elephant herding exercise should look like a great team effort. The white game wardens from the other stations therefore had to participate. I had grave doubts. Apart from one or two game wardens, the others were not as well trained as my Bushmen, and were therefore not as firm in their saddles. The filming started. Many scenes were shot on more suitable terrain, but the actual elephant drive was filmed from a helicopter in flight. At that stage most of the elephants were near Namutoni and on the Onguma boundary, which was the most difficult terrain. The northern area of Onguma, and part of the nature reserve, is very sandy, with a great deal of elephant's-root. Elephant's-root is a creeper which dries out after the summer rain, leaving very tasty nuts which the Bushmen gather. Underneath the creeper, quite deep in the sand, one finds the plant's bulb, which may grow to one metre in diameter. New shoots grow from this every year in summer, bearing flowers and eventually the nuts, and so forth.

The elephants love digging up the bulbs to eat, leaving behind large and deep holes.

During the filming a large herd of elephants we needed to drive was located in the northern part of Onguma. Anglia Television wanted to film this, so we located the elephants and began to herd them back to the reserve. Initially all went well, but then the elephant herd began to scatter. My Bushmen and I kept driving one group of elephants, and forced them back into the game reserve through the breach in the game fence. However, the helicopter was no longer following us, and we began to wonder what had happened to it. We rode back to the camp at a trot. My Bushmen were still with me, but the rest of the company was no longer with us. On our way to the camp, the helicopter passed us and landed near the camp. When we reached the camp and were unsaddling the horses, someone from the film company came to me and said there had been a near-fatality. Apparently one of the game wardens had fallen off his horse and had almost been trampled by an angry elephant cow. I walked to the tent where the game warden was lying in great pain, groaning all the while. He had hurt his back badly, but he was able to tell me the story.

He and the other game wardens stayed with the slower-moving elephants, which included a calf. The calf's mother turned around at some stage and chased the pursuers. She was right on the heels of the game warden from Otjovasandu. When he looked around at the elephant chasing him, he put his weight on one stirrup, and the saddle slid over to that side and under the horse's belly because it had not been cinched properly. The warden lost his balance and fell to the ground almost directly under the elephant's feet. He hurt his back badly, and could not get up. As the saddle slid off the horse's back, the saddle-cloth under the saddle fell right before the elephant's feet. The cow probably thought this was her enemy, and trampled the cloth. As the helpless warden was lying there, he saw a large hole next to him, rolled into it and hid at the bottom, not moving a muscle, while the angry elephant cow was ravaging the saddle-cloth right next to him.

The helicopter crew saw all of this happening, swooped down and quickly drove the elephant away from the helpless man in the hole. The hole was one of those the elephants had dug some time before to get to an elephant's-root bulb.

What a pity that the film crew was so petrified that they did not film the whole thing. That would have been the cherry on top. They had all the time they needed while the helicopter was descending, but they were all in a tizzy at what was happening, and forgot to let the cameras roll.

The injured game warden was taken to hospital, and he recovered.

More amusing incidents involving elephants

Because I had the most experience with elephants at that time, I had to train most of the game wardens in herding or shooting elephants. Most of the men would rather shoot than herd.

At one time we had endless trouble with an elephant bull on the farm Eindpaal, owned by Hertzog Robberts. The senior game warden at Okaukuejo wanted to shoot this elephant under my supervision. Even though he ranked above me at the time, I required everyone during an elephant hunt to do exactly as I instructed. Everybody agreed to this.

The senior was a World War II veteran, who liked everything to be neat and precise. Because I spent most of my time in the bush, my clothing was definitely not to his taste. My shoes were his biggest headache. I walked barefoot most of the time, or with worn tackies with holes cut in them. I have already explained that when I had to track wild animals, I took off my tackies so as to tread as quietly as possible, and then tied them to the back of my belt.

This happened on that specific day when we had to deal with the elephant on Eindpaal. We followed the fresh spoor from a breach in the game-proof fence into the game park.

After about 8 kilometres we saw the large bull browsing about 200 metres from us. I signalled to the senior that he should take off his shoes. He looked at me with a frown, and quietly did so after much hesitation. It was neither the time nor the place for an argument. I took the lead in stalking the animal. Every now and then I heard a muffled, scarcely suppressed curse as the man hobbled over the terrain with bare feet. The senior wanted to shoot when we were still about 50 metres from the elephant. I really wanted to bring him to within 20 metres of the elephant, but his feet could stand no more.

He carefully rested his rifle against a tree to aim, and let fly with the so-called elephant-gun, a .458 Winchester. I was carrying my 9.3 millimetre. When the shot rang out, the elephant went down, but immediately stood up again. I thought the senior would shoot again, but he simply stood there, looking at the fleeing elephant. A wounded elephant with a poor head shot can walk for many kilometres, and sometimes you never see him again. When the elephant was 120 metres from us, he half turned. I took a chance and shot the bull dead with a well-aimed head shot from the 9.3 millimetre.

The senior heartily resented me because he had to walk barefoot. I kept quiet, but felt the sweet taste of revenge for all that nagging about my old tackies and bare feet. I had to hear this incident retold many, many times, even after I had long since left the employ of Nature Conservation.

On another occasion we had to shoot an elephant on Mr Marais's farm Ondera. Ondera is situated east of Namutoni, so it lay within the jurisdiction of the game warden at Namutoni. The game warden at the time had a very high opinion of himself and always told tall tales, particularly hunting tales. I wanted to test him a little.

The game-proof fence ran 10 metres from and parallel to the farmers' wire fences. The gap of 10 metres between the fences was regularly cleared. There was a cleared roadway all along the game-proof fence to facilitate patrolling of the fence, and to control veld-fires.

Inside the gap there were two ridges all along the two fences as a result of soil displaced by the graders scraping the road surface.

When we reached the breaches in the fences at Ondera, we could see the elephants approaching the farming area from Crown Land quite some distance away. They were not aware of our presence. We left the vehicle in the bush and sat down inside the gap, on the ridge on the farmer's side, with our rifles cocked. I sat down next to the game warden with my old .303 and told him he may only shoot when I gave the signal; I would spread the fingers of my left hand. With elbows on knees, we waited quite comfortably on the ridge, in the open. I repeated that we would only shoot when I spread the fingers of my left hand.

The herd's bull approached, and the game warden became excited. He was shifting about on his bum. When the elephants were

30 metres from us, he asked me in a whisper: "Piet, may I shoot?" I shook my head.

An elephant's eyesight is rather poor, and if you sit or stand quite still, he may almost step on you. The bull approached slowly, grazing all the while, and the man next to me repeatedly asked, in a whisper, whether he should shoot. I shook my head. At some stage he was shaking so much that I had serious doubts about his ability to shoot. In the meantime the elephant had reached the game-proof fence, and was about 10 metres away from us. When he lifted his trunk to break the fence, I was certain he was the culprit, and I spread the fingers of my left hand. The .458 roared immediately, and the elephant sagged to the ground, his back end first. The bull's front legs remained stretched out straight in front of him. He held his head high, and tried to get on his feet again. I jumped up, ran to the side, and gave him the final shot with the .303 at a distance of 3 metres.

When I looked at the game warden, he was ashen-faced, and it almost seemed as if his eyes would pop from his head. His mouth was dry, and he spoke incoherently. Eventually he calmed down.

Afterwards, word on the street was that he would never, never, never again hunt elephants with that crazy German.

I never had any respect for the so-called elephant gun, the .458. It was heavy and clumsy. The stock was far too long for me. By far the best rifle I have ever had in my hands was a Hammerli 9.3 millimetre. This rifle fitted my hand like a glove, even better than my own Husqvarna 9.3. When I eventually resigned from Nature Conservation, I tried everything in my power to get that gun, but it remained the Administration's property! I was sorely tempted to steal the rifle. It was originally confiscated from a poacher – someone who surely knew a thing or two about firearms!

There was an elephant miscreant who regularly broke the fences near the farm Renex. Furthermore, he returned time and again to push over a windpump on the farm. The farmer was most upset, and I was sent to shoot the elephant. The Bushman Stefanus came with me. First, we reported to the farmer on his farm. There were eight farmers from surrounding farms with him. When I asked what they were doing there, the owner replied: "To help shoot the elephant!"

It took a lot of persuasion to get them to understand that only I was responsible for taking down that elephant. However, they accompanied me, very cross because I forbade them to shoot.

We followed the elephant's fresh tracks from the breach in the fence, and because the gaggle was not moving silently enough, I made sure they walked a good 20 metres behind Stefanus and me. I was carrying the .458, and Stefanus my proven 9.3. This was the first time I would test the .458. We could see the bull in the valley from our vantage point on a hill, and once again I had to warn everyone they were not to shoot, and that they needed to keep a safe distance behind us.

We closed in on the bull. The wind was unpredictable, and he was standing in a dip with a lot of yellowwood bushes that were almost as tall as the animal itself. Very unfavourable. I had instructed Stefanus to hand me the 9.3 immediately should the elephant not fall after a shot from the .458. We stalked him as silently as possible, and I gave a hand signal to the bunch behind us not to follow us any more. When we were 18 metres from the elephant, he suddenly looked in our direction and began moving his trunk and ears. He must have noticed something. Stefanus and I could get no closer. When I aimed at his forehead with the .458, there were still a few branches in the way. I simply had to shoot. The shot made no impression on the elephant bull at all, and he immediately attacked us. In a flash I handed the empty .458 to Stefanus and grabbed the loaded 9.3, aimed, and shot at the elephant's head. He hit the ground a little in front and to the side of us like a thunderclap.

The farmers were still standing where I had left them. I had absolutely no respect for the elephant cannon from then on, and shot all my elephants with my 9.3, apart from the times I had to use my old .303. Because of the branches, the shot from the .458 was slightly high, but because the shot had made no impression on the elephant at all, I never used the .458 again.

The scorpion attack

Chasing elephants became routine for me, and it worked well. Eventually we got to know the elephants and their habits better, and gained a great deal of experience. To me, these games with the elephants were like rugby to a farm boy.

One day I had to chase elephants from Onguma again. It was a very hot and cloudy day; the rainy season was coming. The first rains fell that afternoon – a perfect occasion for scorpions to come looking for food after their winter hibernation. Which is exactly what happened that evening. The fire was burning, and I was braaiing eland kebabs threaded onto pieces of wire. We had confiscated the meat from some Owambo poachers. As I was occupied in this manner, the first scorpion made his appearance with his spear across his back

I cannot stand scorpions, because they have stung me many a time. A scorpion's sting burns like fire mixed with electric shocks. Furthermore a scorpion has far too many legs, and two ugly pincers to boot. I get the heebie-jeebies whenever I see a scorpion.

When I saw the first scorpion, I immediately killed it with a stick and threw it in the fire. The Bushmen's night fire was about 20 metres away, and when they saw me hurling the scorpion into the fire, they protested strongly, because they reckon the smell of a burning scorpion draws the others. Before long, a second scorpion appeared. His lot was the same as the first one's. Once again the Bushmen protested loudly.

In the meantime I finished one of the kebabs. When the next scorpion appeared, I pronged him with the empty kebab skewer. One scorpion after another made an appearance and met the same kebab death. When the scorpions simply kept on coming, I placed my folding chair close to a large tree and put my feet up high against the trunk. I continued pronging scorpions with my skewer from this position. By 23:00 I tired of this game. I put my mattress and blankets on the service vehicle and went to bed on the back of the bakkie. There were 32 scorpions on the skewer the next morning. I burned them all in the fire. The Bushmen did not say a thing.

I experienced a similar evening near the Groenewald windpump when I was busy building an underground shelter. That, too, was at the start of the rainy season, and furthermore a strong wind was blowing. That evening I killed only 28 scorpions near the fire – but most certainly enough to ensure that I slept on the back of the bakkie!

Over the years I established that when the first rains fell and during a windy night, you can be sure that you will be visited by a horde of scorpions.

A snake in the bedding

Scorpions were not my only bedmates. Near Bitterwater one night it was a large Cape cobra. We were busy erecting a number of windpumps on the 19th parallel. We usually worked from early in the morning to dusk, with a lunch break of two hours from 13:00 to 15:00. It becomes so hot in summer that it is virtually impossible to work with anything made of iron at midday. I had trained a young Bushman as my batman. Early every morning he had to make coffee, pick up and put away all the bedding, wash the dishes, collect firewood, keep in the shade any food that could spoil, cook food, ensure that a supply of drinking water stays cool, bake bread, allow the horses to graze, and look after them, store all personal belongings under tarpaulins should it start to rain, place the horses in their corrals and feed them, and prepare supper and a bed for the night.

He therefore did very important work, with a multitude of tasks and responsibilities. He did not only have responsibilities towards me, but towards the other workers as well.

I trained quite a few young Bushmen this way. All of them were later employed by Nature Conservation.

It was quite a cold night, and I used a few blankets. Early the next morning I drank my coffee, and then left for work with the Bushman workers. We had to build a new drinking-trough that day, and that meant we did not have much time for eating. We took some cooked food with us, because we would be pouring concrete all day until the trough was finished.

At dusk we went back to camp. Bushman Sam was my batman at the time, and as I came to stand by the fire, he asked me quite casually: "And what is that?" while pointing at something on the ground.

When I looked around, I saw a large Cape cobra, rather the worse for wear, and very dead. "Where did that come from?"

"From inside your bedding," Sam answered, and told me that when he picked up the blankets, he found the snake inside. While he was telling the story, I felt my hair stand on end, and cold shivers ran down my spine. A Cape cobra is one of the most venomous of snakes, and one bite can kill you. I slept badly that night. I woke up every now and then to make sure there was no snake in my bed.

A lion causes pandemonium, and I make a big fool of myself

We had quite a few run-ins with lions. Probably the biggest fool I made of myself was one night when we were busy developing the airfield at Halali, a tourist camp between Okaukuejo and Namutoni. Its former name was Tweekoppies (Twin Hills), the only place in Etosha where there are two hills next to each other on the southern boundary; for the rest, it's just flat country.

Almost exactly opposite Halali, north, lies a sluggish spring named Geikoizaub ("fountain of the big people"). This waterhole was drying up because of that year's serious drought. We had to use a bulldozer which was clearing the airfield at Halali to deepen the waterhole.

A short while previously I had shot a zebra for the Bushmen's rations. As the climate is so warm, the Bushmen cut all the meat into strips to enable it to dry more quickly. There were no cooling facilities. Early in the morning one would roll the half-dried meat, closely packed, into blankets and then leave it in the shade during the day. After sunset the meat was removed to dry some more during the night.

On the day we were to leave Halali for Geikoizaub with the bulldozer and its crew, the bulldozer's radiator was pierced by a stick. Gert, the driver of the bulldozer – a large, heavy-set white farmer with a beer-belly and love handles – first wanted to solder the radiator, and asked me and my team of Bushmen to ride ahead to Geikoizaub and set up camp there. He would follow with the bulldozer on a transport trailer.

My team of Bushmen and I left Halali in the afternoon, and reached Gaikoizaub by nightfall.

Gert and his truck arrived later. After having enjoyed a meagre meal, he decided to make his bed next to mine on the flatbed of the Thames. I always slept in the raw. At least Gert was wearing flimsy underpants.

I want to mention here that whenever I was woken shortly after having fallen asleep, I was as disorientated as ten drunken sailors. I went to take a leak just before I went to sleep. The moon was at first quarter. When I finished, I hastened back to camp, because I had that disturbing feeling that I was being watched. Back on the vehicle, I crawled in between my blankets and talked to Gert about lions.

I was just dropping off when a Bushman shouted in fright: "*Chamqua, aijee chamqua, chambike!*" and then the angry roar of a lion sounded, as if it had caught something. I sat up, and saw a yellow streak leaping up by the light of the Bushmen's fire with something in its mouth, and flashing past me. I instinctively tried to grab my rifle, which always lay to the left of my bed. However, it wasn't there, because we had made camp so late, and I had therefore left it in the cabin of the vehicle. I was completely disorientated because I had just fallen asleep, and all I realised was that the lions were among us, and that the Bushmen needed help immediately. My pillow was the closest weapon to hand. I jumped up and grabbed the pillow. Beneath me there was a confused throng of frightened bodies shouting for help: "*Hoeitere, hoeitere!*" ("Help me, help me!") I began lashing out with the pillow at the movements I could vaguely discern in the dark. I have no idea how long this went on, but as I was hitting and kicking, I heard a voice beneath me saying: "Let me go, boss, you're hurting me." Only then did I come to my senses and register that I was standing on the load-bed of the truck, and that the movements below me were the Bushmen trying, in panic, to clamber on board.

Swart Sikspens had also seen something in front of him, and grabbed it in an effort to haul himself onto the load-bed. Unfortunately he had grabbed hold of the love handles near Gert's beer-belly, and he held on to these for dear life. Gert thought a lion had taken him, and began shouting: "He's got me!"

The situation calmed down. The Bushmen were extremely indignant about the hitting and kicking, and we had a lot of explaining and apologising to do. Tobias simply wanted to know what had happened to his blanket. Then I remembered that I had seen a lion with something in his mouth at the start of the commotion, and that this had been the cause of our actions.

My sense of humiliation and shame turned to a thirst for revenge. I wanted to teach that lion a lesson. Gert and I quickly bundled into the front of the vehicle, started it and began looking for the lions. I really wanted them to suffer for their little joke. After having driven in the dark in circles for a while, we saw the lions in the dark. I went for them like a maniac. The lioness still had Tobias's blanket in her mouth – the cause of the consternation – and she was my main target. I was after her like a warthog. I was on her heels at full tilt when I saw her leaping high into the air. Before I realised what was happening, the Thames made a similar leap. It was suddenly dark before my eyes, the Thames momentarily felt like an aeroplane floating through the air, and then it landed in a dry river-bed with a thunderous sound. The inside of the Thames was full of dust, shifting spanners, pliers, hammers, the rifle and heaven alone knows what else, all flying through the air, hitting us on the head and landing on our bare toes.

From the back we heard the indignant shouting of the Bushmen clinging to the sides of the load-bed. I realised I had just suffered my second defeat. Fortunately the Thames had stayed on its wheels rather than capsizing. However, I was frightened stiff, and then calmed down. I left the lions, and drove back to camp. When I got out of the vehicle, I realised that throughout the commotion I had been as naked as the day I was born.

Early the next morning everybody got to work with great enthusiasm to finish everything that day so as to avoid spending another night there. The owners of the Geokoizaub waterhole were a pride of seventeen audacious lions, and the two eldest lionesses were particularly aggressive.

Other incidents at Geikoizaub

The pride of lions at Geikoizaub was known far and wide for their aggressiveness, and many tourists complained that they had to flee for their lives before the threat of a pride of lions at Geikoizaub. Chasing after the cars was great fun for the lions. They became my great allies, because I understood them well, and knew how to handle them. Whenever professional photographers wanted to take photographs of lions, I always took them to that particular pride.

One day an exceptional visitor named Hans-Günther Winkler arrived. Winkler was the German world champion showjumper. He had won gold medals at various Olympics, and was Germany's equestrian hero.

Bernie, a friend from my youth, brought him to us at Okaukuejo with the request that Winkler should experience something extraordinary. They were accompanied by their young wives. I asked Bernie and Hans whether they had strong nerves. "Of course," they answered with great self-assurance.

It was a Saturday afternoon, and the camp was very quiet, as there were almost no tourists. It was an ideal occasion to have some fun. There was a pipe-railing on the back of my Ford 4x4 to enable one to stand easily on the back. It was fairly lion-proof. We went to Geikoizaub, and as if we had made prior arrangements, the pride of lions were soaking up the late-afternoon sun on the bare pan near the waterhole. I alighted some distance from them and asked

140

the people on the back of the bakkie to remain calm and take photographs. To enhance the drama of the situation, I handed Bernie my 9.3 millimetre and told him that he was now responsibile for the people on the bakkie.

I then drove slowly towards the pride of lions. The two aggressive females charged from some distance away, and came to a sudden halt in front of the vehicle, showering it in a cloud of dust and sand. I stopped right in front of them to give the people at the back an opportunity to take photos. The rest of the pride approached at a more leisurely pace. The excited voices behind me made it clear that everyone was extremely tense.

After a brief photo session I warned the people on the back to hold on tight to the pipe railings, because I was going to turn around and spark a lively pursuit. I made a U-turn and pulled away as swiftly as possible. The lions launched their attack, as expected. They ran after the vehicle like a pack of mad dogs, with the two old females in front. It was flat terrain, hard and with no obstructions, so I could pull a few risky tricks. Each time the two lionesses were close enough to leap, I swerved to one side like a fleeing jack-rabbit to throw the lions off. I drove just fast enough to make sure the foremost lion felt it was worthwhile to launch a leap, and so I got the whole pride to run after the vehicle for a fairly long distance. I could hear terrified screams coming from the load-bed. The two women had thrown themselves down between their husbands' legs and were screaming their lungs out. Bernie and Hans remained standing like two brave gladiators, and clung to the pipe-railings for dear life while I careened from side to side.

Lions never keep up a pursuit for very long, and they stopped after a little while. I drove on for a short distance, and when it was all over, I stopped, got out and asked the visitors whether they would like a repeat performance. The two women were still lying down between the men's legs, and all were agreed that they had had enough.

Hans and Bernie were ashen-faced, but they tried to look calm. It did take a great deal of persuasion, however, to coax the women back into a sitting position. They admitted that they thought their last moments were at hand. A long while afterwards Hans-Günther Winkler sent me a letter from Germany to express his thanks, once again, saying that the episode with the lions in Etosha had been the highlight of his life.

The shoe is on the other foot

Not too long after the Winkler episode, my friend Helmut came to visit me. He was a gifted photographer, and enjoyed adventures of all kinds. It was a Sunday morning in the closed season, so there were no tourists in the camp.

We drove to Geikoizaub and soon spotted the pride of lions. Swart Sikspens and Tobias were on the back of the bakkie. Swart Sikspens, Nabekub's cousin, could be quite forward at times, and for some reason Tobias always found himself in trouble when lions were involved. I wanted to give the two of them a good scare. First we played cat and mouse with the lions while the Bushmen made all kinds of remarks.

At one stage I managed to isolate two young males from the rest of the pride, and decided to give them a good lesson. I pursued them with the vehicle, and made them run for all they were worth. When they tired, black spurts appeared from underneath their tails every now and then – a sure sign that they were really tiring, and were giving up.

Just when I wanted to leave them in peace, they jumped up into a thorn bush and began climbing. Normally lions are not great tree-climbers, and it wasn't a very tall tree. I slowly drove to right below them in the Ford. The two Bushmen became hysterical and really cussed me out. While they were still swearing and shouting, I decided to drive matters to a head. Through the vehicle's right-hand window I grabbed hold of the lower lion's tail, and began pulling. The lion clung to the tree in panic.

I did not, however, expect the stream of really pungent excrement that streamed over my right arm and right shoulder! The two Bushmen on the back of the bakkie did not escape this either. What with me pulling the lion's tail, and the lion roaring loudly, the Bushmen's screams reached a peak. In my opinion, everyone had now had a turn. The Ford's cabin stank like a pit latrine with a three-month load. I let go of the lion's tail and slowly reversed the Ford. Unfortunately Helmut could not photograph all of this, because it was too dangerous to get out of the vehicle.

We got out of the vehicle some distance away, and I tried to wash the ordure from my right arm, shoulder and ear with water from the milk-can.

I cannot repeat the Bushmen's comments. Despite many desperate efforts in the shower, the lion smell clung to me for days afterwards. Every dog – or cat – has his day!

Serious lions

The lions I had chased so mercilessly at Onguma later became my play-mates. If one comes into contact with them almost every day, you eventually relax and take chances.

Because we never dared to shoot anything for the pot, we fell into the bad habit of stealing the lions' meat. The Bushmen were always on the lookout for vultures descending, or already sitting in the trees. We then went and had a look. Normally the lions had caught something. If the carcass was very fresh, and there was plenty of meat, we chased away the lions by throwing stones at them, and took some of the meat for ourselves. We always left enough for the returning lions.

One night André, a game warden, returned from the veld with a badly injured Bushman who had been mauled by lions. André reported that they were attacked by lions while they were sleeping in the veld. Somebody took the Bushman to hospital, and André and I drove to the camp. He told me the story on the way. He and his Bushman helper were on a routine patrol when they saw vultures descending. They went to investigate, and found that the lions had taken a gemsbok. They chased away the lions and took some of the meat. At dusk they decided to make a camp and to stay in the veld overnight. They hung the gemsbok meat in the branches above them, which was a big mistake. (When hanging meat, hang it some distance from your camp. Rather have the meat some distance away, than have lions in your camp!) They made a fire, and braaied some of the meat. Then they went to bed, with André on his folding cot and the Bushman on the ground next to him.

It was midnight when André woke with a start because of the Bushman's terrified screams. The moon was shining quite brightly, and he could see a lion dragging away the wriggling Bushman. André took his rifle and ran in the direction of the lion and Bushman. As he jumped up and ran in the direction of the lion, he heard his bed overturning. When he looked around, he saw another lion near his bed, but ignored it. When he was close enough to the lion with the Bushman, he shot at the lion. The lion dropped the Bushman and ran away. The lion had been dragging the Bushman by his right leg, and blood was spurting from deep gashes in his thigh.

André dropped everything and drove back to Okuakuejo with the Bushman as fast as he could.

On reaching the abandoned camp, I began my inspection. Judging by the tracks, a whole pride of lions must have been circling the camp long before the Bushman was taken. When André jumped up with his rifle and ran towards the Bushman, another lion must have thought that he was fleeing. He tried to pounce on André from behind, but landed on the bed, overturning it. When André shot, all the lions ran away. The lion he shot at did not shed a drop of blood, and I believe that André missed him.

Judging by the heap of coals, the campfire was totally inadequate. When I asked him why he hadn't made a bigger fire, he answered that the smoke bothered him. (Another big mistake: a large fire at night causes lions to think twice before attacking.) André was cleared of all blame, but his silly mistakes almost cost two people their lives.

The Bushman recovered, but retained ugly scars on his leg. You could easily insert your thumb into the marks.

At various times the lions almost caused chaos at night. We had enormous problems with veld-fires almost every year. At the end of winter, before the first rains of the new season, the veld was often set alight by lightning strikes, or else poachers set fire to the veld. This is why the entire Etosha was divided into fire-blocks of 10 kilometres each, with fire-breaks of 30 metres wide. One would rather lose one block than to be running fruitlessly after a veld-fire for days on end, accumulating enormous losses in fuel, vehicle wear and tear, and man-hours.

At the start of my career at Etosha these fire-blocks did not yet exist, and sometimes large areas of Etosha burnt down, despite the efforts of the entire game park staff to contain the fires.

In that time we were one day engaged in an enormous fire-fighting effort on the northern Etosha/Owamboland border. We managed to bring the fires under control in the second night, and when my team put out the fires in our section, I decided, at ten o'clock at night, to sleep right there.

At midnight I was woken by shouts of "voertsek" ("go away") from the Bushmen, and I could hear the thuds of a fleeing lion's paws fading away. All the Bushmen were up, and they were shouting into the night like a troop of frightened baboons. When they eventually calmed down, I was able to determine what had happened. Moses, my Bushman foreman, had woken and had lighted his pipe. Tobias lay sleeping next to Moses, and in the light of the match Moses saw a large male lion standing near Tobias's head. Moses immediately sounded the alarm by shouting at the lion, which fled.

On another occasion Tobias was once again involved in a night-time visit by a lion. I was busy pouring the concrete drinking-trough at the Ozonjuitji m'Bari windpump, and we slept near the windpump.

Early one morning Tobias noticed fresh lioness tracks by his bedding. The lioness hadn't just stood next to him, but had lain down like a dog. I wonder what Tobias would have said or done had he woken up with that lioness next to him. Perhaps, in a previous life, Tobias had been a lion. The half-tamed lions of Leeubron were involved in this particular incident. They were fed regularly, and were probably not hungry. Tobias had to endure our teasing the entire day. However, he was very nervous, and emphasised again and again: "And the thing didn't just stand next to me, she lay down by my side!"

Elephant visits at night

I explored the entire nature reserve whenever time allowed. It was like a hobby, and on many a weekend I went to visit my private game wardens – those Bushmen I had left outside the Ombika entrance gate on a previous occasion. After a while I knew where they lived, and I often took them some tobacco, sugar and flour. Eventually they trusted me completely, and showed me their secret waterholes and other interesting things.

The old father and medicine-man, "Tail-and-Neck", talked to me for hours at night about their life, his past, and their mores and customs. I learned a great deal from him. Paul Doodvreet was a cousin once removed of his, and Paul always knew where to find his family.

One afternoon we drove to the waterhole at Guinzeb ("Bubbling Water"). At that time Guinzeb was quite unknown, and no road went there. It was an extremely stony and overgrown terrain, and we were able to make our way through the bush only at some 10–15 kilometres per hour. When Paul spoke of Guinzeb, he was always in raptures about the time he grew up there.

I really wanted to see the waterhole, and reached it late in the afternoon. There was a large congregation of many types of wild-life, and we decided to camp about one kilometre south of Guinzeb. I had, however, not taken into account the swarms of mosquitoes. You cannot imagine the vast numbers of mosquitoes near such a waterhole, and besides, it was a malaria area.

It was full moon, and I wanted to sit near the waterhole to study the nightlife, but the mosquitoes were simply too much. I decided to go to bed, but this, too, was spoiled by the mosquitoes. In the end I wrapped myself completely in my blankets, leaving only a tiny opening for breathing. The mosquitoes even flew in there and bit me on the tip of my nose. It was a warm night, and I was sweating profusely under my blankets. Despite being really tired, it took a long time for me to fall asleep.

By midnight Swart Sikspens and Paul Doodvreet were still sitting by the fire, talking.

If there was something that really drove me wild, it was Bush-men loudly talking by the fire, or lighting their pipes with their tin-derboxes. The Bushmen sitting there, talking so loudly, caused me to tell them brusquely to shut up. "Just look at the elephants, Boss," Sikspens answered quite calmly, and pointed in the direction of the waterhole. Three elephants were standing quite close to us. "Look at them yourselves, and just keep quiet!" I snarled at the Bushmen after giving the elephants the beady eye. Then I wrapped myself up in my blankets again, and tried to get some sleep. Eventually I must have fallen into a deep sleep until it started to get light.

Both Bushmen were up and about, and water for coffee was al-most boiling on the fire. When they saw that I was awake, Sikspens asked me quite calmly: "And what is that next to you?" He pointed to a spot behind my back. I looked around and was instantly wide awake. The whole area was trampled. It was clear the elephant bulls had gathered right behind me, perhaps conferring about what to do about the three humans, the fire and the camping equipment. The nearest elephant tracks were only 1,5 metres away from me. If I had turned onto my back, the elephant's mouth must have been right above me, and his trunk would have brushed my nose.

I felt shivers down my spine, but I kept my mouth shut and looked at the Bushmen meaningfully for a long time. I could only

146

say a silent prayer of thanks, and really appreciated the behaviour of these peaceful elephants. To this day I still wonder what went on in the heads of those animals, because they must have been standing there for quite a while. The entire area was covered in footprint after footprint.

Fortunately all three of us were sleeping soundly at the time. To this day I am still wondering what would have happened if I had woken up, with that elephant looming right over me.

On another occasion we were busy building a large round concrete dam at Olifantsbad. Throwing the concrete for the dam was a task that kept us busy for nearly three days and three nights, with perhaps three hours' sleep per night.

We camped about a kilometre away from where we were working, but because we were so busy, we were not at the camp very often. We cooked our food at the construction site, and because of the many scorpions and ticks, I slept on a foldaway bed, something I seldom did.

When we got to the camp late one afternoon, my bed was gone, the coals of the fire had been raked apart, and blankets were strewn about – it looked like a tornado had whirled through the camp.

The foldaway bed was lying some distance from where it had originally stood, all mangled. In our absence elephants had come to inspect the camp, and were clearly not satisfied with the state of affairs. We had to clean up everything in their wake.

Olifantsbad, a turning point in my life

After a few years at Okaukuejo, I was probably at the physical peak of my life. Apart from horse-riding and the outdoor life, my hobbies were archery, boxing and weight-lifting. I also loved listening to classical music (Mozart, Beethoven, Bach and Vivaldi), but I was particularly fond of my weight-lifting. I had developed my arms and upper body through regular exercise with my weights, and my ability to lift heavy objects was something that most people would not be able to emulate. Because I did a lot of horse-riding, I did not want to develop my legs and lower body muscles too much, because thick thigh muscles just get in the way of proper dressage. I therefore concentrated on my arms and torso.

There are many windpumps in Etosha, and each game warden has a few in his area which he needs to maintain. Dolf, the game warden at Namutoni, borrowed my tools to repair a windpump in his area, but shortly afterwards my windpumps at Olifants-bad stopped drawing water. This was on a Friday afternoon. We had been in the veld for the whole week, and were looking forward to spending the weekend at home. That Friday afternoon I was instructed to repair the windpump at Olifantsbad. My team of Bushmen were most upset, because they were on the point of going home. However, the water-supply at Olifantsbad had been completely exhausted, and hundreds of head of game were milling about in expectation of water. Because I had lent my tools, I had to get all the necessary tools (apart from the automatic winching system) from the motor mechanic.

The borehole pipes were 2 metres long and 635 millimetres wide with a large 127 millimetre suction cylinder. Our team often simply pulled up these pipes by hand – perfectly possible if everyone worked together well. On that afternoon my Bushmen simply did not cooperate. On previous occasions I had pulled a number of pipes full of water from the borehole by myself when the Bushmen struggled. I was very cross at the negativity shown by the Bushmen, so I chased them away from the pipes and said I would do it myself. Because of my anger, I wasn't thinking, and I began pulling up the pipes with an arched back. Then I felt a sharp pain in my lower back, as if something had torn along my spine. Because I had boasted that I could do it, I continued lifting the pipes. The Bushmen then shifted the pipe-clamp downwards, and began to cooperate. I felt a strange numbing pain in my lower body and legs, but kept quiet. We completed the work and replaced the rusted suction-rod. I drove home that evening with a numb and painful back.

When I wanted to get up the next morning, I had no power in my legs, and I collapsed next to the bed. Elke looked at me and laughed. When I tried to stand up, I couldn't. "Don't laugh, something is seriously wrong!" I said. Eventually I stood up, hoisting myself up with my arms. Little did I know, that morning, that I would have to rely on this method of getting up for the rest of my life, and that I would never be able to walk normally again.

That accident at Olifantsbad changed my life. That morning, as I was training my champion dressage horse Alarich at the end of a tether, I fell down three times. I could no longer mount a horse in the normal manner, and had to clamber on board from some platform. My days of lifting weights were over. The days when I could easily walk 60–80 kilometres in a day, were over. I had to adapt my gait. Back pains became an everyday occurrence, and to this day I have no idea what it feels like to be without back pain. Often I could not tie my shoelaces in the morning. But if you want to keep living, you also need to adapt and stop moaning, because that only gets on the nerves of everyone around you.

Self-pity only sours one's life. I believe this accident was sent from Above. I had been too bold, too much of a monarch of all I surveyed, too much focused on myself, too liable to tread on the toes of others without taking their feelings into account. I had to accept that I needed to bear my own punishment without complaint.

Battling poachers

Curbing poaching was probably the most important and most valuable contribution I was able to make to Etosha as a game warden.

My horses and my permanent team of Bushmen were my greatest allies; I would not have had any success without them.

In my first year at Etosha I had to maintain my personal horses myself, and undertake all patrols at my own risk. All went well. I started removing trespassing elephants from the neighbouring farms, and proved the value of horses for nature conservation work.

My first anti-poaching action was bringing in the "trespassing" Bushmen in the game reserve, and that run-in with Nabekub. Eventually all those Bushmen were free again, and they lived in the bush for many years. They were my private game wardens, and thanks to their cooperation I eventually knew Etosha better than any other officer.

I have no hesitation in revealing that I protected those Bushmen all those years, even though it was strictly speaking illegal. In my heart of hearts I was convinced that they deserved to live there in their original state, because we are all born free. Apartheid is something of the past, all the black tribes claim their original place of birth. This handful of Bushmen had no other place to live. They had no one who could speak on their behalf. They were a part of nature which was disappearing. Why could they, too, not be granted their place in the sun? Thousands of head of game died of anthrax every year because of overcrowding. What damage could a handful of Bushmen with bows and arrows do to the overcrowded game? Every year we shove hundreds of head of game into tins (using culling as an excuse), because Etosha has become one large game farm. Yet some would have it that a handful of Bushmen "do too much damage"! I told my Bushmen countless times: "It's a pity I don't have a black skin – I would have run away to live in the veld like a Bushman. I would have been far worse than Nabekub." And I mean it. I care little if people blame me for that.

I am writing these words because of my actions towards poachers in my capacity as game warden, as you will gather from the following stories.

As a former poacher, I always had a soft spot for someone I had to put behind bars. I always enjoyed tracking, following and outwitting a poacher. Yet, after I had put those handcuffs on his wrists, this enthusiasm nearly always left me. I always made a distinction between one poacher and another. The one who shot elephants and rhinos just for the tusks and horns – he should be locked up and the key thrown away! And if he wants to shoot you, then shoot him twice! I would not feel a thing. The person who shoots several head of game simply because he enjoys killing – no mercy, mate. Treat him like the first category.

The person who shoots large numbers of game and then cuts out only the haunches and fillets – treat him the same as category one and two. Someone like that has no respect for God's creation.

Then you get the trophy hunter. He must have this trophy, and that one, but apart from that he loves the wild, and respects it. I will prosecute such a man, but I understand him, because he does not waste anything from the wild.

Then there's the man who hunts because he is poor and is looking for meat because he cannot afford meat. I will prosecute such a man very reluctantly, and depending on the circumstances, I will let him go with a warning – but if the offence is repeated, there will be no mercy.

I was warned, from the start, about the farmers on the boundary. I was once a boundary farmer's foreman, and was well versed in the circumstances that such farmers had to contend with. That is why I listened to everyone's problems. If farmers along the boundaries hunted inside the game park, I always warned them first that I was on to them, and that I would show no mercy if I caught them. Sometimes they told me quite openly that they were after a lion that had repeatedly caught their cattle. If I could convince myself that this was indeed so, I did not act against such farmers.

Farmers complained about lion problems all the time, and I reported this to the Head Warden, but he often dismissed the claims as tall tales. I then had to tell the farmers they had to fend for themselves. Sometimes, in a real emergency, I took the responsibility on myself. This was the case when a lion caught 45 head of cattle on those farms. This was a particularly large lion with a light mane, and it caused havoc on the Lombard, Bester, Du Toit and Coetzee brothers' farms. All these farms were situated along Etosha's southern boundary.

This lion had been caught in a trap before, had eaten poison, and was later wounded, but never left the cattle in peace. Danie du Toit, himself a successful lion hunter, nearly had him one day. He was tracking the animal, and when he spotted the lion, he climbed into a tree for a better view. He climbed quite high into the tree, and spotted the lion. Danie had to shoot from a standing position on a horizontal branch – a very precarious position. He chanced a shot; the recoil knocked him off-balance, and Danie fell from the tree to the ground, breaking his collar-bone in the process. The shot missed. The lion fled without a scratch.

The lion that accounted for 45 cattle meets his match

I was on boundary patrol one morning when I saw Uncle Danie standing on the other side of the Grensplaas boundary fence. When I came closer, I saw there were tears in his eyes.

"He killed seven of my calves last night," he said. "Seven of my dairy-cows' calves, and he only nibbled on one of them. I can't carry on like this. Please come and help me. There are the fresh tracks he left when he went back to the game reserve last night!" Uncle Danie was a strong man with a strong personality, but he was visibly moved. There and then I decided: this far, and no further. I would help Uncle Danie by trying to destroy that lion. I promised him that I would take all the blame, permission or no permission.

I was accompanied by Tobias, a particularly good tracker on difficult terrain, and we followed the lion's spoor. The area consists of the one stone ridge after the other, with thick bush, but we were able to follow the trail.

We followed it for a long while, because the going was often very slow. Fortunately we were always able to pick up the trail again. A fairly strong north wind had been blowing for most of the day, and the lion was heading into the wind. By 14:00 I had almost given up hope, when we suddenly noticed that the tracks were now heading downwind. Fortunately the wind had turned west and was blowing as a cross-wind, so we still had a chance. We followed the spoor some more – very quietly and cautiously – and spotted the lion under a tree about 20 metres ahead of us. He immediately got up with a warning roar, and tried to run away. I took a shot with my 9.3 millimetre. He stumbled, let out another quick roar, and was gone. We hadn't seen him for more than three seconds. He was a large and conspicuous specimen, light of colour.

I knew the shot had hit him obliquely from behind because he had run around a thicket. With that type of wound he would be able to travel a long distance.

We followed very cautiously. Tobias was wary of lions, and I had no idea what he would do if the lion were to attack. The wounded lion had disappeared downwind, and I warned Tobias against large trees and thick bush. If we spotted such a potential hiding-place, we had to leave the tracks, circle around the hazard, and approach it from downwind in order to inspect it thoroughly.

After two kilometres we saw some large, green trees a fair distance away. I told Tobias to leave the tracks for now and to approach the trees from downwind by circling around them.

When we were 30 metres from the spot, we could see the lion lying under a tree next to a large ant heap. He was looking upwind, in the direction from which he had come, and he had his back to us. He was lying in wait for us behind that ant heap. I had my rifle at the ready, but it was much too easy, and I did not want to shoot him in the back. "Here I am, bastard, come and get me!" At the sound of my voice, the lion looked round, jumped up and tried to attack. A quick shot from the front, through his lower jaw and chest, dropped him. He tried to get up again, but a quick shot to his neck finished him off.

After we had skinned him, we followed the long way back to where we had left the vehicle. Then we drove back to Grensplaas, where we stayed the night. Uncle Danie and his wife were overcome with joy. The next morning I first had to wait for gifts of a large gelded goat, a full can of cream and bags of breakfast rusks.

When I reported the matter at Okaukuejo, the chief game warden simply looked at me with a overdone sour grin and said: "I knew you'd do that!"

152

A drop of blood gives away a notorious poacher

On the southern boundary of the game reserve, about 800 paces from the fence, there was a dilapidated little farmhouse on the farm Mooiplaas. This house belonged to Uncle Jopie Robbertse and his son Flip. There was a string of Robbertse brothers and cousins on various farms along the southern and western boundaries of the game reserve. The Robbertse family were descendants of farmers who had left Angola. Almost all of them loved hunting, and did not pay much attention to the game reserve's boundaries. Many tales about their comings and goings did the rounds, and almost every game warden pretended to be deaf when someone referred to them. These much-feared folk interested me a great deal, and in the course of time I counted some amongst them as friends, even though a "green-jacket" (game warden) was never welcome on their farms.

I came to a halt on the boundary opposite this house, climbed through the fence and introduced myself to them. Uncle Joop and Flip initially studied me from head to toe for some time, taking my measure, then mumbled their names and shook hands. Later they invited me inside and we had a good chat over a cup of coffee. I could see these farmers were having a tough time, because they had lost nearly all their livestock in the drought.

Before I left, I offered my help should they experience problems with predators.

From that day on, I stopped opposite the little house during almost every routine patrol, was given a cup of coffee every time, and chatted for a while. I also asked whether they were experiencing any problems. We began to treat one another like friends. Because they were stigmatised as a result of the poaching, I occasionally made sure they understood very well that I would prosecute anyone who did not respect the boundary.

One day a few fence droppers near the house were broken. While the Bushmen were busy replacing the droppers, I walked along the fence as usual, looking for anything unusual. We were on a stony ridge, and any tracks were almost invisible. Some distance away I noticed a rock with a black spot on it. Initially I thought it must be bird droppings. I walked on, but then began wondering whether that spot wasn't blood, perhaps. I walked back, picked up the rock and satisfied myself that it wasn't bird droppings. Rubbing a bit of spit on it, I ascertained that it had to be a drop of blood.

153

The spot was quite small, but there had to be a reason for it. I studied the stony surface and the fence very carefully once again. A little further on I could see black bloodstains on two of the fence wires at shoulder height. I was certain that someone must have passed meat through the wires. I called my Bushmen and said: "Something funny is going on here; look carefully, and tell me what it is." I replaced the rock with the blood on it carefully in its original position.

The Bushmen walked up and down along the wire, but found nothing. When they gave up, I showed them the small black spot. They looked at it with vacant eyes, thinking it must be bird droppings. Then I showed the marks on the fence, and they admitted, somewhat shamefacedly, that something strange must have happened. Moses, the Bushman foreman, told me that Flip's Bushmen had a little hamlet on the other side of the ridge. We could see the tracks of a herd of fleeing gemsbok on a small low-lying marshland with hard, grey soil. They led away from the wire, obliquely north into the game reserve. We followed the gemsbok tracks for about 4 kilometres until we saw vultures circling quite a distance ahead of us. We walked directly to where the vultures were, and found the head and skin of a butchered young gemsbok. There were at least four bullet-holes in the skin. It must have been Flip who had been hunting here. There were blood-stains on the trunk and branches of the tree beneath which the gemsbok remains lay. Pieces of meat must have been hung here.

We picked up six .303 cartridges 50 metres from the slaughtering-place. We took all the pieces of evidence and returned to the vehicle.

I sent Moses to the location. He had to bluff Flip's Bushmen, telling them that we knew everything and that they had to talk, or they would be in trouble themselves. Moses returned after quite a while. He had done his work well, and had pieces of a zebra-skin and a set of springbok horns in a bag. After he had thoroughly scared the Bushmen, they talked quite freely.

They not only gave details of the gemsbok hunt, but revealed that Flip had, on another occasion, shot a zebra and later a springbok.

I wanted to give Flip and Uncle Jopie a chance. I walked over to them and asked whether they knew who had shot the gemsbok that had been butchered in the game reserve. They tried to blame the cattle-inspector who also patrolled that fence. I then warned them that I would report the matter to the police for investigation. Then I drove to Okaukuejo, and reported the matter to the police station commander.

I was not popular with the police, because I had handed many black poachers to them for safe-keeping. They were very jealous of me and tried to sabotage me as much as they could. They raced alongside the boundary fence in their vehicles and found nothing. When they had completed a patrol, I always went on my own horse patrol, and then had a great deal of success. Every time I brought in some poachers, they warned me not to overdo it – they did not look forward to having to search for my dead body.

The next day the station commander placed at my disposal a constable to investigate the matter, and to charge the Robbertses formally. At that stage I was driving the 5-ton Thames. The policeman was overweight, with thick, round thighs. The Thames only had two seats, and the bag full of all the pieces of evidence was in front of the left seat. The contents of the bag were smelling powerfully, and the cabin was swarming with flies. The policeman had to dangle his short, thick legs over the bag, and looked most uncomfortable sitting there. In this manner we jostled over stony ridges on the way to Mooiplaas. I stopped right opposite the farmhouse and told the constable to do his work and to confiscate the .303, as game wardens had very little powers in those days. He walked over to the house and returned half an hour later with a red face, as mad as a snake. "You ruined the whole case by warning them that we were coming. They laughed in my face and taunted me by saying I should cut open the dogs' stomachs to extract the gemsbok biltong. They were very cheeky and dared me to touch their .303. The fists would fly, because I had no evidence. They would not let me take the rifle. You made a fool of me!"

I could hardly stop myself from bursting out laughing. "How much evidence would you like, Sir?" I asked him quite calmly. "Just open the bag and see what's inside, smelling so sweet!" When the policeman opened the bag and saw what was inside, he was even angrier.

"I feel like charging you with obstruction of justice!" he snarled, and waved his charge sheet under my nose. "You have been withholding evidence."

"Stop talking nonsense; let me show you how it's done," I replied calmly. "Ask, and you shall be told," was my last comment.

In my pocket I had the six .303 shell casings I picked up near the gemsbok. On arrival at the house, father and son were standing defiantly in its shade.

"The game is up, Uncle Jopie," I said. "Here are the six cartridges I picked up near the place of the shooting." I showed them to him. Uncle Jopie's eyes grew wide as he stared at the shell casings.

Involuntarily he burst out: "The stupid idiot!" and collapsed.

We helped Uncle Jopie on his feet. "Uncle Jopie," I said, "we got all the evidence from your Bushmen, and we know when, where and how Flip hunted. I already knew everything when I visited you yesterday, but you didn't want to talk to me. Now the law must take its course."

Flip went into the house and brought out the .303 himself and handed it to us. The policeman warned them that he would charge them, and then we drove back to Okaukuejo.

On the morning of the court case I parked my Ford in front of the magistrate's office in Outjo, and offloaded some arrows, bows, knives and other pieces of evidence I had confiscated from a group of black poachers I had caught on another occasion.

As I was doing this, I felt a tap on my shoulder. When I looked around, I saw it was Flip. I first thought he was going to hit me, but then Flip spoke with a voice filled with remorse. "Sorry, Peter, for abusing your trust like that. No matter how the case pans out, and what the result may be, let's stay friends the way we were. Come and visit us, and have a cup of coffee like before."

His case was short and brief, and he pleaded guilty. His only excuse was that he saw the gemsbok standing right alongside the fence, that he could not resist the temptation, and that he shot at them. Flip was fined £100 and was allowed to keep his rifle.

After the court case I wanted to do some shopping, and wanted to draw money from Barclays Bank. Uncle Jopie was there before me. Tears were streaming down his cheeks and his trembling hands trembled even more. "What's the problem, Uncle Jopie?" I asked.

"We don't have enough money, and Flip will have to go to jail. I'm all alone!" he answered.

Without hesitation I arranged with the cashier to pay the remainder of the amount to Uncle Jopie from my account. The fine of £100 wasn't all that much, but it was too much for Uncle Jopie and his son.

The butcher

While on patrol along the northern boundary, I often noticed vehicle tracks from Owamboland crossing the open border to the game reserve.

The Etota waterhole is close to the game reserve's northern boundary, and large numbers of game came to drink there. About 3 kilometres from Etosha the Ekuma River runs south from Owambo and eventually disgorges into the Etosha Pan. Every ten years the Ekuma River flows into the Etosha Pan in full spate, and then dries up again after flowing for two or three months. The Ekuma River is one of the main sources for the Etosha Pan, and thousands of flamingoes breed on the pan when it is full of water.

Children came to me every holiday for advanced riding lessons. Their training commenced very early, before I started work, or after work, late in the afternoon. They almost always went with me when I had to do field-work. This meant the children enjoyed a wonderful holiday, and the house was often full.

One of my regular students was a girl by the name of Ute, a very promising rider who loved nature. Pretty Ute grew up quickly, and it wasn't long before she had a young man by her side, a young veterinarian by the name of Achim. They came visiting over a long weekend, and I wanted to arrange something special for them. It was probable that hunters would come from Owamboland in this period to poach game.

We loaded bedding and provisions on the bakkie on Friday afternoon and went to Etosha. That night we decided to lay in wait for possible visitors in the dry bed of the Ekuma River.

We made a fire to prepare supper. Then I noticed a small spot of light far to the north in Owamboland. A meandering path ran alongside the Ekuma River from north to south, and there are almost no trees on either side of the river; one can see for a long distance. I kept an eye on the spot of light, and saw it had to be a hunting lamp on a slow-moving vehicle. We doused the fire and I prepared my weapons – a .38 revolver and my trusty .303. As we were lying in wait for the vehicle, I gave two crash courses in the handling of weapons. I would be the arresting officer.

The vehicle approached slowly and went by to our left. Fortunately my vehicle was parked in the dry river bed, and we were lying prone on the ground, all agog with excitement. The hunting lamp's beam fell weakly on us every now and then, but we were not spotted.

The vehicle moved further into the game reserve, south.

I knew there was a stand of mopani trees on either side of the road a little further south; an ideal spot for an ambush. I wanted the vehicle to pass us first, and to give the occupant enough time for hunting, so that we would have a watertight case. I would then wait at an appropriate spot in the mopani trees for his return. When the vehicle disappeared in a southward direction, we followed with dimmed lights. It was new moon, and driving was not easy; the grass stood tall, and the terrain was criss-crossed with gulleys and dotted with aardvark holes. We had hardly reached the little mopani forest or the vehicle returned – much sooner than I had anticipated.

The path ran its meandering course through the mopani trees and I picked a suitable spot in the road and waited. When the vehicle's light-beams fell on mine, I switched on the headlights.

Things then happened as in a movie. Something large and tall moved between me and the poacher's minibus, and a large giraffe bull fell to the left of my vehicle and lay still. The vehicle drove by to the right, but came to a halt in the thick growth. I reached the driver's door before the occupants could jump out. I wrenched it open, grabbed someone by the shirt-collar and yanked him out.

Because it was pitch-dark, I wasn't sure how many people were in the Volkswagen minibus. I had to act quickly, drastically and decisively before they got the upper hand. My mother had taught me that attack is the best form of defence, and that remained my motto for the rest of my life. At that stage I did not care very much, as my adrenaline levels were high.

I had explained to Ute and Achim beforehand that they should just cover me with a weapon, and leave the poachers to me.

I made the white driver of the minibus stand against the side of the vehicle with his hands on the vehicle above his head, and warned him not to move. Inside the vehicle a middle-aged Owambo man sat staring at me with huge white eyes. I yanked him out as well, and told him to stand next to his white friend in the same posture.

I quickly searched both of them for weapons, but they had nothing on them apart from knives.

Inside the vehicle a ten-year-old boy was sleeping on one of the back seats, completely unaware of what was happening around him. There were a .303 and a .22 rifle in the vehicle. Right at the back there was a caracal (*rooikat*) that they must have killed earlier.

A climax, followed by an anticlimax. I had expected a whole bus-load of people, but the two I arrested were as meek as little lambs. I had to keep them in custody somewhere, and Okaukuejo was the nearest place. The police station at Okaukuejo was no more, and the only way was to lock them up in one of the tourist huts.

Achim rode in the bus with its owner and the boy. Ute and the Owambo man rode with me in the bakkie behind them. We arrived at Okaukuejo at midnight and locked up the detainees in one of the rest huts under the supervision of a tourist official. The Outjo police fetched them the next morning. Achim, Ute and I went back to our camp, where we loaded everything in the early hours of the morning. Then we had to return to the giraffe. We could not allow all that meat to spoil. I asked the motor mechanic to bring a load of Bushmen to take the last scrap of meat to Okaukuejo. There was enough meat for all the hungry bellies. The men who spent the least amount of time in the veld took the most meat.

The white poacher was a professional butcher at Oshakati in Owamboland who was poaching to get cheap meat for his butch-ery. His case really took a wrong turn for him. His vehicle and all his firearms were confiscated, and he was given a fine of R300. He was hit hard, but the entire Owamboland got a fright.

I catch my former teacher

Every game warden in Etosha had an area of responsibility. Even before every area had its own two patrol horses, I often rode horse patrols along the northern boundary: from Operet at the eastern-most point of Etosha to Otjovasandu, the furthest west; a distance of 320 kilometres.

Every 50 kilometres or so there was a horse-paddock, given a name for identification purposes.

A horse-station consisted of six sturdy camps fenced in with high screens, each one some three square metres in size, to enable the horses to rest properly at night after a long ride, and for protec-tion against lions. Our field staff knew where every camp in their area was situated.

I always picked thickets for shade, and to hide the station as much as possible in order to avoid enemies.

I also had an area of 30 metres cleared inside a thicket, where I practised with my sporting horses if time allowed.

I usually rode my sporting horse if I went on patrol, but if there was time, I practised dressage moves in this 30-metre area. This was the only way I could keep my dressage horses on their toes, and it worked.

The horse patrols also gave me the opportunity to get to know my colleagues' areas of responsibility very thoroughly – much better than the person whose area of responsibility it was!

In this way I found that there were a great many vehicle tracks from Owamboland on the Andoni Plain in the Namutoni area. I decided to investigate.

I hit the jackpot the very first time. Between the Andoni Plain and Poacher's Point I built a horse-station for myself with a good view of the Andoni Plain and across the eastern Etosha to Poacher's Point. This area was as flat as a table-top, and with a good pair of binoculars you could see far and watch all the goings-on. This camp became a trap for many a poacher.

On the first afternoon I sat watching there, a yellow bakkie with two whites as occupants sped by me on the road. Shots began to ring out not far from the camp. We could see the bakkie stopping on the pan every now and then. The two men then got out and loaded a springbok. We let them be. The more game, the stronger the case, and the higher the fine.

After a while the bakkie turned back in our direction. The Bushmen had already climbed on the back of my vehicle, and I switched it on and let it idle. When the yellow bakkie passed us, I burst out of my ambush at the camp and followed them.

I overtook the yellow bakkie at a good spot, turned in front of it and indicated that they should stop.

The two men in the yellow bakkie stared at me in fright. When I walked over to their vehicle, the face of one of them seemed familiar to me, but I could not place it. We introduced ourselves and when the names were said out loud, we all knew who we were dealing with. The driver of the bakkie was my Mathematics teacher in my last two years at school. I felt bad. This man was one of the very few teachers for whom I had any respect when I was still at school. He tried to instil the basics of mathematics in me with the greatest patience, but I never showed any enthusiasm. If I had had to teach such a negative pupil, I would have sent him to blazes long ago, but this man had shown nothing but patience towards me. He was one of the few teachers I liked. Now, as fate would have it, I was arresting him, of all people.

There were eight springbok on the back of his bakkie, and I needed to skin the carcasses in order to present those skins as evidence.

In reply to my question why they were hunting in the game reserve, they said they had not seen the boundary road and did not know they were inside the reserve. It was a very poor excuse. I took their knives and noted the numbers of their firearms and the vehicle. They were most upset and afraid of possible dismissal from their work. I had to make them understand quite clearly that I could not drop the case – if I did, I would never be able to call myself a game warden.

I then sent them home and reported the case at the Tsumeb police station.

There were major developments before the court case. Only then did I learn that this former teacher of mine was the Minister of Bantu Education, and the other person a respected principal.

Both tried to persuade the Prime Minister at the time, Vorster, to have the case dropped, but he gave instructions that it should proceed. In the end they received a relatively light fine, and were able to keep their vehicle and firearms.

Poachers become good game wardens

I had even more success by using the horse-station near the Andoni Plain. There is an artesian bore-hole on the Andoni Plain, with the water bubbling from the top of the pipe. Thousands of head of game concentrate at this bore-hole, and on those bare plains it is relatively easy to shoot the animals from a vehicle.

The poachers just can't get enough, and then their vehicles become hopelessly overloaded. I have seen, many times, how the undersides of some of the bakkies touch the ground as they struggle to get home with a full load of zebra and wildebeest. It is then easy to overtake them and effect the arrest.

The main thing is to act decisively and quickly and not to be drawn into a lengthy discussion, because that gives the poachers new hope, which may give them the upper hand.

The driver of a vehicle will only be caught by someone driving a good vehicle, and a horseman by a better horseman on a better horse. Normally the hunters who enter on horses have about eight to ten horses with them, as well as 30–50 donkeys, and about 20 dogs. They are usually also accompanied by women and children who must process and dry the meat. When they have enough meat, the donkeys are loaded, and then the trek returns to sell the meat in the homeland.

The modus operandi of these horsemen is that all the riders, as well as all the riding and pack donkeys, dogs, women and children, cross the boundary separately and penetrate deep into the game reserve until they reach a large rain-water pan. Each pan has a name known only to them. They usually set up camp in a thicket on a tall sand-dune. This gives them a good view, giving them enough time to flee, or to spot game from the camp.

They usually cross the boundary at night at places where there are people with cattle. The poachers then make arrangements with the cattle-owners to drive their stock across their tracks early in the morning in order to erase them. You therefore do not see any horse or donkey tracks near the boundary.

We always patrolled on horseback 5–10 kilometres south of the boundary and parallel to it, and regularly picked up tracks, because the cattle were never driven that far south. If we found such tracks, we followed them to where the poachers were hiding near the water-pans. They will sometimes remain at such a water-pan for one or two weeks, accumulating a good deal of meat in that time. I have found camps where they had killed and processed six to eight giraffes, eight to ten large eland and many other head of game. The trees were then black from all the dried meat, and from a distance one would think you were looking at a herd of elephants.

In the morning, three or four groups, each consisting of four horsemen, would go in four directions, each group hunting independently. In most cases they would follow fresh spoor until they reached a game herd. Sometimes they chased eland and giraffes in the direction of their camp. When they reached the camp with the tired animals, they were greeted by people and many, many dogs. The already exhausted animals were then surrounded by a group, and spent even more energy trying to fend off the dogs. The trapped animals were then dispatched with bows and arrows, throwing spears or even guns. I still have some respect for a hunter on horseback, because he must be a skilled rider to be able to bring game to a specific place through the bush at full gallop, dodging aardvark holes all the time. However, these riders treated their horses dreadfully hard and cruelly, and some of the animals I confiscated were in such a poor condition that shooting them was a release from their suffering.

If the horses were still good and useful, I let them live. On conviction, all weapons and animals are declared forfeit. The horses and donkeys were usually destroyed, or sometimes the state bought them. I saved the lives of many horses in this manner. They often rendered good service to Nature Conservation, living the rest of their lives in far better circumstances. Some of the horses were wonderful bush animals.

Some poachers' horses therefore became Nature Conservation horses, and likewise Nature Conservation also employed some of the poachers.

One morning we went on a horse patrol in a north-western direction from the Andoni camp. This is a sandy area, and fairly densely vegetated. We were riding parallel to the northern boundary when we saw fresh human, horse and eland tracks. It seemed that the horseman was chasing a large eland bull. We followed the tracks for a distance until we saw two Owambos engaged in cutting up an animal carcass. They were so busy that they did not spot us. The wind was blowing quite strongly, and so they did not hear the approaching horses. We rode up to them at an easy canter and stopped right in front of them. Then I greeted them loudly and clearly: "Morning!" Only then did they see us. The larger of the two almost landed flat on his back from fright. I indicated that they had to stay calm. Then I asked them a number of routine questions, which they quite eagerly answered, strangely enough.

The two Owambos were used by an Owambo chief in the manner of tracking dogs – they had to run along game tracks ahead of the chief's horse. When they came upon game, he then chased the animals, and when the animals were exhausted, he shot them with his .303. The trackers then had to follow him and process the game. Next, they had to walk back to the camp, fetch the donkeys and take the meat back to the camp. When I asked where the chief was, they said he was at a waterhole named Uteres ("Come and get me"). Uteres was a shallow well amongst some sand-dunes at a spot where nobody would expect any water.

Years ago, when I still worked at Onguma, Koos Myburgh, the constable at Namutoni at the time, asked me whether he could borrow some of my horses, and whether Willie and I would undertake a horse-patrol with him to the Weisele Plain. He wanted to tackle some Owambo hunters. He, Willie and I therefore rode to Weisele. There were no roads, and Willie and I were unfamiliar with that region. We had not taken enough water with us, and the only water-bag had been pierced by a gate made of thorn branches.

On that day we went in search of Uteres from Weisele. It was extremely hot, and we could not find the waterhole amongst the dunes. At dusk we were forced to unsaddle, and we tied the horses to the bushes. We had no food, but the thirst was worse. Nobody said a word, because our tongues felt as if they had been pasted to our palates. After a restless night we saddled the horses early, and Willie went off to look for the waterhole. We found the well after about an hour. Instinct had taken Willie to it. It was a shallow sandy well with a little bit of green water, in which some rotted starlings were floating.

Despite the dead starlings, despite the green water, we did not hesitate. Unless you have ever experienced serious thirst yourself, you will have no idea what it's like. We removed the dead birds and simply drank and drank. There were no holders in which we could first boil the water. The green water tasted wonderful, and felt like balm from heaven. We recovered our strength there and rode back to Onguma, where we arrived in the afternoon. I had great respect for Koos Myburgh – he was still one of those old-fashioned cops. I met Koos again many years later when he was a general, and in command of the police in South West Africa.

But let's get back to the tracker dogs. The two arrested Owambos, Jason and Petrus, mentioned Uteres and said the chief had set up camp there. I suggested that we should stalk Uteres that night to overpower the chief while he was sleeping. According to the two Owambos, the chief had a .303 rifle, and he would not simply surrender.

We first loaded the meat of the large eland bull and took it to our camp. That night, after moonrise, we drove along the boundary fence in the direction of Uteres. Jason indicated where we should stop to make sure the chief did not hear our vehicle. We then proceeded through the bush on foot. There was a fire burning at the camp, and the horse and a few donkeys were standing in a thorn enclosure. The Owambo chief was lying on his back next to the fire, fast asleep, with the .303 rifle in the crook of his right arm. I lifted the rifle gently from his embrace, and then Jason woke the chief. When he opened his eyes and saw me standing next to him, he wanted to grab his rifle and jump up. However, Jason pushed him down and indicated that the game was up and that they were under arrest. The chief was very agitated and it took a long time for him to calm down. I had to put handcuffs on him for safety's sake.

We then loaded the half-dried meat onto the Ford, but there was too much, and we had to leave some of it behind. We drove the donkeys and horse in the direction of the chief's territory. They would walk back to their home.

I then handed over the chief with his firearm and all the evidence at the Tsumeb police station. I did not charge Jason or Petrus. Petrus was employed as a camp worker at Namutoni. Jason was a member of my team of game wardens for a long time, a decision I never regretted. He was very loyal and hard-working, and rendered me valuable service. He may have been small and skinny, but he was worth every kilogram of his weight in gold. The chief got nine months in jail for his hunting expedition.

The cheeky Hereros of Onautinda, and Sam plants a knock-out blow

Although we experienced a good deal of trouble with poachers at Andoni and the surrounding areas, most of our problems came from the Kaokoveld in the west. There was a black town named Otjitjekua on the western boundary. We had many, many problems with its inhabitants. A mountain range named Othondunduothordane (meaning "Calf mountains") runs from north to south along the western boundary. I shall rather refer to the Calf Mountains, as the Herero name is a bit long and difficult.

The Hereros of the Kaokoveld and Otjitjekua usually came through valleys in the Calf Mountains in an easterly and southerly direction, entering the Etosha Game Reserve at the Onairo, Onandera, Onangombati and Okatjongeana waterholes. They are good horsemen and a very proud nation, and do not simply allow themselves to be arrested.

Because the poachers were very active there, I gathered a few teams of game wardens and their assistants, equipped them with two-way radios and placed them all along the defiles in the Calf Mountains. I was near one of the routes with my own team of Bushmen – Moses, Hebakoib and Sam – and the two Owambos Jason and Flanjama. Flanjama was a big, strong Owambo and a former poacher whom I had kept out of jail, and had then added to my team. On the very first afternoon we received a radio message from one of the lookout posts that six people with donkeys and horses were riding through one of the defiles in the direction of Onautinda. I instructed the game warden to ride to a place close to Onautinda, where we would meet. We got together after a while, and followed the Owambos' trail. We saw a few donkeys and three men near the waterhole at Onautinda. The horsemen were gone. After a quick gallop on our horses we surrounded and took the three men prisoner. They were too surprised to offer any resistance. After asking a few questions, it was clear that the three horsemen had left to look for game. I handcuffed the three men's hands to their leg-irons, and made them sit beside the fire. I warned them that they should not give any warning, and that they had to sit like that until the horsemen were in the camp. We then withdrew and hid in the surrounding bushes.

The horsemen returned after about ninety minutes. As they were asking the sitting men what was going on, we pounced on them from all sides. They were still mounted, and we ordered them to get down. I walked to one of them – there was a fresh gemsbok tail hanging from the bridle. (The most successful hunters usually tied the tail of the animal they had killed to the bit of their horse's bridle.) This Herero was a large, well-built man, and he shouted to the other riders: "Do not get down!" I can understand Herero, but cannot speak it fluently. I immediately knew trouble was at hand.

I ordered my men to grab them. I then grabbed the cheeky one near me by the arm, and tried to drag him from his horse. Initially he pulled back, then suddenly jumped on top of me from his horse's back. We were both on the ground, the Herero on top of me. We had each other by the throat. As we were wrestling on the ground, the Herero was plucked from me, and near my face I could see a military boot smashing into the Herero's face, followed by another boot to the stomach. As I struggled to my feet, Flanjama and Jason had a good grip on the Herero and were kicking and hitting him quite cruelly. The Owambos were speaking to him all the time: "You want to hit our boss, hey, now we'll show you!" I thought they were going to murder the Herero, and had to intervene and stop them. The Herero's mouth and nose were bleeding profusely.

In the meantime the other two Hereros had jumped off their horses and had tried to run away, with a whole bunch of white and black game wardens at their heels. In the van of the pursuers was Sam, the son of Moses, my Bushman foreman. He was only 18 years old, but very self-assured. I taught him how to ride a horse very well (and even dressage); he boxed well and was always lifting weights for strength.

Sam was after a Herero who was almost twice his size, and was followed by a game warden named Steyn. While the Herero was running, he pulled the bow from his shoulder with one hand and strung an arrow with the other. He suddenly came to a halt and turned round to shoot at his pursuers. As he was aiming, Sam ducked under the bow and arrow and gave the Herero a fist to the face at the same time. It was a classic uppercut to the Herero' chin. Game Warden Steyn could simply not stop talking about it. According to him, the Herero rose into the air and landed flat on his back. Then Sam produced a Smith & Wesson .22 revolver, and wanted to shoot the Herero. Fortunately Steyn was able to stop him just in time.

The other lot, with Andries van Vuuren in command, were pursuing the third Herero and were fortunately able to apprehend him. They had to use violence to handcuff him. The entire operation was a huge success, offering great excitement. The police, to whom we later handed over the prisoners, were not very happy about their condition. In the circumstances we could, however, not have done otherwise. Those Hereros were put behind bars for nine months.

I follow my own rules

In the course of time, catching poachers turned into a cat-and-mouse game. Eventually my team and I were known and feared all over Owamboland and the Kaokoveld. If for some reason I had to visit Owamboland or the Kaokoveld, it normally wasn't long before someone recognised me. This caused a whispering and scurrying amongst the residents, and they all took a quick look. I can understand some Owambo, but unfortunately my knowledge of the language was inadequate. I understood the Herero language fairly well. The Hereros have a sporting instinct. I was often approached by someone who asked whether I didn't know him. Sometimes he had to refresh my memory by recounting an incident where we were involved in altercations during an arrest, or when emotions ran high. In the end we had a good laugh together, without any bad feelings on either side. If we met in the game reserve, I would never allow myself to be beaten. The more arrests and prosecutions there were, the wilier the poachers became, and the more they plotted to outwit their enemies. Although we sometimes had to use force during an arrest to reach our goal, I always treated everyone with dignity afterwards. I could not bear mistreating someone who was lying on the ground or who had been vanquished.

I was supposed to be accompanied only by two trackers armed with bows and arrows when making an arrest. However, because I was involved in a great deal of development work, I often had six to eight Bushmen in my team. We found ourselves in many situations where we were outnumbered by the poachers, and many of the poachers, mostly Owambos and even whites, were armed with good modern weapons. I could not expect that we had to act against firearms only with bows and arrows. At that time blacks were not permitted to handle firearms, nor were they permitted to follow any radio procedures. I knew my Bushmen, and I was led by their intelligence and personal courage to train them in everything they were suited to. Driving a vehicle came first. Moses was my foreman, and a man of very strong character. He was my head driver, could handle any firearm very well, and was a good radio operator. Tobias, my top tracker, could shoot well. Stefanus was also a very good tracker, was a top shot and knew my firearms almost as well as I did. Paul Doodvreet was very intelligent, could drive well and was my head signalman.

Sam was also very intelligent and had great daring. He was my best horseman, could handle firearms well and was always prepared to follow me into any dangerous situation. I was almost like a father to him, because Moses had "given" him to me to raise. Sam was with me from a very young age. At that time there was no school for Bushmen. They were all illiterate. I had a good initial impression of him. When Moses brought him to me that very first time, he probably stood as tall as my belt. He looked me straight in the eyes from down there, standing with feet apart and hands on hips. He rode horses from a young age and never showed any fear. He had a particular talent with horses, and I taught him dressage moves. Later, when my back and hip problems became severe, he also trained all my showjumping horses. I once went on vacation to Swakopmund for the dressage championships with him and another Bushman, Piet.

I had a holiday home at Wlotzkasbaken where I kept my horses. I always transported my horses with my three-ton International truck, and also used it to transport water to the holiday home. I cared for that International as if it were a treasure, because I had paid a good deal for it. It always worked like a Swiss watch, to the day we had to drive to Okaukuejo at the end of the holiday.

I filled it with petrol at Swakopmund, and then the trouble started. It hesitated and spluttered, and eventually stopped. There was nothing wrong with the electrics, so it had to be the petrol. I thought I must have been given dirty petrol at that last filling station, and began cursing the owner and his petrol depot. I was in the desert, in the middle of nowhere, with a wife and children and three horses on the load-bed. Nobody would tow such a large vehicle and three horses. I cleaned the entire petrol line as best I could, but the engine still would not run. Then I used the tyre pump to pump air into the petrol tank. The truck ran for 5 kilometres and stopped again. I now knew where the problem was, and kept on pumping air into the petrol tank through the inlet. This went on and on. It was a Sunday, no garage was open, and I had to do the best I could. The International was heavy on petrol, and I had to fill it at Okahandja, Otjiwarongo and Outjo. Nothing helped – sometimes I managed 1 kilometre, or 4 or 5, and once even 16. With help from Above we reached Okaukuejo at midnight. I was as volatile as a stick of dynamite, and exhausted from struggling so long.

Early the next morning I instructed Moses to remove the petrol tank, pour the petrol into a large receptacle and to clean the tank. When I went home for breakfast at ten, Moses called me. "Look, Boss," he said. "The little buggers are sniffing the petrol. Look at all the pieces of paper and cardboard. They push the paper into the tank with a piece of wire to breathe in the petrol and become drunk. Then the paper falls into the tank, and they can't get it out. That's why the tank is so full of paper." When I asked what was to be done with the two, Moses simply said: "Whack their backsides until it burns!" I was still too angry, and would have done them serious damage, and I did not have conclusive proof. Apart from swearing high and low that they were not guilty, the pair also refused to come closer than 20 paces from me. A few days later I sent Sam to get me something from the stables. I waited and waited, but no Sam appeared. I looked for Sam and Piet at the stables, and found them on the trailer, fast asleep, with petrol-soaked paper still on their faces. I filled a bucket with water, grabbed my quirt and went back to the trailer. My wife, sensing trouble, followed me.

I climbed silently onto the trailer and poured cold water over the sleeping figures. When Sam saw me looming above him, he wanted

169

to jump up to run away, but I grabbed him by the collar, turned him onto his stomach and made that quirt dance on his backside. When he began to scream, my wife also began to shout, pleading with me to stop. However, she was the one who previously had repeatedly begged me to discipline Sam as he simply did not listen to her at all. I had often been accused of treating Sam like my pet.

The thrashing was brief and powerful. Sam became an exemplary colleague and never again took chances with me. While I was dealing with the struggling Sam, Piet jumped up and vanished in a flash. He never returned, and went to look for work on the farms. Which was just as well, because he had a negative influence on Sam, and was unreliable.

Bushmen I would like to mention in particular are Hebakoib and his older brother. Both Bushmen were sons of old Fritz who had also "given" his sons to me as my children. (When a Bushman "gives" you one of his children, you become responsible for that child's welfare. The parent withdraws his control to a large extent.) Initially they were my personal servants and horse-trainers. They went the same route as Sam, and both were top horsemen. However, it was never necessary for me to lift a hand to them. Like their father, both were very good trackers, and were able to handle fire-arms exceptionally well. They mainly helped in driving away elephants.

All these individuals were elite assistant game wardens or colleagues without whom I would not have been able to do my work properly.

As I recounted earlier, the poachers became cleverer by the day, and constantly changed their tactics. Using the motto "know thine enemy", I was also forced constantly to adapt my modus operandi. We were prohibited from crossing the boundary, and the poachers set up camp with their horses and donkeys at watering-points across the boundary. On moonlit nights they rode across the boundary to deep inside the game reserve. Early in the morning they were at the spots where the game gathered. Then they herded the game towards the boundary and killed them there. This meant it was extremely difficult to catch them. We had to make a plan. Initially we went on foot to determine their main entry and through routes. In the rainy season we then picked the best spots from where we would be able to follow their movements. Drinking water was the biggest problem. On rainy days, when tracks would be obliterated quickly, I buried 160-litre drums at the observation sites we had planned, with their bungs at the top. We would then simply scrape off the sand on top and get to the water by lowering a tube through the opening. These observation points were inside the poacher's territory, which they did not expect. My people were not allowed to wander about, but had to hide in the bushes near the drums full of water. They had a radio, and normally also my old .303 in case of emergencies. They took their blankets and dry rations for about a week. We dropped them at the boundary, and then they had to employ the counter-trail method to walk to the observation spots. I gave them a watch, and three times a day, at 07:00, 13:00 and 19:00, they had to contact me. If there were signs of movement, they had to report – in night-time – second hour. In this way we created a very efficient tracking network. Strictly speaking it was all against the law, and many things could have gone wrong. I trusted my Bushmen, however, and could rely on them. We only spoke the Bushman language over the radio, and as briefly as possible. We regularly crossed other Afrikaans-speaking stations on the same channel, particularly in the morning. I then often heard that the "damned 'kaffirs' had to get off the air". My people could not speak Afrikaans, however, and we said what we had to say to each other in Bushman, even though other people were most peeved.

If poachers were approaching the game reserve, by mid-morning we usually knew exactly where they were headed. We were therefore able to surprise them time and again, achieving great success. We would never have been so successful if we did not have the horses.

Operation "Neck Shot"

Some people observed my regular successes with my Bushmen and horses with greedy eyes and a frown. These people also wanted a share of my success. I was not the most popular man amongst my colleagues.

The chief game warden therefore arranged with the police to execute a helicopter patrol. Two helicopters were made available. We would fly over the entire game reserve, and poaching would be eliminated once and for all. It would be possible to cover a much larger area far more efficiently, etc.

I was very sceptical, because all our successes depended on tracking. Unless you fly over a group of horsemen or people by accident, it is difficult to spot any movement from the air. I voiced my doubts. One can hear and see a helicopter approaching from far away, which leaves plenty of time to find a hiding-place.

Because I knew the reserve very well and knew all the main entry routes and camps, I was instructed to sit in the front of the leading helicopter to indicate the direction in which to fly. We flew all along the northern boundary, from Namutoni to deep into the Kaokoveld, circled old poacher camps and visited all possible spots. We flew over a few settlements in the Kaokoveld, causing the inhabitants to scatter as the helicopter dove straight down, as if falling. This caused all the passengers great amusement.

We saw a lot, but not a single hunter. Everyone, the chief game warden in particular, was very disappointed. At one stage he accused me of deliberately misleading the helicopter pilot. This angered me, because it was far from the truth. I also wanted to see how the poachers would react to the helicopters.

Then I told them that I would conduct a horse patrol in my way, and that we would track down poachers at some stage. This was a great challenge, and a bet ensued. The challenge was accepted, and everyone wanted to see how it would pan out. The chief game warden organised everything. In my opinion far too many people and vehicles were involved. Too much noise, fuss, dangers and disturbance. Tourist officials were also taken along, for instance. One of the tourist officials was always on my case – a typical know-it-all. He was a large, strong man, twice my weight. He could simply not accept that I, in spite of being so skinny, could lift the same weights as him. In his own manner he was constantly trying to put me down. I'll call him "Strongman".

The horse-patrol was arranged. We eventually left late that morning, northwards to the left of the Okua Salt Pan. I had a horse-camp there. Poachers were fairly active in that area, mainly from Ongandjera in Owamboland. After our arrival with the horses at that horse-station, I suggested that I would undertake a foot patrol that afternoon, to explore. In all friendliness I asked Strongman whether he would like to come along to look for tracks. "Of course," he said. It was a scorchingly hot day.

"It's already fairly late in the afternoon," I said. "We'll be back soon, so we needn't take anything with us."

I carried my .303, he had his side-arm, and we walked in an easterly direction from the camp. As usual, I maintained a stiff pace. Initially Strongman was able to keep up, but eventually he began to fall back more and more. Every now and then I had to ask him to walk faster. Then we came across fairly fresh horse-tracks, and we followed them just to make things interesting, because the state of the tracks indicated that the people must have crossed the boundary some time ago. After a while I pointed at the sun. "When the sun sets, we must go back to the camp; we must hurry." By this time Strongman was so tired and thirsty that he was able to follow only with the greatest effort. He kept on stumbling after me. We were close to the camp shortly before sunset, and I switched over to fifth gear. When he could no longer keep up, I pointed him in the right direction and said: "Just keep going in that direction to get to the camp, or the wolves will eat you!" When I reached the camp, everyone wanted to know where Strongman was. All innocence, I said. "He should be here shortly." In the meantime I gave Tobias a bottle of water and sent him back on my tracks to fetch Strongman. It was dark, and I was preparing the evening meal when Tobias and Strongman reached the camp. He was moving slowly, very footsore and completely exhausted. Everybody felt sorry for him, except me. He had tried to belittle me too many times, and this was but a small example of what we field guys had to endure out there. Something positive did, however, come from this enterprise – it shut him up, he could not look me in the eye, and for the rest of the project he stayed out of my sight, because his thighs were so raw that to the end he had to sit on the back of a bakkie whenever we moved.

We saddled the horses the next morning. I gave the horse Optel to the chief game warden. This was a very placid but useful bush horse. We rode in a north-westerly direction, and soon afterwards we saw four men each leading a horse. They were moving from north to south, and were following tracks. I stopped, pointed to the horses and men about 200 metres away, and signalled to everyone not to move. At that stage the poachers had not yet seen us. They would have to move past us, and in a low voice I told my people we have to charge as soon as the poachers spotted us. Suddenly the thunderous voice of the chief game warden sounded behind me: "Hey, you! Come here!" Alarmed, the poachers looked up, mounted their horses and rode away.

"Charge, men!" I shouted to my people, and spurred on my horse. We went after those poachers at full speed. Because I was riding a fast horse, I soon overtook the last poachers and was going for the leader, because I wanted his horse. On taking off, I had heard a shot behind me, but did not pay it any attention. I began gaining on the leading poacher after a wild chase through the bush. When my horse's head drew level with the shoulder of the Owambo rider's horse, I shouted for him to give up. Instead, he hit my horse on the head with his whip. When I was right next to him, he tried to hit me. I pulled out my .22 Smith & Wesson and hit him on the head with it. When he nearly fell off his horse, half unconscious, I grabbed him by the collar, quickly pulled him from his horse, and pulled him over onto my horse's shoulder. He hung limp in front of me, like a wet sack, legs on one side and head and arms dangling on the other. I brought my horse to a halt, cuffed the man and took away his weapons. My Bushmen overtook two of the other riders and forced them, too, to submit. One poacher escaped. We went back to where we had left the chief with our prisoners.

When we got there, he was standing by his horse, and I could see something wasn't right. Embarrassed, he showed us that he had accidentally shot his horse in the neck with his .38 revolver. I examined the horse. The shot entered from straight above at the mane, and had travelled down the horse's neck, just past the right main carotid which runs alongside the throat, to the skin at the bottom, where I could feel it. Some good luck with the bad. We went back to the camp, and from there along the boundary west for 50 kilometres to the next camp. The chief, three Bushmen and I rode on our horses. Moses drove my vehicle along the road to that camp, with the rest of the convoy in his wake. They were now in control of the prisoners. The head wound of the poacher I had caught was disinfected and dressed. Strongman preferred lying on the back of a vehicle, as his raw thighs prevented him from sitting, and he still could not walk properly. On reaching the camp that evening, Moses was already there.

Optel, the chief game warden's horse, had to undergo an operation that evening. There were no anaesthetics, and I wrestled him to the ground as one does when castrating a horse. It went well. His head was pressed to the ground. I made an incision of about 2,5 centimetres in the skin above the bullet with a sharp pocket-knife and removed it. We disinfected the wound and kept it open for drainage.

From that day on, the camp was named "Operation".

Because we had to hand the prisoners over to the police as soon as possible, we went home the next day.

A chief punishes his subjects

About 60 kilometres north of Okaukuejo there is an old water-well named Okahakana ("place of the wild dogs"). When South West Africa was a German colony, the Owambos and the German security forces used this well. It then became a drinking-spot for game. The well is to the side of a pan, and as the place was fairly close to Okaukuejo, nobody would have thought that poachers, too, still used the well.

I often noticed human and horse tracks there. When I told the chief game warden about the tracks, he thought they must be the tracks of stray Owambo horses. The human tracks could be those of Owambo runaways on their way back to Owamboland. One day I noticed fresh tracks, and decided to follow them. All the tracks went from north to south, and back again from south to north. I found this highly suspicious. Okahakana is to one side of the pan, and there is a thick mopani forest about 2 kilometres north of the well. When we entered the forest, we came across large, abandoned hunting camps. There were heaps of burnt game bones everywhere under the old trees. Cross-beams had been placed high in the trees, probably used as observation platforms by the poachers. Because the road to Okahakana runs all along the pan, the poachers were able to see approaching vehicles from far away, giving them enough time to flee. It was therefore very difficult to approach the hunting camps unnoticed. I visited Okahakana regularly from then on. One day the fireplaces were still warm. There were signs that three giraffes had been killed, because fresh heads, legs and hooves were still lying around. The poachers must have spotted us and fled, because the horse and donkey tracks showed that they were running, and every now and then a piece of meat had been dropped. I was on a routine patrol, and only had Tobias with me. The signs indicated that a number of poachers were involved, and I decided to get help from Okaukuejo. We quickly assembled a number of men, got some cuffs and radios, and went back to Okahakana, with the chief game ranger in the cab of the vehicle with me. Because the tracks were quite clear in the sandy veld, we had two Bushmen sitting on the front of the Ford. They had to use their arms to indicate the direction of the tracks we were following.

It was fairly thickly vegetated, but we were able to proceed quite quickly, because mopani trees have no thorns. We were all determined to get hold of these poachers. The boundary was overgrown with grass when we crossed it, and a while later the chief innocently asked me: "Piet, aren't we across the boundary yet?"

"I didn't see a thing, Sir," I answered.

"Even if we are on the other side, we are going to catch them and hand them over to Oshona Shimi," he said, and we continued driving along the tracks. The freshly trampled mopani leaves indicated that they were just ahead of us. Oshona Shimi means "Short Calf". He was the chief of the Ongandjera tribe and much feared among his subjects. He worked well with the white government, which eventually led to his demise – he died in a "road accident" during the war years, probably engineered by SWAPO.

We reached the first Owambo settlements after about 20 kilometres. The poachers must have reached it very shortly before us, because they were busy watering their horses and donkeys. The donkeys were still fully loaded with meat.

We asked no questions. We had a number of very sizeable gentlemen with us, and before the poachers knew what hit them, they were cuffed, and landed on the back of the bakkie like sacks of corn. The poachers were so amazed that we came to arrest them in their own territory that they offered little resistance. We left two young boys with the horses and donkeys and went to see Oshona Shimi at Ongandjera. He received us in a friendly manner when we reached his village. We explained the reason for our visit and pointed out the prisoners. He was annoyed when he heard what they had done. He made all the prisoners stand in a row. The poachers were Hereros and Ongandjera Owambos. Oshona was accompanied by his bodyguards – all big, strong, hand-picked men with long palm-frond rods in their hands. The rods were between 1,2 and 1,8 metres long, and still carried sharp spikes on the sides. Only the sections that served as handles were dethorned.

When Oshona began speaking to the poachers, the Owambo prisoners went down on their knees and answered his questions in a supplicatory fashion. The Hereros however, remained standing, showing a stroppy attitude. Oshona lost his temper. "I see you stand when you talk to me?" he asked the Hereros, and without waiting for an answer, he ordered his bodyguards: "*Denga!*" ("whip!"). The bodyguards knew their work. In an instant the Hereros were flat on their stomachs, trousers and shirts removed. The first three blows from the palm-frond rods rained down on their buttocks. The rods were wielded with both hands, and after every blow the bloody welts rose. The Hereros cringed in pain, but said nothing. The Hereros were forced to sit, and Oshona asked: "Where did you come from?"

"From the south, from the game park."

"Did I not forbid you from crossing that boundary? *Denga!*" This time they were all forced to lie down, and everyone got three strokes. They were made to sit, and asked: "What were you doing there?"

The answer: "Hunting, oh King."

Oshona asked: "Did I not forbid it? *Denga!*" Their buttocks and backs were thickly swollen and red from their blood. They now began moaning and pleading, but Oshona was not to be deterred. They received three more strokes after every question. The Owambos each endured twelve strokes, and the Hereros fifteen. I began to feel nauseated, because such treatment was too much for me. Oshona must have read our feelings on our faces, because when it was all over, he simply said: "You white people don't know how to mete out punishment. You just play. The real punishment is still to come. These were just the preliminaries to make sure these people talk readily. Once I have all the facts, you are welcome to attend the trial – I'll let you know!" We were then invited into his house, and in a trice all manner of beverages were placed on the table, from the most expensive whiskey to home-brewed palm beer. We chatted easily, and Oshona showed us his collection of weapons with pride. He wanted to start a shooting competition there and then, but we modestly withdrew. It was a long way back, and the sun was already heading towards the horizon. We left after many hearty goodbyes.

A few weeks later Oshona informed us by radio when the trial would take place, and once again invited us to attend. The chief game warden did attend, and according to him 90 poachers had been rounded up. Apparently Oshona always determined who the poachers were hunting for, and then rounded up those people as well. He then held one large combined trial and fined all the guilty parties by making them pay in cattle. In those parts a black man can, in reality, measure his wealth and status only in cattle. Accordingly this was a very sensitive fine, with the proceeds deposited into the tribe's fund.

Perhaps Nature Conservation could not have asked for better cooperation than that provided by Oshona. Things were quiet in those parts for quite a while. A real poacher does not scare all that easily, and the Hereros living in their own homeland did not pay him much respect, continuing their activities from their area.

A very close shave

Not far from Okaukuejo, to the north, one finds the 19th parallel. Nature Conservation planned to grade a road along the 19th parallel from Okaukuejo to the Kaokoveld boundary. At that time the entire Kaokoveld was part of the Etosha Game Reserve. It was very rich in wildlife, particularly rhinos and elephants. However, the Odendaal Plan envisaged that the Kaokoveld would be given to the Hereros, and be opened up for settlement and occupation. This was the most beautiful part of Etosha, as it was very mountainous and rough, with wonderful scenery.

From Okaukuejo to the Kaokoveld boundary there is a stretch of savannah of about 190 kilometres in width. It was relatively water-poor, and we had to develop it. We planned to erect a windpump every 16 kilometres along the 19th parallel, with a large water-trough alongside. This would create watering points for the game and open up this stretch of savannah for them. We wanted to attract the game from the Kaokoveld in a natural way before everything was destroyed by the occupants of the Kaokoveld. We were particularly interested in the elephants and rhinos, which were, even in those days, protected game and endangered species.

I was given the task to erect all those windpumps and build all those water-troughs. Mynhard Blom, the motor mechanic at Okaukuejo at the time, had to help with the erection of the windpumps. A large portion of the work consisted of carting all the material. We had to get stone and sand from rivers in the Kaokoveld. Stone also had to be collected from the Calf Mountains, and I had to fetch the windpumps and the cement from Okaukuejo. A small grader had previously graded a road along the 19th parallel, but it had become overgrown, and in the rainy season the elephants made deep dents in the surface. Stark was good enough to do all this driving, and furthermore he constantly had to explain why his vehicles broke down. This type of work contributed to the bad state of my back. The road was properly graded only after the last windpump and water-trough had been erected. Then, after many months, my work was inspected.

Mynhard and I also started with development on the Kaoko-veld side. The first windpump we erected was named Duineveld. This was a hilly, sandy vicinity with very deep, red sand – ideal for trapping a double-wheeled heavy truck in the holes made by the mole colonies, or deep sand, or in the mud if it had rained. The entire area was a poacher's paradise, and before I began cleaning up there, hunters must have been camping and processing meat there for weeks. By following the tracks, I eventually found all their camps. Large heaps of burnt bones lay under the trees near a watering-point.

The poachers burn the bones and heap them up in order to attract more game. Game eagerly gnaw these bones to compensate for a lack of calcium. They congregate around the heaps of bones and are then easily tracked and hunted.

In the period when I was developing the 19th parallel, I found a great many of these poachers and arrested many of them.

Although it was tough, this period counts among my best in the service of Nature Conservation at Etosha.

This was unknown territory. I explored the land thoroughly on horseback, and eventually knew it like the palm of my hand. I sometimes went to Okaukuejo for a weekend, mainly to allow the Bushmen to visit their families. Most of the time my wife and small children were in the veld with me. We made our home under a tarpaulin stretched between some trees, enclosed on the sides with fencing droppers or suitable trees and bushes.

This was a happy time, carefree and untrammelled, and the children grew up like little Bushmen. We confiscated meat from the poachers, and lived sparingly from the other rations. I tried to go to Okaukuejo as little as possible. The road from Okaukuejo to my door in the veld was as long as mine to theirs, yet in all that time nobody came to inspect my work.

Moses, my Bushman foreman, often had to transport the building materials, but never from Okaukuejo, because I was strictly forbidden from allowing him to drive.

All of this was at my risk and only mine.

Usually my workers and I brought in all the sand and stone we could on one day, and then Moses had to take over and bring the same amount. This meant that I could exercise good control. In the morning I took my horses and went on a riding patrol with Stephanus to explore the area thoroughly. If we came across poachers' tracks, we followed them. If there weren't many poachers in one spot, we arrested them and took them back to camp. However, if there were many, we returned to the camp to get help, and then effected the arrest.

In this way we did two tasks in the time it usually took to do one, and the construction did not suffer at all. In my view the most important task was to curb the poaching, yet the development along the 19th parallel also continued without any interruptions.

We were busy fetching a load of building sand at Kowares in the Kaokoveld when we saw a large number of fresh horse and donkey tracks in the direction of the Onangombati waterhole. I had Moses, Tobias and Paul Doodvreet with me. We followed the tracks in the vehicle and saw a large number of men sitting under a tree near Onangombati.

They made no effort to flee, and I drove up to them in the vehicle. I stopped, got out and greeted the group. They did not answer my greeting, but looked me straight in the eye. They were all armed, most of them with bows and arrows, and I could see they were poisoned arrows. The other had machetes in their hands. They were all sitting there with frowns on their faces, and I immediately realised the situation was dangerous. When they did not answer my greeting, I asked them what they were doing there. Without answering, they asked me what *I* was doing there.

Their defiant attitude was slowly making me boil over. They far outnumbered us, being eighteen to our four, and almost all were armed with deadly poisoned arrows. Yet I was not about to beat a retreat.

When I explained to them that they were in the game reserve illegally and that I had to arrest them, they just laughed and said: "Touch one of us, and we will cut off your private parts today and hang them in the trees to dry."

When the German security forces fought against the Hereros all those years ago, that is what they did to their prisoners. I knew this was no empty threat, because we had only three firearms.

During the argument almost everyone had notched an arrow to his bow, and some had even drawn their bows. They were ready for action, and were standing before us in a semicircle.

In Bushman I told Moses to cock the .303 and to shoot immediately should one of them attack. I inched closer to a young, tall Herero, the one closest to me. I told Moses that I would grab this youth and that he had to be ready. I argued with the Herero all the time, to distract their attention from my slow forward movement.

When I was close enough to the young Herero, I sprang at him and immediately twisted his arm behind his back, holding the struggling man in front of me like a shield. If the Hereros decided to shoot, they ran the risk of shooting their mate. When I moved, they all lifted their bows and arrows and aimed at us. Moses also lifted the .303 and aimed at their main speaker, shouting in Herero: "Watch out, I'm also going to shoot you, lower your weapons!"

The man I had grabbed tried everything to free himself. He even shouted at his men not to shoot, for fear that they would shoot him. The situation could hardly have been more tense. With the young man as protection, I slowly moved in the direction of the vehicle. Moses was still covering the large group with the .303.

The attitude of the Hereros then changed. They lowered their bows and arrows and said they would come along if I did not shoot their animals. They first wanted to collect the horses and donkeys. I promised this, because I did not have much of a choice. There were simply too few of us, and I had to allow this. In the meantime I cuffed the young man to the vehicle. My hands were free again.

One by one the Herero men disappeared on the pretext of gathering the horses and donkeys, but never returned. We were in a dense stand of mushara trees, and could not see what was going on. A middle-aged man close to me asked that the handcuffed young man be released. Moses spoke to him and indicated to me that it was the young man's father. However, I ordered my Bushmen to handcuff the father as well. Now we had two prisoners. The others had all melted into the bush. In all the arrests I had made over the years, I always made it known that if there were no resistance on the part of the poachers, I would return all the animals, with one or two of their wives or children delegated to take them home. If they resisted or fled, I would confiscate or destroy all their animals.

It had become late, and a few donkeys and dogs were still visible in the last light. Against my will, I shot them. After each arrest I made it quite clear to the people why I had acted harshly or leniently. I wanted to avoid a loss of life in every circumstance, but never excused the real guilty parties.

We returned to the camp near the windpump in the dark, and tied up the two prisoners very thoroughly. I was hungry and frustrated and went to bed without washing. I was disappointed at how the day had turned out. Early the next morning I made coffee, and as I looked at my bare legs, I could see the lines where fear had made me sweat the day before. I did notice, during the arrest, that I was talking with a tremulous voice. I was so excited that I could not control my voice. I must have been dead scared with all those arrows pointed at me like a porcupine's quills, but my pride and sense of honour would not permit me to retreat.

After I had taken the prisoners to Outjo that weekend, I heard a knock on the front door of my house.

It was afternoon, and I wanted to rest after all my efforts. When I opened the door, a large, strong policeman was standing there. He very officially asked my name, and then began to berate me about the arrest of the Hereros. Apparently those that had fled had complained to the Bantu Commissioner at Ohopoho that I had shot their animals in their own territory.

This was a brazen lie, and I immediately felt riled up. The more I tried to explain what had happened, the less this policemen wanted to see reason. When I felt my neck-hairs rising, I slammed the door in his face and walked away before it was too late.

An extensive enquiry was ordered; the powers-to-be at Bantu Affairs, police chiefs, my own bosses and I went to Onangombati, the place where the incident had taken place. Eventually all were satisfied that the arrests had indeed taken place some 27 kilometres inside the game reserve. The two arrested Hereros each received a jail sentence of seven months; the rest of the group were never caught. I reckon this was a bit unfair.

I would have loved to have seen that policeman in my place amongst that bad lot.

A bunch of prisoners and the elephant cow in the night

As I was busy with the development of drinking-places along the 19th parallel, I kept my camp near the Duineveld windpump as long as possible.

This was largely because this was the main hunting area for the Kaokoveld Hereros, but the environment was the main reason.

I will never forget the mornings when I woke at dawn beside my night-fire. I always drank my first cup of coffee in bed. In the evening a small three-legged pot full of fresh water was placed next to the night-fire. A container with coffee, powdered milk and sugar also stood next to my pillow, as did a clean cup with a teaspoon in it.

On waking, my first action, without even getting up, was to place the pot on the warm mopani coals. As soon as the water boiled, I made my first cup of coffee from my bed, turned on my stomach, drank my coffee slowly and marvelled at the scene surrounding me. It was balm to the soul, and an essential preparation for a stressful day.

From Duineveld one can see vast distances across the grassy plains, and almost every morning herds of elephants, springbok, gemsbok and perhaps a few eland would trek past the camp. What could be more beautiful than waking at dawn in pristine nature and admiring its creatures? One can only thank one's Creator for the privilege.

During one of my routine patrols we saw horse and donkey tracks going from the Calf Mountains southeast to the Okatjongeama ("Drinking-place of the lion") well.

We were on foot, and I was accompanied by Swart Sikspens and Simon, a tall, thin, middle-aged Bushman. I was carrying the 9.3 millimetre and two revolvers. The tracks indicated another very large group of poachers. While we were engaged in our pursuit, we passed the Okawao water-well. Okawao is a shallow well dug by the Herero to one side of a pan. The game use this waterhole, so the water is not very clean. The poachers then dig smaller waterholes at the sides of the large hole to get cleaner water. An elephant calf had fallen into one of these smaller holes and could not get out. When we arrived, it was clear that the elephant calf had died only recently. It was not distended, and no elephants were nearby. We pulled the calf from the hole, pulling it some distance away so that it would not pollute the water. Then we followed the poachers' tracks again. It was a warm day, and clouds were starting to form in the sky. It began to rain close to Okatjongeama, and we reached the well in the rain. We saw horses and donkeys standing under some large trees a short distance away, and when we approached, we saw a thick column of smoke. The people were all sitting on the ground around the fire, each with a blanket over his head as protection against the rain, so nobody saw us approaching. Their quivers and bows hung in the trees.

We first collected the bows and quivers with arrows and hid them behind a bush. A dog began to bark, and the Hereros pulled the blankets from their heads, spotting us among them for the first time. They stared at us as if we had just arrived from the moon.

We could hear long drawn-out "thhhh" sounds; sounds the Herero make when they are extremely surprised, or feel trapped. I gestured to them to remain sitting and to remain calm. However, they got up and looked to the tree where their bows and quivers were supposed to be hanging, but the weapons were gone. Still more reason for surprise. The Hereros were not nearly as hard-boiled as the Onajombati lot. One could talk to them.

I did not have any cuffs with me that day because I had not expected any poachers. There were 20 people in total, and we were only three. I had to create some sort of gentleman's agreement. I immediately made them understand that I would not let them get away, but that I would spare their animals if they would come along without resistance. After a lengthy discussion amongst themselves they agreed to this. I left the two youngest there to take the animals home.

We then began walking while the sun was setting. Simon walked right in front, and Swart Sikspens to their right halfway down the column, while I came on behind to make sure nobody disappeared. Simon and Sikspens were laden with all their weapons. Little was said, and only every now and then a Herero would exchange a few words with one of his compatriots. We walked fairly quietly, and a half-moon hung in the sky before us, providing a glimmer of light. When we were almost at Okawao, the Hereros stood still and pointed forward to the Okawao well. A very strange, long drawn-out sighing sound could be heard from that direction. "The elephant cow is mourning her calf," explained the Herero near to me. "If she charges, we will have to run!"

"I will shoot dead the first one to run," I answered under my breath. "Nobody runs; I will protect you." The elephant cow must have heard us, because the ear-piercing trumpeting of an enraged elephant could be heard from the well. I cocked my 9.3 millimetre and said as calmly as I could: "Nobody runs." Of course this presented the Hereros with a wonderful opportunity to flee, and I would not be able to do anything about it. I was alone with them, because the two Bushmen made tracks when the elephant cow began trumpeting. I directed my attention ahead of me, because I expected to see the cow's silhouette in front of us at any moment. Miraculously the cow did not come, and the Hereros did not break ranks.

I gestured that the Hereros had to walk around Okawao in a wide circle. I therefore had to take the lead, because my two brave Bushmen had disappeared. This was another golden opportunity for the Hereros behind me to desert, but they did not. When we reached the footpath on the other side, I could walk behind them again. While we were skirting Okawao, I could hear the elephant cow's heart-rending sighs every now and then. It is difficult to describe the sound, but few things symbolise a mother's distress at the death of a baby as clearly as that sighing sound. I almost felt like crying with her.

My two brave companions joined us again. I did not want to talk to them in front of the Hereros, but later I let them understand quite clearly what I thought of them. But I suppose one has to take account of the feelings of frightened people!

I began to have great respect for the Hereros. I found it very difficult to load them onto the truck and take them to the police at Outjo that night. I almost let the whole lot go. They had a golden opportunity to murder me that night when I was left alone with them! Only my inherent sense of duty compelled me to deliver them to justice. I charged them only with trespassing without permits. They were free after three months.

This was another case where I would rather have excused poachers.

The helpful poacher

As the game reserve developed, we gained more field staff. We now had game wardens at Namutoni, Halali, Otjovasandu and myself at Okaukuejo, and each was responsible for his own area. Two horses were assigned to each game warden; they all had to learn to ride, and had to undertake efficient horse patrols. On completion of very basic horse-riding training at the end of a lunge, it was decided to undertake a lengthy horse patrol all along the boundary, from Namutoni in the east to Otjovasandu in the west. The men received their baptism of fire on the very first day. I was riding my personal dressage horse, Alarich, a particularly large, warm-blooded bay. I liked riding him on patrol because of his obedience and ability to cover good distances, even though he was a valuable horse. His sire was an imported Hanoverian, his dam a thoroughbred, and he went through thick bush like a steamtrain. That afternoon, after we had offloaded the horses from the trailers near Omuramba Owambo, we moved west along the south side of the boundary. I was at the front of the cavalcade, thanks to Alarich's walking prowess. Every now and then I had to ask the other guys to keep up, or they would lose sight of me. Then we came across some fresh human and donkey tracks which entered the game reserve southwards from Owamboland. We held a brief council of war, and I instructed every man to catch his own poacher if we should overtake them, or come across their camp. We followed the tracks at a stiff walk. I was way ahead, and had to hold Alarich back every now and then so that the rest could catch up. Then the tracks entered a very thick stand of yellowwood. I suddenly saw something falling out of a tree about 50 metres ahead of me. Initially I thought it was a baboon, but there were no baboons in this part of the game reserve. It could only have been a human. I shouted: "Charge, men!" and Alarich raced through that thicket at full speed. I suddenly found myself in their camp. There were bundles of clothes underneath various trees, and donkeys were standing all over the place. Some way ahead of me, I saw someone running through the bushes. I went after him without hesitation. As I approached, I saw more people running. One was way ahead of the others; his loose shirt flapped about his head, and it looked like his heels would touch the back of his head.

When I was almost on top of the fleeing man, I held Alarich back slightly to make the moment last a little longer. The poor guy looked around every now and then, and was screaming for help. He began to tire after a while, and when I came up alongside him, I grabbed him by the shirt collar and indicated that he should halt. I could not help laughing heartily, and when the poacher saw that I was not about to kill him, he calmed down. To this day I can still see the whites of his wide eyes as he looked around every so often, and when I grabbed him. He was ashen-faced, and was trembling like a reed. I indicated that he should return to the camp with me. Some of my men were standing around game warden André, who was lying on the ground, holding his knee and groaning. When I asked what had happened, I heard he was pursuing an Owambo, but when he tried to grab the man, he lost his balance and fell down in a heap in front of the poacher. André was a large, portly gent weighing about 100 kilograms, and must have landed at his quarry's feet with a thunderous thud. André said that the Owambo stopped running, turned around and helped him to his feet. I couldn't believe my ears. When he pointed out the man to me, I asked him about it myself. In broken Afrikaans the Owambo explained: "Oh, I ran, I saw the boss falling hard, I saw he was hurt, I helped him up!"

I had never seen anything like it in my life. What a gentleman, I thought. I then asked the man I had caught: "So, why were you all running like that?"

He answered: "Oh, I just saw the lion coming on the elephant, I had to run, because I thought I would die today!"

We all burst out laughing. At the time I sported a long, straggly red beard which I combed to either side of my face. This made the beard appear even bigger. My chief had given me the name *Kaiser Rotbart* ("King Redbeard"). The enormous beard and my large horse bursting through the bush must have resembled a maned lion sitting astride an elephant.

There was only one old muzzle-loader in the camp, and no meat. The Owambos explained that they had taken along the muzzle-loader as protection against lions, and that they were looking for mopani worms.

I felt a good deal of sympathy for these hungry people, but I had to detain them because they were inside the reserve illegally. I explained this to them, and took the entire group to our camp, where we had left the vehicles and trailers. I summarily sent home the man who had helped André, together with the donkeys. When the Owambos realised we were actually quite friendly, they began to talk freely, telling us of other groups of Owambos who were looking for mopani worms in the game reserve. It was full moon, and I asked them whether they would help me to find the others in the dark. They agreed. After we had had a bite to eat, we walked in the direction that they were leading us. I took along most of the adult Owambos, my Bushman trackers, and some of the game wardens. I left André and another white game warden at the camp to guard the remaining prisoners and to watch the vehicles.

We walked from camp to camp almost throughout the night, and encountered no problems. However, we had to spend a good deal of time at each camp, because I made them all gather their donkeys, mopani worms and possessions. Those who had been in the reserve longer, had sacks full of dried mopani worms. The people were all disappointed, but friendly. By midnight we had gathered together a mass of people and animals, and reached our old camp only in the early hours of the morning.

At first light we were able to do a head count – altogether 311 men, women and children. Nothing like this had happened in Etosha's history. Our camp looked like a large Owambo settlement. I informed my chief at Okaukuejo by radio. He contacted Nature Conservation in Windhoek, and in turn they negotiated with Bantu Affairs.

In the meantime I sent home the women and children with their animals. They posed too much of a logistical problem. In the meantime there was a tug-of-war between Bantu Affairs and Nature Conservation. Bantu Affairs wanted us to let them go, Nature Conservation wanted to prosecute them.

By the afternoon I had made my own decision, sending them back home with a thank-you for their cooperation. I felt relieved, even though I was expecting a reprimand from my boss. In my eyes they were not poachers. They were hungry people looking for food. In any case, there were millions and millions of mopani worms at the end of nearly every rainy season.

One should allow them to enter the reserve without weapons in the time of the mopani worms and permit them to leave when they have finished harvesting. Looking for mopani worms is a traditional activity of the natives, and some sort of system should be worked out to maintain control.

When all the people had left, I informed Nature Conservation that the problem had been solved and that I had sent all of them home. My chief was not very happy with this, but the bad feelings faded. If I had not undertaken this patrol at the time, nobody would have realised there were so many people in the reserve illegally.

An unexpectedly large catch

As I was busy transporting building material for the windpumps along the 19th parallel, I was using the 5-ton Thames Tipper to bring sand from the dry water-courses at Kowares to build the drinking-troughs. I took along two Bushmen, Simon and Swart Sikspens, to load the sand. They were good workers, but not of the bravest.

As they were loading the sand, I walked about as usual, doing a little tracking. I found fresh horse and donkey tracks in a game trail leading from north to south. Because it wasn't my area, I did not know the Kaokoveld well at that time. The tracks were deep inside the game reserve, however, and I decided to follow them. We halted the loading of the sand for the time being, and followed the tracks. We only had my old Remington .22 with us, and no food, water or cuffs. I never expected that we would walk so far that day. Uphill, downhill, along dry water-courses, across ridges.

We found the dried-out carcass of a black rhino bull in a dry river-bed. All the ribs to one side of his spine were broken. Either the rhino had fought an elephant, and the broken ribs were the result of a blow from the elephant's trunk, or the rhino had fallen down a steep cliff. The horns were still attached, and I fetched them the next day and took them with me. I still have those large horns to this day.

By afternoon we were climbing another hill when we heard sounds ahead of us, like someone chopping wood. We crept towards the spot where the sounds were coming from. We found four Herero men in a thicket busy removing mopani bee honey from thick branches. A mopani bee is not much bigger than a midge, but a real nuisance, because it crawls into your eyes, ears, nose, mouth and clothes. This bee is at its busiest during the hottest hours of the day, and you can forget about getting any rest where they are working; they will torment you without end.

The four men spotted us only when we were in amongst them, and of course they were greatly surprised when a white man appeared from the wilderness. Without much ceremony I made it clear to them that I was arresting them and that they had to take me to their camp. There were four women, donkeys, dogs and two horses at the camp. The sinews and pieces of skin of giraffe hung from the trees, and there were plenty of bows, arrows and machetes. There were bundles of bedding everywhere under the trees. I took some thongs from the bedding, tied the men by the arms, two by two, and made them sit by the fireplace. My two Bushmen and I took shelter near the closest trees and waited for some others who had gone to get water. The first lot soon arrived, with containers of water on their heads. They were all quickly captured, tied two by two, just like their mates, and made to sit. In their absence we had hidden the weapons they had left at the camp. They were very surprised to see a white man there, and because they had no weapons, they offered no resistance. We hid once more and waited for the next lot of water-carriers. The same happened when more of them arrived. This was just too easy. By late afternoon a horseman arrived with a fresh giraffe tail tied to his bridle. We quickly helped the surprised man off his horse, because he had his weapons with him. He was riding a sturdy, beautiful black stallion, and I really wanted it. It takes a man and a horse to round up giraffe in these rugged mountains, and then shoot them with a bow and arrow.

The sun was low on the horizon, it was a long road, and this was elephant, rhino and lion country. We now had 22 Herero men in custody, and I had to get them to our vehicle armed only with a single-shot .22 rifle. Once again I found myself in a perilous situation. There could have been enormous problems had we encountered a single angry elephant or rhino on the way back.

Because the arrest had gone so smoothly and peacefully, I sent the women home with all the animals apart from the black stallion.

It was a wearisome, slow trek through the dark night, over mountains and along rivers. I expected the snort of an attacking rhino or the trumpeting of an elephant at any moment. We were still quite close to the Herero camp when we came across the fresh, still warm giraffe carcass, and I felt great respect for the hunter and his horse. There were arrow wounds in the giraffe's chest, and between its shoulders, and it seemed as if all the arrows could have hit its heart. I wanted to fetch the giraffe meat the next day, and it was only a miracle that we did not encounter any rhinos or elephants. On reaching the vehicle, we made an enclosure of thorn branches to protect the black stallion. I wanted to get him to our camp on the 19th parallel the next day.

We then drove to our camp in the vehicle and reached it at midnight.

At daybreak the next day my people and I drove to Kowares with the prisoners. When we reached the enclosure of thorn branches, the black stallion was gone. At one spot the thorn branches had been torn apart. The Herero women must have sent someone to fetch it. I was very disappointed, but would probably have done the same.

We all returned to the giraffe and rhino carcasses on foot. I took the rhino horns, and as much giraffe meat as everyone could carry.

As we were engaged in processing the giraffe, two more Hereros (a middle-aged man and his wife) appeared, having walked on their compatriots' tracks. We welcomed them with open arms. He had to share the fate of the others, and sit in jail for nine months.

The rhino charge

Following this big catch of poachers, Japie, the game warden responsible for that area, wanted me to show him the spot. In those years Japie, a bachelor and nature expert (particularly with regard to insects and spiders and things), was getting on a bit. He sat by the campfire every night while his play-mates, the sun-spiders, scurried about him, and he fed them pieces of lard. He would not mount a horse to save his life, much less climb a windpump, because he suffered severely from vertigo. Well, that was his excuse, anyway.

Japie, his Damara workers, my Bushmen and I went, on foot, to the camp where we had caught the large group of Hereros. There were twelve of us in all.

We were quite close to the hunting camp, and I was leading, when I saw fresh rhino tracks in the path ahead of me. I motioned to the men behind me to walk very quietly, and pointed to the fresh rhino tracks on the ground ahead of me. The footpath then disappeared into thick bush, an ideal hideout for rhino. We soon heard a rhino's warning snort. This caused all and sundry to scatter, and it sounded like a herd of startled zebra running across stony ground. At the time my left leg was already weakened, and for the life of me I could not run, even when faced by great danger.

I stumbled across the stones as best I could, and ducked under the nearest stamper-wood bush, ignoring the thorns and hoping for the best.

There was a small mopani tree close by, and the Bushman Hebakoib, who had been carrying my 9.3 millimetre, had scrambled into it with my rifle and all. The thin trunk began to bend down, however. Japie, who had been walking behind Hebakoib, ran towards the mopani tree with him. Being a white man, he probably thought he had first dibs on the tree, pulled Hebakoib down and began climbing it himself. However, Japie was rather larger than Hebakoib, and the tree bent down even quicker. Having arrived at the tree first, Hebakoib claimed privilege of discovery, and in turn pulled Japie down.

In the meantime the rhino had burst from the bushes like a steam train. Snorting and puffing all the while, it passed about four metres from me, went past the two wrestlers at the mopani tree, and thundered past the other fleeing men at full throttle. The rhino had long ago disappeared over the horizon when the two were still fighting over possession of the tree. Even though it was a grave situation, I was rolling on the ground laughing. The Damaras and Bushmen returned in drips and drabs, their eyes wide and white and looking more like saucers than human eyes.

When everyone eventually calmed down, everybody burst out laughing. Japie and Hebakoib looked somewhat shame-faced, and were the butt of jokes for the rest of the day.

In general rhinos have very bad sight, but very good hearing and smell. Because they are so aggressive, they usually charge blindly at a sound or smell, and then just keep going.

Like a baboon on a rock

While we were occupied with the basic development of the Otjo-vasandu Camp, I decided to study the wildlife at the Otjovasandu waterhole one night with a full moon. After supper I walked to the water, a very faint river course which formed water-pools lower down. I picked a suitable hide downwind and next to a rock near one of the pools that was used most often. The rock was a little over two metres high and sloped at an angle, an ideal seat. As there were few lions at Otjovasandu, I did not take a firearm with me.

Animal activity increased after sundown. First came the night-jars with their special night noises. Then the large animals, mainly the noisy, forever fighting mountain zebras, quite a few kudu, and every now and then an isolated jackal and a small herd of giraffe. Shortly before midnight a large rhino bull came to drink, about ten metres away from me. He drank long and slowly, and later rolled about in the wet river sand. Then, suddenly, another large rhino bull stood on the somewhat elevated side of the river. Both rhino bulls began throwing sand with their forepaws and noses. It seemed they knew, but did not like, each other. They made a strange, threatening bleating noise in their throats. I felt uneasy, because I was at the same level as them. If they started fighting, they could very easily tread on me. Yet I held out on my seat on that rock. The two approached each other threateningly until their noses almost touched, and then a to-and-fro shoving match ensued. They used their horns to good effect in the fight, and all the while they were moving in the direction from where they would pick up my scent. I knew I could be in for real trouble. And so it happened. First the one, and then the other, made warning grunts. They both stopped fighting, stood dead still, and stared intently in my direction. They were 15 metres away from me at the time.

The only escape was to scramble up the rock. I clambered up like a baboon as they stormed closer with snorting and grunting sounds. If they were able to stand on their hind legs, they would have been able to pick me off the rock. Fortunately they couldn't. One tried to push over the rock with his forehead, but the rock held firm. And then, as suddenly as their initial charge, they fled with a warning snort. Only a large dust-cloud remained.

I realised that I would not be able to do the same with elephants, and ended my night-sitting at the waterhole. I walked back to camp to get a little sleep.

Wild dogs at Okawao

We were busy with developments along the 19th parallel when I decided, one Sunday morning, to photograph elephants. I left the Thames two kilometres from the well and walked to Okawao, armed with my .303 and and 16-millimetre camera.

I sat in a bush below the wind near the well, and waited. An old elephant bull came to drink first, and I took a few pictures of him. A little before noon a pack of wild dogs put in an appearance. The first few halted under the trees on the opposite side of the well and scouted the area thoroughly. Then they jogged to the well and jumped down to the water. The sides were about 1,2 metres above the water-level, and the animals who came to drink had to jump down the steep sides to get to it. Smaller animals like wild dogs therefore disappeared completely in the well for a while. The water-level in the well was very low.

More wild dogs followed, and eventually they totalled 32, a good show. As they were drinking, one would jump from the well every now and then to spy out the scene, looking for trouble, and then disappear in the well again. I wanted to photograph them, so I suspended the .303 from my neck by its strap, and crawled closer. The area around the well was quite bare, without any cover at all. I held the camera in my left hand and supported my torso with my right hand as I approached the well in a hopping motion on my knees and right hand.

A wild dog suddenly jumped from the well and looked around. When he spotted me, he stood on his hind legs and made a great warning noise. In a flash all the wild dogs had jumped out of the well and were looking at me. Almost all of them stood on their hind legs and made the weirdest noises, ranging from excited bird-twittering to dogs barking. They reminded me of an excited Bushman kraal, but my instincts warned me that I was in a life-threatening situation. I was only 25 metres away from them, and had only just placed my camera on the ground when they charged. As I stood upright, I unslung the .303 from my neck and cocked it.

Wild dogs move very fast, and the first was on me in a flash. To this day I can still see the flattened ears, the slightly grinning lips, the white canines and the light of murder in their eyes. I knew what hungry wild dogs were capable of. Now you see a living animal, the next moment you see only a skeleton. Wild dogs on land are like piranhas in a river.

There was no time to lift the rifle, and I fired a shot into the bunch from the hip. At the same time I came upright and shouted – nervously – "Voertsek!" ("Go away!"). I was seized by fear for my life.

The bunch in front of me divided into two, ran past on either side of me, and fled wildly.

I was trembling like a reed, and had trouble breathing normally. Everything happened so unexpectedly and quickly.

Generally wild dogs fear people. When they saw me approaching on all fours, they must have mistaken me for a crippled animal and thought I would be easy prey. They must have gotten as big a fright as me when they saw this crippled animal transformed into a large man. I certainly stood up in the nick of time. If they had caught me still in a crouch, it would have been too late.

It made me realise once again that one should never walk about in the game reserve without a weapon. A good resolution, yet one becomes negligent, and then you make the same mistakes again.

Moses qualifies for a medal for bravery

I was on an inspection trip to the windpump at Adamase when I saw warthogs drinking water at the water-trough. A strong wind

194

was blowing, and they were standing with their upright tails in the direction of the vehicle, unaware of our presence. A notion flashed through my head, and the devil whispered in my ear. There was a thick raisin-bush close to the hogs. As the wind was blowing strongly, I wanted to stalk the hogs from behind the bush and catch one. I stopped the Jeep and got out, and had to walk in a semi-circle to get to the bush. Doing so, I had to walk a short distance through a dry pan close by. The pan was thickly overgrown with large leadwood trees and raisin-bush. Some instinct warned me, but I ignored it. When the raisin-bush came between me and the warthogs, all hell broke loose. A large lion charged me with a loud warning roar. I got the fright of my life and spun around to face the lion, with my back to a bush. The lion put on the brakes about five metres from me, in a cloud of dust. His tail swept from side to side along his flanks, and he stood before me in a threatening manner, as if he was about to leap. However, his eyes did not show that hate-filled expression of a cornered lion; it was almost as if he was showing amusement.

I shouted at Moses like a madman to shoot the damned lion, and I kicked sand in the lion's direction, making sure not to lose sight of him for a moment.

My .303 was in the Jeep, but instead of shooting, Moses came running towards me with the rifle in hand. When the lion saw someone else coming, he turned around and slowly trotted away. Without hesitation Moses pressed the loaded rifle into my hands, even though it was no longer necessary to shoot. The lion spotted a lioness from a bush a little distance behind us, and the manner in which he trotted after her indicated that she was in heat.

I really admired Moses's actions. If any medals existed for such bravery, I would most certainly have recommended him. In my eyes that medal will always be dangling on his chest, even if no one else sees it! The warthogs must have hosed themselves.

The rotten tusk

When we erected the first windpump, we were close to the Kaokoveld and far from Okaukuejo. Because it was so far from home, and the track leading there was so bad, Mynhard and I decided to stay in the bush at the site the first weekend and to complete the first waterhole as quickly as possible. I was very bored on the Sunday afternoon, and drove along the track in the direction of Otjovasandu

195

in the Thames Tipper. At that stage there was only a borehole at Otjovasandu, and a foot and mouth disease veterinary control post was situated on the boundary with the farming areas.

It was interesting that the elephant paths were quite well-worn, which indicated that there had to be water somewhere, even though the chief game warden maintained that it was dry throughout. I wanted to make sure about this, and followed the elephant paths. About five kilometres from where we were working, I stopped the Thames and got out to see how fresh the elephant tracks were. There was a fresh human footprint on top of the elephant tracks. It was a small, delicate print, almost like one a Bushman would make, but this wasn't Bushman country, as the Hereros and Bushmen were sworn enemies. A Herero regards a Bushman as nothing more than a dog, and in earlier times the Herero hunted the Bushmen. They decapitated them or kept them as inferior servants. On the other hand, the Bushmen were always stealing the Herero's cattle. Initially my Bushmen were afraid of the Hereros, and refused to accompany me. That track could therefore not have been made by a Bushman.

I took my .303 and followed the trail. The bush thinned out after six kilometres, and I came upon a very large lime pan, with large limestone rocks scattered about. This was a typical game drinking-hole, and doves and other birds flew about in the middle of the pan. There had to be water.

On the opposite side of the pan, in amongst the bushes, I saw a dark object that looked like a black man sitting in front of his hut.

I stalked this supposed hut and its occupant by taking the long way round. The closer I approached, the stranger it looked. And then I was able to identify it! Before me lay a dead elephant bull with a fantastically large tusk. The bottom tooth was equally as impressive, but had unfortunately been broken in half. The elephant must have collapsed suddenly and with great force. The carcass was in too great a state of decomposition for me to see any bullet-holes. What I had taken from a distance for a sitting black man, was in fact a large triangular hole that the vultures and predators had gnawed between the elephant's haunches to get at the animal's insides.

Because I had just recently spotted human footprints, I was concerned that someone would hack off the tusks and steal them.

I returned to the Thames. There was a long, strong chain on the back that we used for pulling upright the windpump tower structures. I affixed one end of the chain to the undamaged tusk with a triple knot and the other to the Thames's tow-bar, and began pulling slowly in first gear. The tusk came loose, and I removed the second, broken tusk in the same manner. The end of the tusk which had been lodged in the skull was still wet from blood.

Because the wet end stank terribly, I embraced the tusk firmly so as not to dirty my hands. I had to lift the tusk high above my head to tip it over the railing onto the Thames's load-bed. In doing so, a large chunk of rotten nerves cascaded down onto my head, face, shoulders and the rest of my body. I had clean forgotten that the nerve mass would still be inside the tusk, and I was literally covered from head to foot in rotten tooth marrow. I had not eaten anything that day, and my stomach was empty, so I vomited pure bile. I couldn't stand the stink, and tried to scrape off the rotten marrow from my hat, beard, shoulders and overalls with a stick as best I could. The urge to vomit overcame me every now and then. I was actually glad that I was on my own. No water to wash in, no soap, only a miserable little stick for scraping.

I had lost my appetite for the second tusk, and left it there for the next day. Somebody else could come and pick up that second tusk. It would most certainly not be me.

After having removed most of the gunge, I drove back to camp. The smell once again became unbearable in the close confines of the cab, and I had to proceed slowly with my head stuck out of the window.

Back at camp, Mynhard would not approach within ten metres of me. He simply admired the beautiful tusk on the back of the truck very briefly, and then remained standing upwind from me.

A large three-legged pot of boiling water and a large chunk of soap had to do the trick. Every now and then I heard a stifled giggle from where the Bushmen slept. They were simply unable to help themselves. Still, they knew they were in for a lot of trouble if they laughed at their boss in such circumstances.

I slept very badly that night, because the stink woke me time and again. The smell clung to me for almost a week, and I felt clean only after a number of baths at home.

I left my overall in the veld for the wolves.

Today that tusk, weighing in at almost 60 kilograms, is part of my collection of other hunting and horse-riding trophies in my sitting-room.

The wall of punishment

On completion of the windpump project, I had put a large number of poachers behind bars. I arrived at Outjo with another batch of prisoners almost every week. As a result I spent a good deal of time in court. These constant arrivals with prisoners caused the chief warden to hold his head in his hands one day, leaning back in his chair, looking at me intently, and asking me in frustration: "Don't you ever work? What's going on out there – it seems to me you're only chasing after poachers!" I explained that my Bushmen were well trained for their tasks, and that the work was continuing without a break. He then warned me that I was fully responsible and that if anything went wrong, I would have to take all the blame. I was angered, because I took it to be self-evident that I would accept full responsibility. To his warning I replied that he should get up off his chair for a change and see for himself what's happening out there. I turned on my heel and walked out.

He had his revenge later. On conclusion of the developments along the 19th parallel, I was assigned routine tasks. Then some lions caught and killed a kudu cow in amongst the rondavels in the camp. Stupid tourists took photographs of the incident, unaware that the excited lions were quite capable of attacking them as well. We had our hands full to keep the tourists away from the danger, and in the process we had to take quite a few insults.

The chief warden then decided to build a large security wall of natural stone between the Okaukuejo waterhole and the rest camp to deter the lions – just the job for Stark, and a good way of keeping an eye on him. Another reason for this punishment was that I had burned down the old, ramshackle rondavels around the waterhole without his permission. In my opinion those rondavels should never have been built around the waterhole. They kept the game from the waterhole, and the people in them were unsafe because lions, wolves and jackals played football with their pots and pans and cutlery at night, which gave rise to never-ending complaints from the tourists. We then had to search for those pots and pans in the bush, and return them to their owners.

I was given instructions to dismantle the rondavels neatly so that the material could be re-used. This was impossible. The brittle old thatch crumbled at any touch, the wooden poles were eaten away by woodworm, the binding-wire was rusted, and all the material was useless.

There was a far quicker and more efficient method which would save a great deal of time and labour. A jam-tin of petrol and a match would get the process going. Petrol was dirt cheap at the time, and was often used as cleaning material.

The entire process would last ten minutes at the most. As the reed huts were burning and black clouds of smoke rose heavenwards, the chief warden, Mr De la Bat, arrived in his green Land Rover. Despite the speed limit in the game reserve, the Land Rover swooped down on its prey like an eagle, coming to a halt near me in a great cloud of dust. From the vehicle alighted a man with a purple face, protruding eyes as large as saucers and a neck swollen like the hood of an angered cobra.

Out of breath he wanted to know what was going on. When I tried to explain to him that the building material was completely useless and that it would take a great deal of time to knock all this useless material down, he shouted: "You will pay for this, Stark!" got into his Land Rover and gouged deep holes before leaving as rapidly as he had come.

"That man is furious," I thought. The result was that I had to endure many months of hard and frustrating work.

Strangely enough, it seems that whenever someone really had it in for me, I was sent to a quarry to break rocks and build something constructive with them. First old man Wiese, after a particularly successful horse-jumping competition, then Mr Böhme, after I had rid his farm of lions, and now the chief warden at Okaukuejo, after I had rid him of poachers!

Every day for three months I worked on that great wall between the waterhole and Okaukuejo. We first had to break the stones from the sandstone formation, then transport them, and lastly build the wall with them. I was frustrated, angry and disappointed, and the frustration gave me extra strength and stamina. From the middle of that wall towards the left there is a spot where I incorporated a few particularly large sandstone blocks in an upright position.

I loaded those blocks onto a vehicle by myself, offloaded them and built my wall. My black helpers bet me I wouldn't be able to do it, but I did it all on my own. It serves me as a monument to the time when I still had my health, and shrank from nothing.

As I was busy building that wall, my friend Japie arrived from Otjovasandu to tell me about a dead elephant he had just come across. The elephant had six bullet wounds in his shoulder, and had died very recently.

Japie's Damaras were poor trackers, so he came to ask me for help. But no, Mr Stark was not permitted to go, as Mr Stark had a wall to build. The matter of the dead elephant was never solved. When the wall was finished, I called it the Chinese Wall of Okauku-ejo. Should the reader ever visit Okaukuejo, remember that Stark, that mad German, built that wall!

The rabid lioness

I was suffering badly from the flu, and in my case this was always complicated by tonsillitis and heavily congested lungs, quite apart from the normal flu symptoms. The worst flu I ever sufferred, was the year I worked for old man Weigmann in Windhoek as an apprentice bricklayer. At that time I earned only £1 per hour. It rained, and because I did not want to forfeit even that meagre wage, I worked in the rain all day long.

Two days later I could not get up because of joint pains and headache.

In the end, after fourteen days in bed, I got pneumonia to top it all. After days of struggling to drag some air into my lungs, I was almost off my rocker from the effort, and about ready to put an end to it all. I then removed and hid all my mother's weapons and other objects I could possibly use to end my life. In desperation I ran full-tilt into a wall head first. However, I was a coward and wanted to drink myself into a coma first. There was a bottle of red wine in the refrigerator. I drank the entire bottle as quickly as possible, and because of my poor condition, I fell into a deep sleep. When I woke, my mother was beside my bed, and she said I had slept for two days and two nights. I felt much better, and recovered soon afterwards. It was a potent lesson.

For not wanting to forfeit a day's wages, I spent the entire month of May in bed; and to my mind May is the most beautiful month.

It was a Sunday afternoon when I was sitting on my stoep with a heavy bout of the flu. I felt really nauseated, and had a bad headache. I could see large parts of the tourist camp from my verandah.

Suddenly I was aware of a great excitement and scurrying about among the tourists, and all of them hurried inside their huts. Then I saw a lioness running about aimlessly. It was quite unnatural for a lioness to enter a tourist camp in broad daylight. The manner in which she was running about aimlessly immediately made me suspect that she was rabid. At the time we experienced a good deal of rabies amongst the predators and even the kudu. For this reason I always had my old .22 with me to shoot suspect animals, and to deliver their heads to the veterinarian for analysis. At that time jackals, too, suffered a good deal.

When I saw the suspect lioness in the camp, I quickly got into my car, drove to my chief's house and asked his permission to shoot the suspect animal. My request was denied. Perhaps he thought I just wanted to shoot a lion for fun.

The lioness left the camp and went back into the bush. It would have been very easy simply to destroy the animal there and then. On Monday morning, however, I was instructed to track the animal and shoot her. I was still suffering badly from flu, and really was very ill. I'm no friend of staying in bed, but on that Monday morning I would much rather have stayed in bed than to go running around in the bush to find a rabid lioness. I knew from experience that rabid animals are capable of covering vast distances.

From the Okaukuejo camp the lioness first ran in the direction of the Gemsbokvlakte. Tobias, Simon and Stefanus were with me – my best trackers. I did very little tracking on that first day of the pursuit. Because of the sharp light and my flu, I could hardly keep my eyes open. I stumbled along in the wake of the trackers like a zombie, and had great difficulty keeping up.

We had problems picking up the tracks on the Gemsbokvlakte, as the many animals who drink there had obliterated her spoor. However, any tracker worth his salt does not let something like this put him off, and after having completed many full circles, we were able to pick and follow her footprints. We had already completed a good 20 kilometres on foot.

When we picked up the tracks again, they led in the direction of the Ombika waterhole. My legs were as heavy as lead, and my headache was almost unbearable.

I know from past experience that rabid animals run from one water-source to the next. Because they are unable to swallow, they become extremely thirsty, until they eventually sink into a coma and die.

It was about 20 kilometres from the Gemsbokvlakte to Ombika through the bush. The lioness's tracks indicated she was running most of the time.

Eventually we reached the Ombika waterhole by 14:00, when the day's heat was at its worst. Then we encountered more problems. Apart from her tracks having been obliterated once more, she had at some stage joined a pride of lions. The Bushmen followed these tracks. Once again, experience had taught me that sick animals do not mix with healthy ones. In nature the healthy animals do not accept the ill ones, and either kill them, or drive them off. I therefore did not follow the Bushmen, but went to look for the tracks of the solitary lioness on my own.

The Bushmen were quite a distance away, following the tracks of the other lions, when I noticed some lion footprints here and there among the rocks. I now had to follow tracks on stony ground and across limestone ridges. I could call back the Bushmen to help me, but my pride started to take over. The character of the prints told me I was on the right track. After tracking slowly for half an hour, I found the lioness. She was lying in thick bush, and looked at me with vacant eyes. If this were a healthy lioness, she would have run away or charged long ago.

When the lioness tried to get up, I dispatched her with a shot to the neck. You do not shoot a suspected rabid animal in the head, because you then damage the brain which the vet needs to examine.

The lioness was dead some time before the Bushmen, who had heard the shot, came running up. They looked at me and the lioness in wonder, and constantly made hissing noises through their teeth.

I know Bushmen well. They were shamed to a degree, but also full of admiration. No one said anything.

I walked from Ombika to Uncle Roy Sterley, a friend of my father's, at the Tsaanas Gate. I summoned someone from Okaukuejo with a vehicle to come and fetch us and the lion.

The lioness's head was sent off, and tested positive for rabies. If I had been permitted to release her from her misery in the Okaukuejo Camp the day before, it would have saved us much trouble and effort.

The lone Bushman from Ombika

In the vicinity of Ombika there lived a young solitary Bushman. He always had his bow and arrows with him, and used them every now and then to shoot a zebra for himself, but did no other damage.

Unfortunately I have forgotten his name, and will call him Jan for the purpose of this story. Almost every Sunday that I spent at Okaukuejo, I went looking for honey in the vicinity. In time I had marked all the honey trees thereabouts, and harvested the honey as required.

I came across Jan's tracks while on one of these honey expeditions, and followed them until I saw Jan's "house", which consisted of a few mopani branches placed at an angle to the ground. A tin canteen with water hung from a tree, and there was another canteen in which to cook meat. A piece of kudu skin on the floor served as mattress, and there was a rolled-up piece of treated skin which served as a blanket. That was the total of Jan's furniture. Pieces of dried zebra meat hung from the trees all around.

I hid behind a bush and waited for the occupant. It was late in the afternoon before Jan arrived. He immediately noticed my tracks near his shelter, and as he was examining them, I spoke to him. He did not get too much of a fright, because I addressed him in his own language, and he quickly calmed down.

From our conversation I could gather that Jan knew about me, and was not afraid of me. He had often crossed my trails before, and had even seen me on previous occasions when I was gathering honey. This just proves once more that the bush has ears and eyes. You may fancy yourself alone, but usually this is not the case. On my question what he was doing there, he answered that he had worked on farms before, but that his previous boss had attacked and badly beaten him. He showed me some old scars on his face. He must really have been worked over.

The manner in which he spoke to me made me suspect that he must have been slightly retarded, yet he was clever enough to survive in this world amongst many lions. The Lord protects His own, I thought.

I warned Jan to stay out of sight of the tourists and other white people, and left him there in the veld.

A little while later a visit by John Vorster, the Prime Minister at the time, was announced. As with all other ministers, he was to be given special treatment. On the day of his arrival, a pride of lions had to be available. Because there were so many lions near Ombika, I went to look for them there. On the way to Ombika I took a long way round a pan with very little vegetation, where one is able to see quite far. Close to the pan I was fortunate to meet a large pride of lions near a zebra carcass, and I reported as much to my boss.

That afternoon at 15:00 we drove to the spot in two vehicles – John Vorster and the chief game warden in his luxury green Land Rover, and I in my Ford. We drove up to the lions quite slowly, and Vorster calmly took photographs.

While we were observing the lions, Jan arrived and walked across the plain not too far from us and the lions. I was praying that my boss would not spot him, but then an indignant voice rang out from the green Land Rover: "Stark, who's that?" while he pointed in the direction of the Bushman.

"I don't know, Sir, I've never seen him before," I lied.

"Fetch him; bring him here," came the command.

I drove to the Bushman, who made no effort to run. I was angry because he was walking around in full view of everyone.

When I asked him how he could be so stupid, he just smiled and said: "But your car is here as well." I did not really understand the logic, and told him that he would have to pay for his foolishness and would have to go to jail because the chief game warden had also seen him. He climbed onto the back of the vehicle with a somewhat bewildered expression in his eyes, and we returned to the green Land Rover.

A long argument ensued when we got there. My chief was incensed and wanted to know who had given Jan permission to walk about there. Jan could speak or understand almost no Afrikaans, so I had to interpret the entire argument. I tried to twist the translation in Jan's favour.

The chief game warden would not budge, however, and wanted me to arrest and charge him on the spot.

When the Prime Minister heard this, he said in a very calm manner: "Wait a bit, this man deserves his freedom; let him go, this is his world, he is a man of nature, and I say let him go, he deserves his freedom!"

The chief was annoyed. Being a spontaneous man, he would have argued with the Prime Minister on the spur of the moment. However, he kept himself in check, realising who was in the vehicle with him, and kept quiet. I felt like hugging the Prime Minister for his wise insight.

I translated the Prime Minister's words very literally to Jan, telling him that the "Big Boss" of all the white people had given him his freedom. At the same time I made him understand very well that he needed to stay out of sight of all white people in future.

Jan looked at the Prime Minister with appreciation, mumbled "thank you", turned on his heel and walked past the lions at a distance of 50 metres as if they did not even exist.

The chief game warden was quite red in the face from anger, but said no more. I had completed my tasks, so I excused myself and drove back to Okaukuejo. What transpired in that green Land Rover will forever remain a mystery. I never received any other instruction to find and apprehend Jan, and I do not know what happened to him.

Follow-up operation involving escaped jail-birds

Six prisoners had escaped from jail in Windhoek; they had all been sentenced to life for serious offences.

They were hardened criminals who cared nothing for people's lives. After their escape, they terrorised the population all around. Wherever they went, they broke into people's houses, taking weapons and food. A large number of policemen followed their trail for weeks, without any success.

The pattern of their break-ins indicated that they were heading north. Aircraft and helicopters were used, but the fugitives kept evading them. The last break-in that was reported occurred on a farm near the gate to the Etosha Game Reserve.

The boundary farmers' Bushmen followed the fugitives to the spot where they climbed through the fence and entered the reserve. The law stipulated that a game warden had to accompany the police, and I received instructions to go, along with my trackers.

It was winter, and dusk had already set in when we joined the police, who were waiting for us at the boundary fence. They were tired and dispirited after weeks of fruitless pursuit, and we decided to sleep near the boundary.

We started tracking early the next morning.

My trackers followed the spoor of the fugitives at a trot, over limestone ridges and through thick stands of mopani trees. At times my Ford had to pretend it was a bulldozer in its efforts to keep up with the trackers. Two trackers always ran on either side of the spoor, and constantly used their tracking sticks to point in some direction, or to indicate large rocks or holes. Not a word was spoken. We understood each other.

The entire police force followed us in their vehicles. Two trackers were always on the ground, and the rest rode along on the back of my vehicle. When the two on the ground tired, they scrambled onto the load-bed, and two rested men took over the pursuit. The trackers were running most of the time. Every now and then the terrain became hard, and the tracking difficult. Tobias and old Kiewiet ("Plover") would then take over. They simply never lost the trail, and we made very good progress. The aircraft and helicopters thundered overhead every now and then, but did not find a thing.

This transpired the whole morning. We had passed through the entire bushy southern region, had crossed the hard, bare Groot-vlakte, and had passed Okahakana, where the northern sandveld with its covering of thorn and mopani began.

Suddenly we were greeted with a volley of gunfire. Stefanus and old Kiewiet, who had been running ahead of the Ford at that time, disappeared like wraiths. I later learned that they dove for cover in a large ant-eater hole.

The vehicles halted and the fugitives' fire was returned. The shooting was ear-splitting.

The police captain who was sitting up front in the cab with me, and a black sergeant on the back, began shooting. I opened the Ford's right-hand door, and stood watching the entire episode from behind that door. The escapees were shooting at us from behind the shelter of some bushes.

To my side a large, dark-haired police sergeant was walking quite openly with his .303 at the ready, loading and shooting. After almost every shot he shouted: "Got him!" and then let fly with some choice expletives. I simply had to admire the man's courage and fearlessness as he advanced into the hail of bullets, shooting all the while.

As I was standing beside my Ford, watching all of this, a bullet whistled past the hair at the back of my head. It was close, very close, but I could not fathom why this bullet had come from behind me.

The fire-fight did not last very long. The escapees shouted that they were giving themselves up, and the policemen were ordered to cease fire. Only three of the escapees stood up, the others were dead. Of the three who stood up, only one could hold his arm up; the others' arms were shot to pieces, and their backs and buttocks looked bad from bullets grazing them. Two of the dead had head wounds, and the third was still breathing, but died shortly afterwards.

The hunt was over. The dead and wounded were loaded, and we returned to Okaukuejo. It was another tracking triumph. After the police had tried to capture the criminals for weeks, we were able to track them down in six hours, thereby ending their reign of terror.

I kept wondering who had fired that shot from behind which missed me so narrowly. Later, at Okaukuejo, I asked my Bushmen about it, and they told me.

During the fire-fight the excited police captain looked across the body of the vehicle for a moment, and prematurely pulled the trigger of his .303. The shot rang out, ricocheted off the rim of a petrol drum, and whistled through the hair on the back of my head and past my right ear.

Big fight at Leeubron

I have already told of the lion parties I sometimes had to organise. Whenever I spent long periods in the bush, someone else had to do it. If I was at Okaukuejo, however, it was my responsibility to ensure that everything ran smoothly with regard to the lion parties.

The number of lions in the Leeubron pride varied. If the pride was at full strength, there were 15 lions in total, but often only old Kastor, the leader at the time, pitched up. Depending on where the lions were and whether they had caught something themselves or not, they either arrived, arrived in part, or did not arrive at all. If the latter transpired, you simply had to drive back to Okaukuejo with all the tourists by 23:00. If the lions arrived at the carcass only at 22:50 or so, you had to sit there until 24:00 at least.

If you had worked hard all day and felt tired, this wasn't always a joke. We had to make sure that the tourists were parked in a semi-circle around the carcass at least half an hour before sunset. They all had to remain very quiet, and radios or unnecessary noise or sounds were forbidden. Nobody was permitted to get out of a vehicle, and every driver of a vehicle had to be in possession of a valid permit to join such a lion party. Only twelve vehicles per session were allowed, as parking space was limited. Lion parties were held every Wednesday and Saturday.

Because only twelve vehicles per session were allowed, there were often grounds for unhappiness, and visitors had to book for a lion party well in advance. Before departing for Leeubron, one had to go to the tourist office to pick up a list of all the vehicles with permits, and the people in them. This facilitated control over the vehicles and eliminated unnecessary enquiries about permits.

When I walked into the office one Wednesday, the tourist official was very worked up, and white in the face from anger. He was arguing with three large bullies and tried to make them understand that the lion party was fully booked and that there was no space for them. The three men were clearly under the influence of alcohol, and cursed and insulted the tourist official, the game reserve and Nature Conservation.

The three men threatened to go to the lion party despite having no permission. Trembling with anger, the tourist official took me outside where the three men could not overhear us, and asked me not to allow them at the lion party under any circumstances.

In those days I was no angel myself, and wanted to ask the three men in the office a few questions in order to assist the poor tourist official. However, because tourists had to be treated like Crown Game, the tourist official stopped me.

I walked to my vehicle, which had a zebra carcass on the back, and drove to Leeubron.

There was enough time to drive at the usual speed of 100 kilometres per hour. The Bushman Simon was with me. We were halfway to Leeubron when a blue Ford with the three men in it passed us like the wind.

When I arrived at Leeubron just before sunset, all the tourists were waiting in their vehicles in their assigned spots, and the full pride of lions were also waiting in anticipation. To the left of Leeubron, on the road to Adamase, there was a thick cloud of dust. The large Ford was not amongst the visitors' vehicles, so the driver must have charged past Leeubron in his haste.

The carcass is always dragged from the bakkie by means of an anchored chain. One person attaches the chain to the front legs of the carcass, while the second person stands next to him with a cocked weapon, to protect him in case of an emergency. Then both persons get into the vehicle and drive forward a few paces until the carcass falls off.

The lions began eating just after the carcass had fallen off. I parked my bakkie in position, in line with the tourists' vehicles, and immediately afterwards the roaring blue Ford arrived and stopped next to us in a cloud of dust. The three men quickly got out of the Ford, set up a camera tripod and began photographing the lions amid much noise.

I was raging inside, but I calmly asked the leader of this pack for his lion permit. Red in the face, he answered in a loud voice: "You know we have no permit, and what are you going to do about it?"

"Sir, you are outside your vehicle! Get back in before we can discuss this matter!" I ordered.

"Look here, I'm from the Cape and I'm now photographing the lions, and there's nothing you can do about it," he said, and walked towards me in a threatening manner. He was big, probably half a head taller than me, and well-built – the very model of a rugby player.

"Sir, you will immediately get back into your vehicle and leave this place," I once again ordered him.

He then began cursing and shouting something terrible. "You and your game reserve can go to hell, you can stick your game reserve up your arse," and so forth.

In his anger he kicked out at me, and I caught his foot and yanked his leg upwards, causing him to fall backwards across the hood of his Ford. When he got up, he attacked me with full force, and I defended myself with my fists.

He would normally have fallen, but because he was big and strong, he stayed on his feet. He then tried to hit me with his fists, but I was able to evade his blows. In-between I was able to plant a few hay-makers of my own. Both his eyebrows were split open, and he began bleeding freely from the nose and mouth.

He grabbed me, and the boxing match turned into a wrestling match. We both landed on the ground, and were rolling on the ground, about ten metres from the very surprised lions.

Despite the wrestling, I kept an eye on the lions. Isabella, the grumpy lioness, was lying flat on the ground and was eyeing us intently, as if she wanted to leap up. Fortunately she didn't. Most of the lions had begun to retreat, but Isabella was lying there with her tail flicking from side to side, watching us.

Now the bully was on top, and then he was under me. As we were grappling, some of the tourists began screaming hysterically. Then the bully was suddenly plucked from me by a nature conservationist – the biologist, holding a revolver – and another man in civilian clothing. This man identified himself as a police captain. The police captain ordered the bully to get into his vehicle immediately, to leave the scene and to report to the Okaukuejo police station, where they would continue the conversation and where I would have to make a statement. Then the bully left Leeubron under police escort, and the biologist took control of the lion party.

At the police station, there was a tremendous commotion, and the three men almost spent the night in the cells. They escaped incarceration because the cells were not furnished with beds.

The next day Mr De la Bat, the chief game warden, summoned me to his office. The frown on his face and his flashing eyes told me: I'm in for it!

Quite livid, he asked me: "What happened? Is this the way we treat tourists around here? The man looks like he landed under a tractor!" This was followed by a harsh reprimand and threats. He refused to listen to me, and I left his office furious.

I then learned that the bully was an old friend of De la Bat's, and that he had sought him out at Okaukuejo the previous night. However, the chief game warden was at Namutoni, where he slept that night. The three strong men drove to Namutoni the next morning, and met him on the way there.

During this meeting they told the chief game warden that I had roughly assaulted them and that they were poor, innocent little angels.

De la Bat's attitude towards me changed only after he had heard the true story from the the police captain.

In the end the police themselves charged the three men. They had to pay fines for all their misdemeanours, and were prohibited from entering Etosha again.

I often wondered why I seem to attract problems like that.

A ride to save my children's lives

It was a year of terrible heat and drought; nothing unusual in South West Africa. The natural springs were drying up, or had already run dry.

This also happened to the waterhole at Onangombati, about 130 kilometres from Okaukuejo near Etosha's western boundary. This waterhole is situated in a lime pan, and when it dries up, it leaves deep gulleys filled with water that only the elephants can eventually reach with their trunks.

As the water is exhausted quite quickly, but seeps back in time, the elephant herds often stand about these lime gulleys for hours, patiently waiting for the water to trickle in. This means there is a thick layer of elephant dung around the waterhole. To improve conditions for the elephants, I wanted to clear the waterhole by carting away and burning all the elephant dung.

Because I also wanted to clear the Onaiso and Onandera waterholes nearby, I would have to be in the veld without a break for at least two weeks. I therefore took along Elke and the two eldest boys, Udo and Ingo.

Drinking water was a big problem, because the intense heat meant that man and beast drank inordinate amounts of water. I took along drinking water for the kids from Okaukuejo in well-cleaned petrol drums. Elke and I, the Bushman workers and the horses would use water from the waterholes. The water had a slightly greenish tinge, and tasted of elephant dung. On patrol we regularly had to use this water, so it was nothing unusual. I took along three service horses in order to undertake some horse patrols, because I regularly had run-ins with Herero poachers in this area.

I used the large 5-ton Thames as my service vehicle to transport the horse-trailer and camping equipment. The trailer meant we could only drive along the 19th parallel, then we had to unhitch it at an appropriate spot and ride the horses through the veld for the last stretch.

We made camp near Onangombati. This enabled us to walk to the waterhole in the mornings for the clean-up.

On the drive from Okaukuejo to Onangombati I noticed the red generator light burning. This meant the battery would not last long, because the alternator's brushes were finished. I would not be able to repair this in the veld.

I had to use the battery very, very sparingly, and start the Thames as little as possible. As the days went by, it became more and more difficult to start the Thames. In the end I did not use the truck at all, and we carted away the dung and mud with wheelbarrows.

We were almost done with the work when the children began to get sick with diarrhoea. Their health deteriorated rapidly. We worked overtime to finish, as we wanted to go home after only one more day.

We loaded all the tools and camping equipment onto the Thames, but when we were ready to leave, the Thames would not start. We were able to push-start the heavy vehicle on the hard limestone only with the greatest effort, and everyone's cooperation. I immediately drove to the trailer that we had left at the Toebiroen windpump. The two Bushmen, Hebakoib and Sam, rode the horses through the veld to where the trailer was. It was already late in the afternoon, and normally I would not have driven back at that time of day, but I had to, in view of the critical health of my eldest son, Udo.

On arrival at the trailer, the Thames died. For no love or money could we push-start it again; the battery was completely dead. There was no radio in the Thames. Udo looked like a skeleton, with no strength left in his body. All I could do, was to ride to Okaukuejo on horseback as fast as I could.

I saddled Bento, my former showjumping mount. He was the most suitable candidate to complete the 130 kilometres in the shortest possible time.

My wife had to stay near the windpump with the five Bushmen, the two sick children and the Thames. Many elephants congregated around the windpump to drink, particularly at night, and cows with small calves can become very aggressive.

Each windpump in the game reserve had to be protected from elephants with a deep and wide ditch, or they would push over the installation if there wasn't enough water in the trough.

The windpump therefore stands on a little island of about five metres in diameter. For safety's sake I had them put all the bedding – for wife, children and Bushmen – on that little island. The Thames did not offer enough protection, and they had to keep a large fire going throughout the night to fend off lions. For the moment that was all I could do for their safety. There was not enough time for supper, and after having issued all these instructions, I mounted Bento, armed with my two revolvers. I left the 9.3 millimetre with my wife in case of emergency.

I constantly felt a fear for my children's lives gnawing at me. One hundred and thirty kilometres is a long way for a horse – you need to save your strength and that of the horse to make sure you reach your goal. Fortunately, I had a useful horse to try to do it as quickly as possible. But it was new moon. The very last quarter-moon would rise only after midnight, and until then I had to ride in complete darkness. I could stumble upon a herd of elephants, a pride of lions or a wandering rhino at any moment.

If my horse threw me in panic, I would have to run to Okaukuejo – if I was still alive! Only Udo's deathly pale, sunken, half-closed eyes spurred me on. Because I could not see a thing, I constantly spoke aloud and made noises like someone driving an ox-wagon, in order to make any wild animals aware of my approach, and hopefully make them turn tail. I had to rely entirely on Bento's sense of smell.

By midnight it was still dark, and near the Bitterwater windpump I decided to give Bento and myself a break. There was an old horse enclosure at Bitterwater where I wanted to unsaddle and give Bento a chance to pee, or I would run the risk of "riding him beyond his kidneys".

However, the camp no longer existed. The elephants must, in the meantime, have used it as a concertina.

I had hardly lain down when a large lion began roaring quite close by. The sound of roaring made it clear that he was moving closer all the time. It seemed to me that the lion was following our tracks. I had to saddle up hastily and make for the road via a roundabout way. At that time the road was simply two worn tracks. Soon afterwards, a little scrap of moon came up. I could now see a little better, and felt slightly more at ease. However, every time Bento threw his head back, pricked his ears and made a snorting sound, I knew, for the umpteenth time that night, that predators were close by. I then had to "drive the ox-wagon" loud and clear, spur on my horse, and ride past the danger. Bento was wonderfully obedient.

When day began to break, I was riding past the windpump at Ozonjuiti m'Bari. There were fewer elephants and rhinos here, but definitely more lions.

As soon as I was able to see better, I dismounted Bento more often, loosening the right-hand reins at the snaffle-ring, so as to have available a double length of rein. This meant I still had control over the horse, but was able to drive the tired animal obliquely in front of me quite efficiently.

I jogged behind my horse like this for long distances without wasting any time. I could also leave the tourist road behind and make directly for Okaukuejo through the bush.

There was still a long distance to cover – some 60 kilometres. By 10:30 that morning I eventually arrived at Okaukuejo with an exhausted but quite healthy horse.

I gave myself no time at all. The Ford was filled with petrol in a trice, and with a bottle of water for the day I was on my way back to my wife and kids.

I took the mechanic and a spare battery for the Thames with me. He would have to battle with the Thames on his own. I reached them again by the afternoon, in scorching heat. Udo's condition was even worse. He lay in my arms without moving.

As quickly as possible I made my way back to Okaukuejo with my wife and children, and I left Elke and Ingo there. With Udo on the seat next to me, I made my way as quickly as possible to the hospital at Otjiwarongo. Outjo was closer, but on a previous occasion I had harsh words for the doctor there at the time over the manner in which he had treated a Bushman child of Simon's for diarrhoea. The child later died. I was extremely angry at the doctor for the way he acted towards Simon, and the way he showed no interest in the case.

There were good doctors and nurses at Otjiwarongo, and I preferred to drive that little extra distance.

I can still remember that Udo's name and room number were written on a blackboard near the entrance to the Otjiwarongo Hospital after I had left him there. I had little hope of seeing Udo alive again. On the way back, I asked the Lord again and again to spare my child.

I later almost fell asleep from fatigue, but the worry kept me going. When I eventually reached home, Elke told me that Ingo's condition had in the meantime deteriorated to such an extent that she considered it to be critical. What illness was this that had such a serious and implacable influence on his body? I could not understand it. We often had cases of diarrhoea because of the brackish water at Okaukuejo, but it usually passed after two or three days. This was something quite different.

It was time again. This time Elke came with me. As if in a horrible nightmare, I drove back to Otjiwarongo that same afternoon.

When we eventually got there, Udo's name was no longer on that blackboard! "He's lying in the mortuary, he hasn't made it!" I thought, and it felt as if my world was crumbling about me. I went on with rubbery legs, holding Ingo in my arms. I could hardly carry Ingo, who felt immensely heavy, even though his body was hardly more than a bundle of bones.

When we handed Ingo over to the duty sister, I immediately asked whether Udo was still alive, and where he was.

She answered with a slight smile. "He's in the intensive-care ward. He needs special care, but his condition has improved slightly, and he should make it."

I cannot describe my relief. The world was a happier place, and I could not thank everyone enough.

After we left Ingo at the hospital, Elke stayed with friends at Otjiwarongo. I went back to Okaukuejo, arriving there in the early hours of the morning.

I had spent 48 hours in chasing to and fro, on horseback, on foot and in a vehicle, without any sleep or food. Body and nerves now began to take their toll, and I felt like a wet rag. A long, refreshing sleep followed.

The children recovered fairly quickly, thanks to the intravenous drip administered in hospital. Blood tests later showed lead poisoning had caused all the trouble. This was caused by lead in the petrol drums.

All of us who had drunk the dirty water from the waterhole, stayed healthy. The kids who had drunk the "clean" water from the drums, became ill. They had been at death's door!

Stories about the kids

I would like to conclude with a few stories about my kids. In the end there were four sons, and their names all end with the first letter of Okaukuejo. They all arrived unexpectedly and on their own steam. No prophylactics were effective, and eventually I simply accepted it whenever Elke told me she was pregnant. They were born in the following order: Udo, Ingo, Heiko and Nico.

Udo

Udo was a quiet and withdrawn child. One day my neighbour, André, was walking home when he heard my kids playing quite raucously. Because his son, Andrew (not exactly an angel) was great friends with my sons, he smelled a rat and went to investigate.

I had planted reeds beside the fence along the boundary of my property to serve as a natural wall. André carefully separated some of the reeds to spy on the kids.

They were playing Bushman and lion. Udo and Ingo, armed with bows and arrows, were dancing all around Heiko. Heiko was still in nappies, and was crawling about on the lawn. He was the lion. The other two were Bushman hunters, armed with children's bows and arrows that the Bushmen had made for them.

As Udo and Ingo were dancing around Heiko with great fanfare, they aimed a blunt arrow at him every now and then. When they hit him and he began bawling, they quickly silenced him with some mopani worms.

Heiko had always had a healthy appetite, and was always ready for a snack. They had collected live mopani worms just for this purpose. The green juice ran down on either side of Heiko's mouth as he sat chewing on those tasty mopani worms.

Ingo's birth

I was occupied with building experimental grazing camps along the 19th parallel for research purposes. It was shortly before Christmas, and I wanted to finish the work. When I left for the camp, Elke, who was heavily pregnant, gave me the assurance that I could go: it was not yet time for her to give birth.

We had hardly started working, and were busy putting up fences for the camp, when Mynard Blom, the mechanic, arrived to congratulate me on the birth of my son.

I heard the whole story from Elke's mouth. Her own version: "When I woke this morning, I felt an urgent need to go to the toilet. On the toilet I realised I was giving birth. There was no time to lose. I took the 8 millimetre Mauser, went outside and squeezed off two quick shots into the air." This was the pre-arranged signal should one of us find ourselves in difficulty. Jack, the biologist, heard it and hurried over to my house. He found my wife there, in bed, having almost completed giving birth. He helped my wife to the end. Fortunately he was there, because the cord was wound around Ingo's neck, and he was choking. Jack unwound the cord and cut it quite professionally. Elke's subsequent stay in hospital was only in the nature of after-care in order to avoid infection.

As a child Ingo loved smaller animals such as ants, spiders, scorpions and other insects. When the time came for the two eldest lads to go to school, we sent them to the German private school in Karibib. From then on we would see the kids only during school holidays, or whenever we visited Karibib. As a result, we insisted that they should write to us. One letter from Ingo read:

> *Dear Parents*
>
> *How are you? Everything is fine with me! There's a tin full of scorpions under my bed. Regards.*
>
> *Your son Ingo*

Heiko

From the start Heiko was a stolid, grumpy little bullock. He followed his own head, even as a very small child. He fared well in many types of sports, particularly soccer, running, high jump and swimming.

At six years old he happened to be walking past the swimming-pool at Okaukuejo when he heard the hysterical screams of a Bushman woman. There was a great splashing from the pool. Heiko reacted immediately, ran to the swimming pool and dived in to rescue the son of the chief tourist officer at the time. He swam to the side with the drowning child, where the woman helped to fish him out.

I actually think Heiko should have received a life-saver's medal, but he had to be content with a brief report in the paper.

Heiko is a big, strong man today. He stands back for no one, and looks after his dad very well!

Nico

Nico always remained short of stature in comparison with his brothers, and I do not know why. Perhaps the mother's milk dried up too soon.

However, of all my sons, he suffered the most punishment. He would not yield, even to his own father. Elke, the children and I went to Ekuna one Sunday. The Ekuna River was in flood, and we fished and swam all day. The three Baas girls, Ute, Gundel and Anette, were with us. They came for horse-riding lessons almost every school holiday.

We all drove home late in the afternoon. The road to Ekuna had been damaged by water and was badly rutted, with many holes and much dust. I was driving my International one-tonner, with bars at the back to enable horses to be transported. There was a thick plank on top of the bars so that people could sit there and enjoy a better view. This was a little dangerous, but one simply had to drive carefully. However, the smaller children were prohibited from sitting on the plank; they had to stand on the load-bed. I was in the cab on my own, and was driving. Nico had joined the girls on the plank. While driving, I shouted at Nico to get down. He did so, but moments later he was sitting on the plank again.

He got down once more, only to scramble up again. I told Ute not to allow him to do this. Ute answered: "He doesn't want to listen!" I began steaming.

When Nico climbed up the third time and I gave him a final warning to get down, he simply kept sitting up there. Instead of getting down, he shouted at me: "Pappa, du Arschloch!" ("Papa, you arsehole!") At that stage Nico was probably about five, but I had had enough. I slammed on the brakes and got out. I calmly ordered him to get down and to cut himself a rod. To emphasise the point, I gave him my pocket-knife.

He returned with a flimsy little stick, typically Nico. I simply looked at him hard and long, and went to cut a better one myself.

Nico the elephant

Andrew was Nico's great friend. They were known far and wide for their mischief. I had a soft spot for a vegetable garden, and one year I had a promising stand of maize next to the area where I exercised my horses. This piece of land was well protected against wild animals, and was the only maize patch at Okaukuejo. The maize was forming seed, and in my mind's eye I was already cooking and eating corn on the cob. Corn on the cob was a gourmet meal at Okaukuejo, and only a handful of farms sold a few of them at very high prices.

As usual when I went out, I made sure to drive by the maize when I came back. I looked and looked again, but my maize had gone. Only a few dry stalks were lying on the ground.

The elephants had paid a visit, I thought. I was extremely disappointed, but in the game reserve the elephants were the boss, and one simply had to accept that. Strangely, however, all the fencing was undamaged. I stopped, got out, and began tracking. No elephant tracks, only small footprints. There were signs of the stalks having been hacked. What was this all about? As I was investigating, and walking about my maize patch in disbelief, Hebakoib appeared. He was able to keep an eye on my garden from his house near the stables. Quite angry, I asked him: "What happened here, Hebakoib?"

"The small whites, Nico and Andrew, did you the dirty," he answered in Bushman.

I wanted to give Alarich some exercise before sundown, and

218

asked Hebakoib to saddle him for me quickly. Nico was nowhere to be seen. I told Elke: "I can see Nico in the exercise yard. Send him to me with the dressage whip!" I turned around and went to the yard.

I had Alarich trotting for a good while to warm up. Then, when I wanted to mount, little Nico came running with the dressage whip in his hand.

When I saw him, I knew what was going on. As usual, his torso was bare. He looked like a well-endowed Nama woman, only much smaller. He wore one of his mother's shorts. The pants were bulging in all directions, stuffed to capacity with his own pants and underpants. When this little man with his bulging posterior came running up, I first had to turn away quickly to hide my smile. Arms akimbo and legs apart, he stood there looking at me with his dark brown eyes wavering a bit, and said: "So, Papa, you can hit me now!" I was totally disarmed.

I glared at him intensely for a long while, and could only say: "Get out of my sight!"

Nowadays Nico is a well-educated young man.

A dark period

The years as a game warden at Okaukuejo had come and gone. I lived a hard but in my opinion wonderful life. Almost every day had its own excitement, and I never knew any boredom.

Even though my serious back pain caused my left leg to wither more and more, I was relatively fit and was still able to walk all day. Not so fast any more, but still fast enough to leave fellow-hikers behind at the end of the day.

After thirteen years of service as a game warden at Okaukuejo, the top structure underwent radical changes. I was approached to apply for the post of chief game warden at Etosha. I was very sceptical, because I knew this would involve a great deal of administrative and other paperwork. I rather wanted to apply for a post as senior game warden, because that meant you would still quite often be out in the veld with your men.

Reluctantly, I eventually accepted an appointment as chief game warden for the north of Namibia. Initially I was still posted at Okaukuejo, but before long there were hints of a move to Windhoek.

My transfer to Windhoek

On my promotion to chief game warden, thunderclouds with regard to my work at Nature Conservation began to gather on the horizon.

I should never have become chief game warden. I was absolutely happy in my previous work – I was a free, uncrowned king in nature. I had enough money to make a living, and the work made me happy. Work never felt like work; I could be on duty 24 hours a day and still not get enough.

Things began to sour between Elke and me. I was married to the bush. I should have paid her and the children more attention, but when I came to my senses, it was too late.

Then the promotion came on top of it all. I did not want to accept the position, but was talked into it.

Before I accepted the post, I was given the assurance that I would stay at Okaukuejo. That was acceptable to me. All the guys ahead of me had already been transferred to Windhoek. The Etosha Game Reserve was my home. About three months after I became chief game warden, rumours of a transfer to Windhoek began flying about. At first I thought it was a joke and that they were pulling my leg, but in time I found out that it was very much in earnest.

When the farmers on the boundary heard that I would be transferred to Windhoek, they actually drew up a petition to keep me there. Even people whom I had caused to end up in court, signed the petition. I may not have tolerated any transgressions, but I did understand the problems faced by the farmers on the boundaries, and tried to help where I could. The main reason, however, was the aspect of security. Very little ever happened in the game reserve without me hearing about it, and doing something about it.

Nature Conservation was, however, adamant that I had to go to Windhoek.

I occupied a large office in Windhoek. One of my tasks was to approve or refuse permits. All the outside work was done by the game wardens; I had to sit inside and delegate.

I was told: "Gone are the days when you did all the work yourself. Sit back and simply delegate."

I was extremely frustrated, and furthermore found myself in an unhappy marriage!

I did control four large game reserves, and during my inspections there I found many irregularities, particularly at Etosha. The monthly reports I received did not accord with the realities. My old Bushmen told me what was really going on. My two white stalwarts, Andries and Johann, also resigned because of the unhealthy working climate.

When the Defence Force asked me to undertake a tracking and survival course, it therefore felt like a welcome holiday. As soon as one survival course was completed, I spoke to the course leader and reminded him not to forget about me for the next course.

To rid myself of my frustrations with Nature Conservation, I bought myself a smallholding at Brakwater about 24 kilometres north of Windhoek. It was a very pretty little farm in the Komas Hochland. The kudus stood on the surrounding mountain-tops almost every evening and early morning and looked down on me. I soon built a natural drinking-trough for the kudu and baboons, and found much delight in the bird and animal life.

I planned the property in such a way that it would one day contain an indoor riding-school of 30x80 metres with 25 stables, store-rooms for feed, and a nice house. In the meantime I had already built the store-rooms and was living in them.

I join the Army

I was conducting a survival course in the desert. Everything was going smoothly. After the drive back, the usual end-of-course function was held, this time at the Commando Headquarters in Windhoek near the Eros Airport. I was dirty and tired from all the walking during the course, and I wanted to have a quick bath at home.

I asked Captain Pinkie Coetzee to take me to my home in Akademia. The captain was a good friend, and one of the instructors on the tracking course.

On arrival at Akademia, I saw a blue Volkswagen Kombi parked in front of the house. I knew whose Kombi it was. I hated the man at the time, because he stood between me and Elke. My emotions threatened to boil over.

I asked Pinkie to turn around on the spot. Quite perturbed, he stopped and looked at me with a question in his eyes. I simply said: "Don't ask, Captain, if you leave me here, I will commit murder; please, just drive back to the function!"

The function was jolly and a good spirit reigned. I was standing to one side, miserable, and caught up in my own thoughts. As I was sitting there, Colonel Roos walked over to me and asked in good spirits: "Come on, Piet, why are you sitting here with a long face? I don't know you like this!"

Feeling miserable, I answered: "I've had it, Colonel!"

"Then leave Nature Conservation and join us; when can I sign you up?"

On the spur of the moment I answered: "Now, Colonel, right now!"

The colonel did not expect this. He asked, in disbelief: "What are you saying, Piet? Are you serious?"

"Yes, Colonel," I answered.

"Just hang on a bit and wait right here; don't go away; I'll get the Brigadier." At the time Colonel Roos was Brigadier Geldenhuys's adjutant. He returned ten minutes later with the Brigadier. "What's this I'm hearing, Piet, do you want to resign from Nature Conservation?" was the first thing the brigadier asked.

"Yes, Brigadier!" They both came and sat at my table and ordered me a drink.

Many questions were asked and many answers were given, amongst others what my requirements were. I answered that rank was not important to me, but that I did not want to give up my present salary, for which I had worked very hard for 16 years. The brigadier agreed. This was another important turning point in my life. From that moment on, I was a soldier.

I resigned from Nature Conservation the next morning. The controlling game warden could not believe his ears. He stood up and walked over to the director. He summoned me and spent some time trying to persuade me to change my mind. However, I had made my decision, and that was final.

My resignation was handled at the highest level, eventually serving before the Administrator of South West Africa.

My resignation was considered to be in the national interest, and departmentally I was transferred to the South African Defence Force. My previous years of service therefore remained in force, and I was appointed in the Permanent Force with the rank of major.

One evening in Windhoek, shortly before my departure for Potchefstroom, Mrs Ani Schmerenbeck came to me and said she was determined to leave her farm Claratal to me. Ani's husband, Kurt, was already deceased, and she had no children,

As I had spent almost every holiday with them at Claratal as a child, and she knew I loved that farm and its rich wildlife, she must

222

have regarded me as the best heir. However, she wanted it to be a family farm for Elke, myself and the children. If I insisted on a divorce, and joined the Defence Force, I would not get the farm.

At that time Claratal was 15 000 hectares in extent, with sixteen dams, fully developed, and only 50 kilometres from Windhoek. It was worth millions. This was a very, very difficult decision to make, particularly when I thought of my children.

My transfer to the Defence Force had already gone through, and I had no desire to return to Nature Conservation with my tail between my legs. Neither did I see my way open to continue with an unhappy marriage.

Nature Conservation held a farewell function for me in the Daan Viljoen Game Park near Windhoek, organised by Stoffel Rocher. As farewell gifts I was given the large elephant tusk which I had pulled from the carcass at Onandera, and the large rhino horn taken from the carcass at Otjovasandu. I also received a magnificent painting of an old lion by Koos van Ellinckhuizen. The lion is looking back over his shoulder, which was symbolic of the way I viewed my stay at Etosha. Furthermore, there was a brown paper bag of prepared mopani worms, and a bag of first-grade elephant dung. I could hardly have received gifts that would have moved me more profoundly.

I then moved to South Africa to join its Defence Force.

But that is another story.